Contents

CW00663704

Tables

Corrupt Capital

This book offers a deep dive into the social, political, and economic forces that make white-collar crime and corruption a staple feature of the nightlife economy. The author, a former bouncer-turned-bartender of party bars and nightclubs in a large U.S. city, draws from an auto-ethnographic case study to describe and explain the routine and embedded nature of corruption and deviance among the regulators and the regulated in the nightlife environment.

This text offers a contemporary and incisive theoretical framework on the criminogenic features and structural contradictions of capitalism. The author both describes and explains how the dominant political economy is rife with structural contradictions that, in turn, generate various manifestations of white-collar crime, organizational deviance, and public corruption. The author uses the bar and nightlife environment to empirically anchor these claims. Methodologically, the research is innovative in advancing inquiry into ethically and logistically challenging environments. The style of writing and framing of the text is one that punches upward and avoids the voyeuristic and reductionist tropes historically associated with "dangerous fieldwork."

Through a range of disciplinary perspectives, *Corrupt Capital* offers both scholarly rigor and inviting prose to advance our understanding of crimes of the relatively powerful and powerless alike. An accessible and compelling text, this book will appeal to readers in criminology, sociology, law and society, political science, and all those interested in learning about the relationship between power, law, and routinized corruption in the nightlife economy.

Kenneth Sebastian León is an Assistant Professor of Latino and Caribbean Studies and a faculty affiliate of the Criminal Justice Program at Rutgers University – New Brunswick. He specializes in crimes of the powerful, empirically studying how criminal justice policies contribute to racial capitalist harms and state-corporate crime. Previously, León was a Visiting Assistant Professor in the Department of Sociology at George Washington University (GWU) and a contracted researcher of transnational organized crime at the U.S. Department of Justice, Office of Justice Programs – National Institute of Justice (2016–2017). León serves as the Managing Editor for the *Journal of White Collar and Corporate Crime*, a peer-reviewed publication affiliated with the American Society of Criminology.

Crimes of the Powerful

Gregg Barak
Eastern Michigan University, USA

Penny Green
Queen Mary University of London, UK

Tony Ward
Northumbria University, UK

Crimes of the Powerful encompasses the harmful, injurious, and victimizing behaviors perpetrated by privately or publicly operated businesses, corporations, and organizations as well as the state mediated administrative, legalistic, and political responses to these crimes.

The series draws attention to the commonalities of the theories, practices, and controls of the crimes of the powerful. It focuses on the overlapping spheres and inter-related worlds of a wide array of existing and recently developing areas of social, historical, and behavioral inquiry into the wrongdoings of multinational organizations, nation-states, stateless regimes, illegal networks, financialization, globalization, and securitization.

These examinations of the crimes of the powerful straddle a variety of related disciplines and areas of academic interest, including studies in criminology and criminal justice; law and human rights; conflict, peace, and security; economic change, environmental decay, and global sustainability.

State Crime and Civil Activism
On the Dialectics of Repression and Resistance
Penny Green and Tony Ward

State Violence, Torture, and Political Prisoners
On the Role Played by Amnesty International in Brazil during the Dictatorship (1964–1985)
Renata Meirelles

Corrupt Capital
Alcohol, Nightlife, and Crimes of the Powerful
Kenneth Sebastian León

For more information about this series, please visit: www.routledge.com/Crimes-of-the-Powerful/book-series/COTP

Corrupt Capital

Alcohol, Nightlife, and Crimes of the Powerful

Kenneth Sebastian León

Routledge
Taylor & Francis Group

LONDON AND NEW YORK

First published 2021
by Routledge
2 Park Square, Milton Park, Abingdon, Oxon OX14 4RN

and by Routledge
605 Third Avenue, New York, NY 10017

First issued in paperback 2022

Routledge is an imprint of the Taylor & Francis Group, an informa business

Publisher's Note
The publisher has gone to great lengths to ensure the quality of this
reprint but points out that some imperfections in the original copies may
be apparent.

British Library Cataloguing-in-Publication Data
A catalogue record for this book is available from the British Library

Library of Congress Cataloging-in-Publication Data
A catalog record for this book has been requested

ISBN: 978-0-367-18581-7 (hbk)
ISBN: 978-0-367-55479-8 (pbk)
ISBN: 978-0-429-19698-0 (ebk)

DOI: 10.4324/9780429196980

Typeset in Bembo
by Apex CoVantage, LLC

Disclaimer

This book makes reference to Metropolis East, a medium- to large-sized city located in the Eastern Standard Time Zone of the United States. Publicly available information from various jurisdictions is used to provide supporting evidence and supplemental context. Any resemblance between Metropolis East and specific people, places, or practices is purely coincidental.

In memory of Bill Chambliss and Steven "Wizard" Broderick

Acknowledgments

When Josh Groban's "You Raise Me Up" plays on my computer, a few people immediately come to mind. The largest share of credit and blame goes to Maya P. Barak, whose friendship is responsible for converting an obscure idea into a dissertation proposal. I am indebted to Ed Maguire, who supported my research and graduate school trajectory and set an example for the kind of dissertation adviser I hope to be. David Friedrichs and Gregg Barak each provided invaluable subject matter expertise, personal guidance, and professional mentorship in ways that made this book possible. This project has been my attempt to honor the influence of Bill Chambliss, who passed away during my doctoral studies and whose mentorship and writing still guide me to this day. When Bill died, I might have been academically lost at sea had it not been for Ivy Ken and Marty Schwartz. Ivy and Marty shepherded my path in a way that validated my own intellectual struggles and curiosities. They knew many of my biographical and personal quirks and biases and encouraged me to always play to my strengths and take stock of my limitations. Fran Buntman, Maranda Ward, and Daniel Martinez also inspired and supported me in ways that made my book and academic journey both possible and enjoyable. Thank you to Ana Castro, Jon Gould, Shelley Morris, David Pitts, Vicky Wilkins, and the faculty, administrators, and support staff of the American University (AU) School of Public Affairs and the Neil and Ann Kerwin Doctoral Fellowship, which generously supported this research. A special shout-out is owed to my colleagues in the Department of Latino and Caribbean Studies and the Program in Criminal Justice at Rutgers University for giving me the professional space to see this project through to completion, and for providing a stimulating and supporting intellectual environment for me to continue developing as an interdisciplinary scholar. Pernille Chambliss, Carlos Decena, Laura Gimenez, Robert Holup, Ivan Marchena, Lauren Martin, Jody Miller, Juan Osuna, Mariana Pereira, and Normandie Peterson each offered critical forms of advice, encouragement, and wisdom that helped me navigate different phases of this work. Many thanks to the Editorial Team at Apex CoVantage, Jennifer Bonnar, Brian Craig, Bharat Bhatt, and Janani Thirumalai, and to Penny Green, Tony Ward, Jake Rainbow, Jessica Phillips, Tom Sutton, and the Routledge Series on Crimes of the Powerful team for their support, enthusiasm, and understanding of the various challenges inherent in writing my first book.

I am both grateful and resentful for the level of care and understanding that my parents, Lourdes and Jorge, my sister, Carmen Sofia, and my grandma, Teddy Roosevelt, shared with me. I left South Florida at 17 years old for college in Tallahassee, and I have moved farther and farther away from my family ever since. To complete the research and writing for this book, I added to an already long list of missed birthdays, holidays, family reunions, and important life events. Not once did they ever guilt me for being absent due to stress or work-related exigencies, although I sometimes wish that they did. True to their own work ethic, they always and at every opportunity encouraged that I grind it out and finish what I started. Writing was not an entirely solitary endeavor for me, as this book was also made possible through the mental health and lifestyle-related support of Tiberius and Juneau, my two rescue "pit bulls" who locked their jaws around my heart. They do not know how to read, but I perpetually show them how they have been my lifeline in so many ways. Finally, words cannot capture how much I treasure the time spent with the people and friends of the nightlife industry. You know who you are, and this book is for you.

Preface

How long would it take to become a detective or a police chief? Those were my guiding questions when I first began a terminal master's degree in criminology. A law enforcement career seemed like a reasonable path to middle-class security and an interesting way to cope with my phobia of working behind a desk.[1] Upon arriving at George Washington University, that orientation was quickly subverted through the mentorship of Bill Chambliss, who until the time of his passing was as a prolific scholar in Marxist criminology and state crime. As one of Bill's students, my reintroduction to criminology would begin with this thing called *the sociological imagination*. No disrespect to friends and family in law enforcement, but I became less interested in becoming a cog in some machine, and found the socio-legal machinations of law, order, and power far more interesting. What sealed the deal was realizing how little state troopers get paid in my home state of Florida, and it seemed entirely reasonable to ditch the plans of being a "Field Agent" and aim for something closer to "Field Researcher" instead.

Bill was single-handedly responsible for my decision to pursue a doctoral degree in the social sciences. Not only was he the first person to suggest that I *could* do it, but treated this previously alien concept as the easy, logical, and self-evident step in my own journey. Through mentorship and support from GWU Sociology faculty, I began my doctoral journey in 2013 in Justice, Law and Society in the School of Public Affairs at American University. While technically forbidden by the stipulations of our funding package, I needed additional opportunities to make money, because DC rent was *too damn high*. In the first year of the program, I secured the proverbial side hustle in the form of being an adjunct lecturer by day and a doorman (or bouncer) and bartender by night. It would take many months before I made a clear connection between what I was studying by day and what I observed after hours. I realized that there was a world of both extraordinary and mundane white-collar crime and corruption, and that such phenomena were largely under-represented in both academic literature and public media. Over time, I realized that such practices are not merely hidden, but actively and structurally obfuscated by criminological theory and criminal justice practice. Our ability to both describe and explain crimes of the powerful is structurally hindered by two things: 1) the way that academics study crime, law, and order and 2) the actual practices and functions of criminal justice systems. As a structural critique, criminological theory (what academics say and write) and criminal justice practices (how institutions work) have not only underemphasized powerful actors and organizations but also serve as sites of reproduction for powerful interests, ideologies, and practices.

I wrote this book to confront these two limitations and offer a political economic account of white-collar crime and public corruption in the nightlife economy. I view the nightlife economy as a theoretical and empirical microcosm for various forms of corruption and social harm that we find in other systems of material, social, and political exchange. Unlike perspectives that focus on "bad apples" or "bad barrels," this is really a study about powerful *systems*. The systems that I reference are varied and perhaps unwieldly in scope, but I anchor them in the nightlife economy so readers might enjoy a more accessible explanation of *criminogenic capital* – or the various crimes, harms, and conflicts that are inseparable from the conventionally legitimate systems associated with capitalism.

This book is made possible by the collective efforts of past and present scholars who have collectively built the *crimes of the powerful* subfield within criminology and sociology of crime, law, and deviance. Importantly, not everyone who studies the harms, features, and functions of the political economic system commonly associated with capitalism will label their own work as being within the *crimes of the powerful* genre, and Table 0.1 is far from exhaustive, comprehensive, or even defensible in terms of adequately capturing the interdisciplinary breadth and depth of this topic. Nevertheless, the table is provided so that specialized readers might know how to situate the intellectual trajectory of this book with the perspectives and works that have influenced its author.

Some readers might immediately notice the relative homogeneity within the formal boundaries of crimes of the powerful (and critical criminology). Phrased differently, this is *qwhite* a list! Race is hypervisible among criminological *subjects* but relatively invisible among criminological *authors*. Chapter 2 of this text will refocus our discussion on the relationship between academic projects and racial projects, which transcend critiques of any one discipline or subfield.

While business is booming for scholars of white-collar crime and corruption, the field's political and empirical center remains aligned with state-centric approaches to defining and studying harm. More so than reverting to a "cop shop" field of study, academic criminology risks becoming complicit in emergent neoconservative and neo-fascist projects if junior cohorts of academics and current graduate students do not have an opportunity to engage with perspectives and positions that have long been relegated to the margins, or treated as though they are outside the purview of criminology and criminal justice scholarship.

Whether this material is brand new, or you are already well versed in the structural critiques of capitalism (and criminology's dirty laundry), my aim is to ultimately bring what might otherwise be a theoretically dense and far-reaching argument into a more accessible framework by keeping our feet grounded in an

Table 0.1 A sample of guiding texts on crimes of the powerful

Author	Title	Year
Louis Proal	*Political Crime*	1896
Edwin Sutherland	*White Collar Crime*	1949
C. Wright Mills	*The Power Elite*	1956
Richard Quinney	*Critique of Legal Order: Crime Control in Capitalist Society*	1974
Frank Pearce	*Crimes of the Powerful*	1976
William J. Chambliss	*On the Take: From Petty Crooks to Presidents*	1978; 1988
Noam Chomsky	*Pirates and Emperors, Old and New: International Terrorism in the Real World*	1986
Nils Christie	*Crime Control as Industry – Towards Gulags, Western Style*	1993
Biko Agozino	*Counter-Colonial Criminology: A Critique of Imperialist Reason*	2003
David Whyte (ed.)	*Crimes of the Powerful: A Reader*	2008
Mark Fisher	*Capitalist Realism: Is There No Alternative?*	2009
Jock Young	*The Criminological Imagination*	2011
Gregg Barak (ed.)	*Routledge International Handbook of the Crimes of the Powerful*	2015
Steve Tombs and David Whyte	*The Corporate Criminal: Why Corporations Must Be Abolished*	2015
Dawn Rothe and David Kauzlarich	*Crimes of the Powerful: An Introduction*	2016
David Whyte and Jörg Wiegratz	*Neoliberalism and the Moral Economy of Fraud*	2017

accessible setting. For readers in the Global North, this location could be the bar, tavern, or nightclub in any metropolitan city nearest you.

As a former employee in this environment, I studied the nightlife economy to better connect institutional forces to my biographical experiences, and understand individual relationships to broader cultural, economic, and political features of criminal law, local governance, and social structure. Importantly, I'll be doing this without replicating the historical critiques and limitations of class-reductionism. By complicating traditional narratives, theories, and perspectives associated with crime and deviance, I offer insights into the relationships between nightlife consumption, crimes of the powerful, and contemporary capitalism.

Obfuscation and crimes of the powerful

In any harmful or exploitative system, the relatively powerful and the relatively disempowered negotiate an array of distracting myths or narratives that obfuscate the true nature of that system.[2] As Lynn Weber has argued, "One of the greatest obstacles to understanding the system of race, class, gender, and sexuality oppression is that its continuation *depends* on ensuring that it is not clearly seen or understood."[3] The immediate follow-up question to this kind of argument might be: Not seen or understood by whom? In quoting Patricia Hill Collins, "On some level, people who are oppressed usually know it."[4] While it might appear as though Collins and Weber are at odds with each other, I would apply Weber's claim to those who are somewhere in the middle between the "all powerful" and "all powerless." Those who benefit *most* and those who benefit *least* from a given arrangement are likely to be most informed on the nature of such a system. In this book, I make the case for recasting crimes of the powerful as harms that are systematically generated by the political economy known as "capitalism." As such, there are marginally and relationally powerful actors. Like a layered triangular hierarchy, each rung on the ladder exercises a degree of power and coercion over the group below it, while being subject to the power and coercion of the group above it. Those at the pinnacle (or at the very top) — like those who experience what it's like to be at the very bottom — are likely to be most aware of what such a hierarchical structure is truly about. It's those of us in the middle that might need some help in making sense of where we exist in this structure and why. Being neither the most privileged nor the most disadvantaged, it would seem reasonable for there to be some uncertainty or even reluctance to admit that systems of oppression and privilege simultaneously coexist and are enacted through our everyday rituals.

Conventional criminological inquiry has generally been underwhelming in addressing three salient features of U.S. society: Institutional racism, socio-legal patriarchy, and the criminogenic features of capitalism. By under-examining these structural forces, we — as in criminologists — are largely disciplined to rely on a smorgasbord of criminological theories that, when taken together, represent a fanciful tautology, describing limited correlations while laundering them into narratives of causal inference.[5] Empirical claims about crime are conditioned by 1) what is defined as criminal and 2) how criminalized actions are policed, enforced, and measured. In the same way that Cesare Lombroso used *incarcerated* people to develop a flawed theory of trait-based criminality, much of the criminological research base continues to rely on ahistorical frameworks and cross-sectional research designs that sample from populations that are formally and socio-culturally tagged as criminal. We often differentiate between criminal and non-criminal actors and actions on the basis of whether they are formally caught, detected, or identified by justice institutions (i.e., police, courts, corrections). This means that we aren't necessarily studying criminal behavior at all, but *identified* criminal behavior. The data that we use are problematic, but that's not really the issue. The problem is a collective inability to articulate the fundamentally flawed nature of the data generation process and the insipid commitment to pretending that our work is value-neutral or "social scientific."

If we were from another planet and used criminal justice data as an accurate reflection of the serious and systematic harms that are knowingly and intentionally generated, we would be woefully flawed in our understanding of how things actually are and how they got this way. Domestic criminal justice data in the U.S., after all, would suggest that crime is something in which the wealthy and powerful have no interest in committing.[6] Wealthy people generally do not end up in jails and prisons relative to their working class and impoverished counterparts. Academics and non-academics alike are familiar with biases and injustices in the criminal justice system. But let me ask a rhetorical question: When was the last time you came across a compelling theory that *explains* crimes of the powerful? I'm not talking about a descriptive and revelatory case study about "under-examined" or "hidden" practices or incentives. For academic readers, when was the last time you read or observed a compelling theory in a mainstream journal that explained crimes of the powerful? Such omissions are far from accidental.

Criminology has historically provided micro- and mid-level explanations for *officially observed* legal offenses. Influenced significantly by behavioral psychology, there is a robust literature base that offers psycho-social explanations for phenomena conditioned – if not driven – by the political economy and material features of the social order. Phrased differently, criminology is consistent with the longstanding intellectual and academic practice of converting European racism into race; or taking what are racist and unscientific beliefs and laundering them into the discourse of racial differences. In studies of crime, deviance, and power, a similar process has taken place where the burden has been placed on the criminalized subject to help explain criminality. Why not flip the question: What is it about our socio-legal structure that contains criminogenic tendencies? What kind of violence, subjugation, coercion, and intellectual hegemony is needed to sustain our systems of production and consumption?

Even within the Crimes of the Powerful brand,[7] there is unintended obfuscation in how we dichotomize labels of power. We often look upward at higher echelons of power, privilege, and influence, focusing on how elite actors and institutions contribute to harmful outcomes – some of them explicitly legal and some illegal. There are pros and cons of this approach, and one drawback is the implicit suggestion that there is an "us" and a "them" – or the non-powerful and the powerful as coherent locations. An analogy to the Occupy Movement, which coined the "we are the 99%" slogan to raise awareness of the disproportionate clout of the top 1% of the socioeconomic distribution, is useful here. Dichotomizing the 99% and the 1% in this way helps to accomplish a series of objectives, but it is reasonable to assume that the top 10% wishes they were in the top 2%, and those in the top 40% wish they could move up the ranks and be in the top 10, and so on. In real life, consider how the working poor still – through participation in rituals like Black Friday shopping and other forms of consumer spending, demonstrate that they, too, want to possess the latest brands that are endorsed by the celebrities and influencers of the day. If we could have Apple Air Pods, that would be nice, and if we could have the Apple Air Pods Pro, even better. In this way, "the powerful" are simultaneously critiqued and emulated. Resentment towards the ultra-privileged co-exists, without any obvious contradiction, by a desire to be as close to *them* as possible; not necessarily in our social relationships but in our lifestyles, patterns of consumption, and value systems. This is different from the lifestyles, patterns of consumption, and value systems conventionally represented among non-powerful individuals who are represented in arrest, prosecution, conviction, and incarceration data.

The sociological imagination

This book celebrates the process of connecting, and then explaining, our personal experiences as they related to broader institutional arrangements and structural forces. The benefit of this approach is that it will help us describe and explain how we, as individuals, interact with and are shaped by specific systems: Systems of consumption, recreation, regulation, criminalization, and control. From this perspective, we can more personally engage with big picture questions of criminogenic capital, or how our mode of economic organization and our *social* economic practices manifest themselves in everyday life. This is a qualitatively different kind of approach than beginning with definitions concerning who owns the means of production, or how neoliberal governance results in the increased commodification of everyday life. The analysis that I encourage you, the reader, to consider is one that takes the mundane and the relatable, and situates it within a sociological framework.

The dominant cultural and ideological ethos in the United States is historically one of self-determination and rugged individualism. Yet, we also generally understand that there are societal influences, institutional practices, and historical forces that shape how we act, think, and move through the world. The relationship between both structure and agency is a two-way street, where each "side" conditions and influences the other, just as the specific patches of soil and the specific roots and leaves of specific trees condition and influence the ecosystem around it, and vice versa. The world we are born into shapes us, but it is the actions and decisions of individual beings that also shape the world in turn. For this reason, whenever we attribute any human-related phenomena to *just* structure or *just* agency (or individual pathology), we risk providing a woefully inadequate (or reductionist) account.

Alcohol, bars, and normalized corruption

Major categories and instances of crime are inseparable from normal business.[8] In discourses of organized crime, for instance, there are words like *criminal underworld*, *black markets*, and *shadow economies* that suggest some meaningful difference between the licit and illicit spheres of commercial activity. Empirically speaking, however, any durable shadow market or systemic form of corruption fundamentally rests on a symbiosis between licit and illicit actors, organizations, and processes that implicate everyone from "petty crooks to presents."[9] More relevant to the present study, the prohibition era offers a salient example of the relationships between organized crime, political corruption, and even the trajectory of federal law enforcement entities.[10] All across the spectrum, from reputable figures to stigmatized folk devils, a symbiosis existed across multiple hubs and spokes of power, privilege, and authority. Joseph Kennedy Sr., the Kennedy family patriarch, is (allegedly) one of the most high-profile benefactors among them. Always known for his savvy investments and business acumen, Kennedy, along with the oldest son of Franklin D. Roosevelt, worked directly with Winston Churchill to negotiate a coveted liquor trade deal.[11]

> The crooked connections between lawbreakers and law enforces ran all the way to the top in Washington. Jess Smith and Gaston Means had a lucrative sideline at Justice, selling government-confiscated whiskey to liquor smugglers. . . . The White House itself was a speakeasy during the Harding Administration.[12]

None of this should be genuinely surprising to contemporary readers. By definition, economically motivated crime reflects the pursuit of material interests, which all people share. Advancing one's material interests can be done via licit and illicit activities. Material interests, however, do not randomly appear.

> For capitalism to work, people must be taught to want to purchase, acquire, and consume vast amounts of products and services. . . . [In the class distribution of a society], some people will not have enough money to live up to the minimum standard of consumption deemed acceptable by the culturally defined values.[13]

Sociologist Robert K. Merton is often credited with explaining this in conceptual terms. Many of us share these culturally prescribed goals concerning material security, upward economic mobility, and social validation.

The institutional means – or the legally and socially recognized opportunities to work towards these goals – will vary for reasons outside of our control. We all are in a rat race or triangular hierarchy of some kind, and not all of us are equally situated to climb the ladder at the same pace or with the same prowess. As such, individuals will innovate in both prosocial and antisocial ways to advance the material and economic interests that are common to many of us. Culturally prescribed goals and institutionally available means are inseparable from the broader system of economic, political, and cultural arrangements where they exist. Our political economic systems are structured in a way where "it's winning that matters, not how you play the game."[14] This overarching ideology and its corresponding practices, are, as I will demonstrate in this book, criminogenic.

Political locations and the "critical" of critical criminology

Calling a political economic system *criminogenic* is important to put into context. In other words, if capitalism is problematic, how helpful is it to recognize it as such? If capitalism is inherently criminogenic and therefore responsible for the bulk of what we call crimes of the powerful, we are left with nothing more than a tautology, or circular form of reasoning. In a practical sense, this would mean that capitalism, and its corresponding political economy, are responsible for everything that might qualify as harmful. This, in turn, is an orientation that in attempting to account for everything, specifically explains very little.

Theory is not "an end in itself but a tool for analyzing substantive social problems."[15] The very existence of a subfield called crimes of the powerful presupposes that there are academics concerned with the harms that are generated by powerful actors, organizations, and systems. This is a political location that some readers might identify as being social justice oriented. I draw, in part, from the critical theory tradition, which examines the exploitation, repression, and alienation endemic to Western civilization.[16] As Stephen Bronner, puts it, critical theory

> refuses to identify freedom with any institutional arrangement or fixed system of thought. It questions the hidden assumptions and purposes of competing theories and existing forms of practice . . . [and] insists that thought must respond to the new problems and possibilities for liberation that arise from changing historical circumstances.[17]

Much has been written about the degree to which Marxism can make sense of crime.[18] A particular mode of Marxist analysis is necessary but insufficient for understanding crimes of the powerful.[19] More specifically a Marxist approach is less helpful for explaining crime events, but offers the most utility in providing a coherent theory of both criminal justice and distributive justice. The works of Karl Marx cannot, on their own, offer any meaningful explanatory narrative for crime, criminality, and criminalization in the United States or in the Global North more broadly. However, the dialectic approach, or a historical materialist analysis, can and does offer insights into theories of criminal justice.

At a time when critical race theory and critical legal studies are enjoying an interdisciplinary reinvigoration, I want to note here that critical theory engages very differently with any particular Marxist perspective. It focuses less on materialist conceptions of economic forces and more on the political and cultural machinations of a social order. Critical theorists – particularly those most closely aligned with the Frankfurt School – historically focused on alienation and reification, its complicated relationship with Enlightenment ideas, its utopian idealism, and the role of ideology in shaping individual subjectivity. Despite a checkered track record of "success" (i.e., relevance, intelligibility) for North American audiences in and beyond academia, critical theory remains the province for clarifying conditions of oppression, opening avenues of inquiry, and stimulating alternative ways of thinking and being.[20] Through this book, I hope to offer a criminological perspective that is reasonably consistent with these ideals, but perhaps communicate them in a way that moves beyond the tired tropes and critiques of the Marxism or critical theory of yore. That is the political project embedded here.

As a final caveat, this book is not written with some sense of ethical virtue or a self-serving notion of being on intellectual or moral high ground. Nothing about being an academic qualifies any given researcher to be an authoritative source on being morally correct.[21] Despite the proliferation of social justice discourses in formal academic spaces, I am not writing this book to provide prescriptive or forward-looking preferences for what *could* or *might* be. It is not my place nor my mission to claim – in any direction – whether capitalism should stay or go, or whether any simplified notion of the *isms* (specifically capitalism, socialism, communism) are more or less problematic than any other. Nor is it my place to give readers any comfort on why they should approve or disapprove of any particular set of political or economic arrangements. It would be bold to think that I have something meaningful – let alone coherent – on what we *should* be doing on any systemwide scale. Plus, who cares what one person thinks, particularly an academic? In other words, I'm not arguing for how things *should* or *could* be. If sociology is "the study of why things don't have to be this way,"[22] then this book is my attempt to explain how some things actually are.

Notes

1 The irony of being tethered to a chair to write this book is not lost upon me. Indeed, the hardest thing about writing this book was physically sitting my ass down to write it.
2 Ken, Ivy. 2010. *Digesting Race, Class, and Gender – Sugar as Metaphor.* Palgrave Macmillan, p. 26.
3 Weber, Lynn. 2001. *Understanding Race, Class, Gender, and Sexuality: A Conceptual Framework.* McGraw-Hill, p. 15. Cited in Ken (2010:26).
4 Collins, Patricia Hill. 2008. *Black Feminist Thought: Knowledge, Consciousness, and the Politics of Empowerment.* Routledge, p. 11.
5 Tautologies – or a self-reinforcing argument that defies falsification – are deeply embedded in the way that academics use conventional criminological theories, which are the causal narratives for why some people commit crime and others do not. When one intellectually shallow theory does not apply, another equally limited theory is used to provide justification for utility of these theories as a whole. For example, if rational choice theory cannot account for some crime event, then perhaps it was low self-control, or association with delinquent peers, or being born to anti-social parents, or lead in the water, or low quality early childhood education, or the prenatal environment, or abnormal brain chemistry, or too much testosterone, or being born into a subculture of violence, or general strain, or residing in a gang "infested" social context, or just some unfortunate combination of existing in a social context where the only viable paths to upward economic mobility are criminalized as part of a racialized and political economic system of labor and caste control (e.g., prohibitionist drug policies, anti-vagrancy laws). The tautological nature of criminological theory is a critique that has been raised in other ways. For instance, Williams III (1984) raised the concern that criminological

theory was moving "towards a tautological position where knowledge will be gained primarily from what we measure, which in turn will be based on what we already know" (p. 92). See Williams, Frank P. III. 1984. "The Demise of the Chronological Imagination: A Critique of Recent Criminology." *Justice Quarterly* 1:91–106.

6 Godwin, William. 1793. *An Enquiry Concerning Political Justice*. Vol. II. London.

7 I am intentionally using the word *brand* instead of *subfield* or *area of concentration*. All subfields, to various degrees, engage in forms of branding, which reflect, in part, how a set of ideas are perceived, experienced, and organized.

8 Chambliss, William J. 1988. *On the Take: From Petty Crooks to Presidents*. 2nd ed. Indiana University Press, p. 53.

9 Chambliss (1988).

10 Sandbrook, Dominic. 2012. "How Prohibition Backfired and Gave America an Era of Gangster and Speakeasies." *The Guardian*. August 25 (www.theguardian.com/film/2012/aug/26/lawless-prohibition-gangsters-speakeasies).

11 Maier, Thomas. 2015. *When Lions Roar – The Churchills and the Kennedys*. Penguin Random House; see also David Nasaw. 2012. *The Patriarch: The Remarkable Life and Turbulent Times of Joseph P. Kennedy*. Penguin Press.

12 Weiner, Tim. 2012 *Enemies – A History of the FBI*. Random House, p. 52.

13 Chambliss (1988:210).

14 Box, Steven. 1981. *Deviance, Reality and Society*. London Holt, Rinehart & Winston. See also Braithwaite, John. 1988. "White-Collar Crime, Competition, and Capitalism: Comment on Coleman." *American Journal of Sociology* 94(3):627–632.

15 Matthews, Roger. 2014. Realist Criminology. Palgrave Macmillan. p. 30.

16 Bronner, Stephen Eric. 2017. *Critical Theory: A Very Short Introduction*. Oxford University Press, p. 1.

17 Bronner (2017: 1).

18 Cowling, Mark. 2011. "Can Marxism Make Sense of Crime?" *Global Discourse* 2(2):59–74.

19 Lasslett, Kristian. 2010. "Scientific Method and the Crimes of the Powerful." *Critical Criminology* 18(3):211–228.

20 Bronner (2017:8).

21 See Nair, Yasmin. 2017. "The Dangerous Academic is an Extinct Species." *Current Affairs* (www.currentaffairs.org/2017/04/the-dangerous-academic-is-an-extinct-species).

22 Ivy Ken defines sociology as "the study of why things don't have to be this way." See https://sociology.columbian.gwu.edu/ivy-ken.

1 Alcohol, nightlife, and crimes of the powerful

Academics, in particular, like to use words like *neoliberalism, carcerality, ideological hegemony, racial capitalism, necropolitics,* or the *racial capitalist patriarchy* to describe complex relationships, processes, dynamics, and configurations of power. Sometimes we use these words without defining them,[1] or we use them expecting their meaning to be clear to the reader. These words refer to complex, historical, and evolving *systems* and *processes*. They also signal the political location of the writer. Because I use similar words to capture a series of complex processes, this chapter first beings with outlining my approach to defining key terms and concepts that occur throughout the text.

Socio–legal contradictions, at the core

The United States is founded on a social contract philosophy organized around protecting life, liberty, and property. In a country that struggles to openly discuss class,[2] the very preoccupation with *tyranny of the majority* must be reconceptualized. This phrase is often portrayed in class-neutral terms as a safeguard against the possibility that, say, the Anti–Federalists, or some majority party that constitute 51% or more of the populace, would trample the rights of the remaining 49% or fewer, who happen to be Federalists or some minority party. Such a phrase, though, is not really about whether one party over-dominates the other in a two–party system. The Founders and Framers, like the Greeks and the Romans, were fundamentally preoccupied with an age-old dilemma: How can a political system retain both stability and legitimacy when the *dispossessed many* could one day mobilize against the *propertied few*? As Johnson (1995:644) writes,

> One aim of the framers was to create a representative form of government that ensured against the democratic excesses resulting from the passion and self-interest that so troubled Madison. As the concern with "self-interest" suggests, the primary concern of the framers may have been with the tyranny of the majority over the *property rights* of the minority. With the experience of government under the Articles of Confederation, including the famous debtors' uprising known as Shay's Rebellion, fresh in mind, the

Federalists feared that, unless checks were put in place, the *debtor majority* might trample the rights of the *creditor minority* in the political process, as well as in the courts.[3]

(emphasis mine)

James Madison emphasized what he perceived to be fundamental flaws in true democracies, which he characterized as "spectacles of turbulence and contention" that "have ever been found incompatible with personal security, or the rights of property; and [that] have in general been as short in their lives, as they have been violent in their deaths" (Federalism No. 63, at 425). To some, it might seem obvious that the "creditor minority" might represent the bourgeoise and the "debtor majority" the proletariat, although this analogy is imperfect and comes with its share of liabilities. In this dichotomy between the non-working rich (bourgeoise) and the laboring poor (proletariat), the functional role of the middle class is to serve as a buffer between these structurally opposed groups. The working poor – via upward mobility – could gain access to a middle-class identity, and are indoctrinated to support the prevailing belief systems that legitimize the institutions created for the primary benefit of the bourgeoise. The middle class is a functional buffer between these two groups and gives legitimacy to a political economy that extracts from the many to support the capital accumulation of the few.

These relationships are not abstract but cemented into the very Constitutional fabric of the United States. To account for this probabilistic outcome, the Framers and Founders intended for the U.S. Senate to be comprised of wealthy landowners that were purposively chosen by state legislatures. The Framers and Founders settled on the language found in Article 1, Section 3, concerning the selection of Senators. It would take the 17th Amendment to free the U.S. Senate from the insulation that the Founders and Framers did not need to justify or debate in any meaningful way. It would have been unnecessary to specify – and unsurprising to the social order of the time – that both eligible and actual Senators would be white, male, and land-owning, and be vetted by the elite networks of the various state legislatures.[4] In no uncertain terms, the 17th Amendment has been criticized by the Republican Party in recent years under the rhetorical cloud of state's rights and curbing federal power despite recognizing how corrupt Senate elections were *prior* to the 17th Amendment's existence.[5] In short, repealing the 17th Amendment would further curtail "excesses of democracy" and provide a protective institutional barrier for curbing the masses.

Of course, these power dynamics are neither deterministic nor absolute. They produce outcomes that are probabilistic. Laws and political systems appear stable and fixed until they are not, and there have been incremental and structural reforms at various historical points. Exceptions to the rule (or structural trend), however, do not negate the existence of the structural trends. My starting point is that this country's socio-legal infrastructure is aligned with the logics of capital accumulation, and therefore subject to the same contradictions of capital that have been studied by everyone from Karl Marx to David Harvey to Patricia Hill Collins to Boots Riley to Aviva Chomsky.[6]

Prior to the Declaration of Independence or the viability of a constitutional convention, the 13 colonies themselves were, functionally speaking, corporate forms.[7] With the U.S. Constitution being so central for actual U.S. governance and symbolic, socially constructed American identity, it is important to audit the kind of power structure that it legitimizes. I share these examples because they communicate what the state is fundamentally about. If we understand that state-corporate power is central to the very Constitution of this country, and that ours is a system of attempting to legitimize, through appearances, structurally contradictory objectives (foremost being the equality of people versus the fundamentally unequal requirements of capital), then we can abandon any pretense about the state being some neutral arbiter for competing claims. State power and corporate power are and have always been intimate bedfellows. With this overarching view in mind, I now turn to what it means to study the state in criminological terms.

Operationalizing the state for criminological analysis

The *carceral state*[8] and the *racial capitalist patriarchy* – or any other terms used to reference configurations of power[9] – are not monolithic entities that *do* things. The law does not, as Donald Black's well-known thesis suggests, *behave*,[10] and society does not expect or demand anything of anyone. The U.S., or "the West," or the 1%, do not wake up in the morning, brush their teeth, and impose a coherent 1-year, 3-year, and 5-year agenda on others. It is specific people, both as individuals and as organizational representatives, that do things. Human beings are the ones who make both conscious and unconscious decisions that influence what dominant groups will seek to recognize as "history." The patterns of their actions are what we label, diagnose, and study, and subsequently organize into words or labels like "McDonaldization," or "gender-based violence," or "institutional racism." In short, any coherent source of power, like the carceral state, white supremacy, patriarchy, or settler colonial violence, are references to the collective actions and reactions of individuals and groups, who are participating in various forms of conflict and cooperation to advance their respective interests. The study of systems, then, is the study of how the corresponding interests in such systems are influential in what people do and why they do it.

Whether it's a study on border militarization, or of European colonialism, or American chattel slavery, or contemporary capitalism, none of these *systems* refer to static epochs of societal organization in which humans are reduced to automatons, merely carrying out the logics of their position(s) (e.g., we are not reducible to whether we own the means of production). Such systems also have intra- and inter-group dissidents and supporters. Street-level bureaucrats, educators, farmers, political sycophants, and political dissidents existed in every one of these contexts and their individual agency actively contributed to the contested evolution of such systems. Subjugated groups did not merely internalize or adopt the logics that others sought to impose, but repurposed and reconfigured them for their own use.[11] A structural analysis is therefore one that accounts for the contingent and contested nature of powerful systems, and how everyday people make sense of their own self-interests in relation to structural forces. How events play out are ultimately about what people decide to do, but human decisions are generally patterned in ways that we can understand in explanatory terms.

But it remains insufficient to attribute all kinds of harms or negative outcomes to "the state." The state, like the business class, is not a monolithic entity that thinks, acts, or responds to anything in any coherent or consistent way. Intra-group divisions do not negate the existence of that overarching group, and their collective role in a class society.[12] Group divisions exist *within* elite private and public capital because "their distinct location in the economy creates requirements that are manifest as political interests that are incompatible with the interests of other capitalist class factions."[13]

Due to this intra-group competition, political capital generally retains leverage over economic capital, as it retains the discretionary authority to prioritize one industry or set of actors of others (e.g., prioritizing coal versus solar tax subsidies and incentives, prioritizing rail transportation or bicycle infrastructure, whatever). The state retains power over any individual corporation within the ecosystem of industries, but can buckle to the demands of an organized collective of businesses.[14] Organized private enterprises can take the form of chambers of commerce industry trade groups, where they might leverage their collective private capital *against* existing political leaders by supporting challenging candidates, or make campaign finance contributions contingent on the adoption of a favorable policy agenda. The business of government is business, but business is a contested arena. The ruling ideas are those of the ruling class, but this "class" also has competing visions for how to materially organize our social world. In short, it should not be surprising that there "is no close personal friendship between the top executives of the major distilling corporations . . . their relations vary somewhere between friendly rivalry and intense personal antagonism."[15]

Nightlife economies

Some might wonder why I use the term *nightlife economy* instead of *nightlife industry*, or just *nightlife*. After all, we – as in people who have worked in nightlife – use terms like "industry night" and ask questions like, "Are you in the industry?" to negotiate insider/outsider status. As a stylistic decision, I view *economy* as a broader and thus more inclusive word compared to *industry*. It also lends itself to the presumption of inherent stratification and conflict among various regulatory and commercial actors, whereas *industry* might conjure an idea of some relatively homogenous group of private sector actors.[16] Nightlife *economy* also implicates the modes of governance that, in turn, can be understood not only as the formal *on-the-books* regulatory structures, but also "the outcome of subtle organizational and interpersonal power-plays."[17] From this system-level orientation, one can better engage with how "interorganizational network[s] may be conceived as a political economy concerned with the distribution of two scarce resources, money and authority."[18] The nightlife economy therefore refers to the individuals, groups, and both formal and informal structures that surround the consumption of alcohol in commercial settings. My empirical focus is on bars and nightclubs, and I study them with an emphasis on how political economic structures influence how patrons and employees experience bars and nightclubs, both as places of ritualistic socialization and alcohol consumption, but also as occupational settings and subcultures.

Political economies and structural analyses

The components of a social structure can only be understood as they relate to one another.[19] To fully understand crime, criminality, and criminalization, we must appreciate their relationship to broader features in our political economy. Defining *political economy* varies by context and application.[20] I use the term to reference the social interactions between politics and economics, or how individuals and groups of people organize themselves around material interests, negotiating various forms of conflict and compromise. Bars and nightclubs are organized around the ritualistic consumption of a specific product, alcohol, and the aesthetic consumption of lifestyles. To study alcohol *consumption* is to study systematic practices, like the manufacture and distribution of these products, their supply chains and markets. To study aesthetic consumption is to also focus on the rituals, cultural associations, and the formal and informal rules that influence how, why, and where people gather in groups big and small to socialize in these spaces. Nightlife is home to a wide array of interests, and this economic sector exists in both cooperation and conflict with a variety of agencies, "including police, local authorities, health trusts, the licensed trade, security companies, residents groups, and charitable/voluntary agencies."[21] The role of the state, the processes of lawmaking, and the symbiotic and conflicting interests between these various public and private enterprises, are all part of this ecosystem. Replace the word *ecosystem* with *political economy*, and we are now on the same page.

What is crime?

There is no inherent connection between *legality* and *morality*, so there should be no inherent moral associations with the terms *crime* and *criminal*. In plain English, just because something is legal does not make it right, and just because something is illegal does not make it wrong. For some readers, our undergraduate students might agree that triple posting photos of your mediocre breakfast might constitute a "crime," and charging for the use of overhead bin space on an airplane should be "criminal." These words are used in ways that reflect social norms, mores, taboos, and conventions, but for a social scientific analysis we must be as specific as possible with the terms that we use. As such, much of what belongs squarely in the domain of "crimes of the powerful" actually reflects things that are, technically speaking, perfectly legal. Calling something *legal* a *crime* is contradictory, but only if using a legalistic definition of *crime*. Calling something legal a *systematic and intentionally produced source of harm* readily fixes that technicality.

Legalistic definitions of crime are inherently political and contingent on who gets to define crime. Some of the most harmful systems are not really crimes at all, at least from the technical or legalistic sense. European colonialism, settler colonialism in North America, genocidal actions against indigenous peoples, chattel slavery, Jim Crow laws, the electoral college, poll taxes and ID requirements, drone-strikes on civilians and non-enemy combatants, the mere existence of Guantanamo Bay, redlining and gerrymandering, discriminatory sub-prime lending, curtailment of reproductive rights, the exclusionary politics of protection for women of color, anti-sodomy laws, and covert drug experimentation on incarcerated subjects are all examples that come to mind, but you might have many more of your own. In light of the legalistic shortcomings for defining crime, we must be open to a *sociological* definition that includes not only those activities that are formally designated as misdemeanors and felonies at a given time, but those actions, systems, and practices that generate *avoidable* harm and suffering to human beings. In an ideal or prescriptive framework, legality and morality should at least correlate. In the empirical, descriptive world that we live in, it's safe to claim that legality and morality have no inherent relationship. This is important to cover at the outset, considering that some of the materials featured in Chapters 5 and 6 of this book include both technical violations of the law, and normatively deviant actions that nevertheless comply with the law.

A mentor and friend, Ray Michalowski, articulated crime as a label for actions that 1) are of public concern and 2) are criminalized by the state.[22] This second requirement can be challenging for crimes-of-the-powerful scholarship, since state crime and state-corporate crime are, by definition, unlikely to be criminalized by the state. Activities that are central to normal state functioning, or the logical imperatives of state-building and state power, are most likely to be beyond the purview of criminological analysis, and will certainly be omitted from U.S. criminal law (which U.S. court would try George H.W. Bush or Dick Cheney as war criminals?). State and corporate power, both independently and together, are organized around the logics and imperative of capital accumulation. So, it should follow that there are harms, including activities that many might understand as both criminal and corrupt, are not merely omitted from the criminal law but are actively incentivized, protected, and legitimized by regulatory structures and ideological belief systems.[23]

It is an empirical question (that is, it is knowable) to ask if large-scale, organized systems of corruption and social harm are embedded and enabled through legal and political institutions. To study this empirically, one must examine the political economy that contains such institutions, and the ways that real human beings experience and negotiate their varied interests within these institutional arrangements.

Unlike the ways in which we come to understand gravity, photosynthesis, ocean currents, and mitochondria, our criminological phenomena are made, as opposed to being found in naturally occurring phenomena. Concepts of crime – like the criminal – must be socially and legally created before they can be said to exist.[24] In other words, the felon and felony are human-made labels that reflect the existence of authorities that name, claim, and assign these labels of criminality. Taken together, my orientation focuses on criminalization – or the processes by which specific actions and actors become subject to the purview of formal social control. Most importantly, criminalization is not random. There are knowable forces and processes that guide law-making, which in turn guide the existence of crime events and criminal actors. These forces – or configurations of power – reflect economic institutions, political structures, and the embedded contradictions therein.[25] In short, crime can be understood as a function of how political, economic, and social systems are arranged in a given society. By extension, the ways that criminal laws come about and the ways that criminal justice systems are designed are similarly reflective of particular configurations of power, order, and control.

What is power?

"Is the criminal born or made?" "What is the nature–nurture dynamic in explaining the criminal offender?" These questions are as old as they are misguided, since such questions imply that an answer can be found in the pathology, traits, or biographies of individuals. We might have started from a different perspective entirely, and instead ask whether our everyday institutions are structurally generative of mass-scale harms, which include interpersonal injuries and transgressions. Crimes-of-the-powerful scholarship, in many ways, offers an understanding of how "crime is not a byproduct of an otherwise effectively working political economy [but] a main product of that political economy."[26] If we take into account how New York City and London would not have been logistically or materially possible without the respective institutions of chattel slavery and colonialism, and how the material prosperity of the industrialized West relies on the continued subjugation of other peoples and places, we could be more inclined to view crimes of the powerful as "a cornerstone on which the political and economic relations of democratic-capitalist societies are constructed."[27]

I make additional references to colonialism in Chapter 2, but we cannot reduce everything to colonialism or any other era of systematic violence and forceful dispossession. Systems of oppression evolve and devolve, and human history can be understood in part as a story of rise-and-fall cycles of imperial advancement, which includes conflicts over material resources. Power is exercised and configured in temporal-spatial ways, and capital similarly varies. Both are experienced differently across time and place. This is why I refer to political economies and nightlife economies as plural contexts that are similar but also different from each other. Variation does not mean "anything goes." Power is both structural and interpersonal; it is in the relationship between who gives orders and who receives them, and it is in the algorithms and standard operating procedures of any type of system and organizational structure. Power, like legal force and political capital, is something that can be bought, sold, and subverted in the regulatory and political landscape of Metropolis East and its corresponding nightlife economy. The ways in which power is configured in the nightlife economy is thus a central focus of this text.

In tying it all together, there are studies of power, corruption, and nightlife economies that predate my own. In the 1970s, sociologist Norman Denzin found that crimes of cooperation and competition were widely prevalent in the liquor industry. Specific norms governed how individuals would negotiate price fixing, mutual concealment of violations, and advanced notice of anticipated regulatory actions. In a contingent process, the regulators and the regulated were part of an ecosystem of conflict and symbiosis. These actors understood that the laws were either designed in an unfair or unrealistic manner, and that legal compliance was a game-like function. "We break the law every day. If you think I go to bed at night worrying about it, you're crazy. Everybody breaks the law. The liquor laws are insane, anyway."

Denzin also found robust evidence of "bribery, kickbacks antitrust violations, payoffs and the circumvention of legal codes," and makes clear that these practices "may or may not be specific to this industry" (p. 919). I am unsure whether it is a good thing or a bad thing that I will be telling a similar story, but from research conducted 40 years later. But no matter *our* age (so long as you're of age), a wealth of both sociological and criminological theory and praxis awaits each of us at the nearest bar, nightclub, or tavern – whether we go to these spaces as patrons, employees, or curious observers. By examining a nightlife economy as a site of conflict and symbiosis, we can come to better understand and explain the corruption that is endemic both to nightlife and non-nightlife economies and understand the form and function of *corrupt capital*.

Alcohol and crimes of the powerful – a historical sampling

It is usually preferable to use observable things to bring theoretical abstractions to life. From the design of the Bombay Sapphire Gin bottle (or just the history of the gin and tonic)[28] to the logo and images on a bottle of Captain Morgan, there are countless invitations to engage with crimes of the powerful. Colonialism and the colonial era offer multidisciplinary platforms for studying the evolution of views about both alcohol and people. The production of spirits, like rum, and the raw materials required, like sugarcane and molasses, were just some of the commercial interests sustained via direct military force and colonial rule, which were robustly advanced by the Dutch, the English, and the French.[29] The impacts of these material practices extend far beyond the confines of economic structure or political economy, but include how people made sense of their own world and material relationships to alcohol.

The colonial era was one where "access to alcohol was a prerogative of dominion" as its consumption among subjugated peoples was viewed as a risk factor for insurrection and rebellion.[30] Both then and today, big business remains robustly defended by militarized forms of protection and coercion. Labor is not organized in strict colonial frameworks, but we can't say that our labor systems today are totally divorced from them, either. Alcohol – or really, the physical product, the mode of producing it, and the regulatory and social regimes of consumption – thus offer a diversity of entry points into studying capital, crime, and power.

Alcohol and crimes of the powerful today

Alcohol affects the lives and livelihoods of those who struggle with various kinds of addictions; there are people whose lives have been permanently disrupted and prematurely ended due to DUI/DWI related events; there are children who have traumatic memories concerning aggressive and depressive behavior from alcoholic family members; and there are sexual assaults and harassments that occur across various types of environments that correlate with how alcohol is used. The public health costs associated with alcohol-related illness and pre-ventable disease is one way of framing this in dollars and cents, as is the cost of criminal-justice-related events that are also patterned by alcohol consumption (e.g., intimate partner violence, aggression).

It is here where it makes sense to talk about the winners – or the beneficiaries – of how we consume alcohol. It took a lot of work for our consumption of alcohol to become what it is today. Some examples are warranted here. The alcohol lobby, along with restaurant chain partners like Hooters, TGI Friday's, and Red Lobster, once agitated against a White House measure that imposed stricter drunk driving laws for the country. In criminology and in scientific inquiry more broadly, statistics and data-driven analyses can be heavily politi-cized,[31] and the direction of this politicization often aligns with commercial interests, as is the case here. The restaurants specifically claimed such regulation "would cut into their alcoholic beverage sales without appreciably reducing drunk driving."[32] Never mind that at the time, public health data showed that approximately "40% of all highway fatalities [were] alcohol-related."[33]

Similar to Big Tobacco and Big Soda, the alcohol industry has funded scien-tific research to promote the view that "moderate drinking" is healthy.[34] While this conveniently provides me with a defense mechanism for that daily glass of wine that I'm, scientifically speaking, *supposed to be having*, it is a practical example of how science is politicized in furtherance of commercial interests. To be clear, public and private interests have significant influence on what and how something is studied, and the regulatory frameworks that might govern the relevant product, technology, or practice. Whether or not someone identifies with Mothers Against Drunk Driving, or joins a temperance movement, or participates in "Sober October" or "Dry January" will be a function of these political, legal, and economic forces.

Alcohol is thus an arena where businesses generate positive outcomes for some and high-risk consequences for others. For companies and industries that generate these "pros" and "cons" – it takes a lot of effort to get to a place where the "pros" are viewed as so important that the industry becomes accepted as part of the natural state of things. Viewed in another way, it is not by *chance* or *accident* that we come to possess these material and social relationships with alcohol, in the same way that it is not *by accident* or happenstance that Coca-Cola and PepsiCo dominate the junk food and carbonated beverage industry, and it is not by chance or accident that public transportation is woefully underdeveloped in the United States while U.S. consumers are encouraged to change their cars every three to five years. To secure this material prosperity, a global ecosystem of raw materials, labor inputs, and consumption must be cultivated, sustained, and reproduced. The line, then, between legitimate and economic *best practices* and criminogenic systems must therefore be studied sociologically and not legalistically. We must be open to the possibility that actions defined as formal crimes are insufficient for sociological analysis, when actions defined as legitimate practices are also generative of significant social harms and human misery. While there are indeed some dry counties and some limitations on the extent to which alcohol companies and alcohol industry business operate, today the alcohol industry – like virtually all other "Big Industries," remains highly consolidated, powerful, and omnipresent in both private life and public policy.[35] This connection between alcohol and patterns of *consumption* – and the broader projects they support – is therefore a central theme of this book.

Zooming out for a moment, consider the phrases Big Agra, Big Auto, Big Coal, Big Pharma, Big Soda, Big Tobacco, Big Tech. What do such big industries have in common? What makes industry . . . well . . . *big*? These powerful industries emerged as part of a historical process of specific actors and organizations. Their efforts, many of which were contested, generated enough economic and political clout that when the harmful effects of their practices were made salient, their commercial interests nevertheless prevailed. Specifically, when there have been conflicts between private profit and the public interest (e.g., public health or effects on the public commons like water, air, soil quality, or the habitats of other living beings), these *big* industries have employed a wide array of both harmful and criminal strategies to secure their ever-increasing pathways to market control, which in turn augments their growing political, economic, and social capital. Of course, this is not a unidirectional process, or one that goes unchallenged and uncontested, which is what Ivy Ken (2010) meant when she underscored how it not only takes a lot of work to *generate* some institutional arrangement, but a whole lot more to *maintain it* in the face of various conflicts and challenges to that same arrangement. Similar to the agricultural sciences and farming practices that generate what we call *food*, there are systems, processes, sciences, and cultural norms that contribute to the conversion of raw natural materials into commodified food products available at a grocery store near you. These systems, whether of food, crime control, financial markets, electoral politics, city governance, and nightlife activity, require active management for their continuation, especially in the face of efforts to change or modify them. Before we proceed any further, let us take a step back and reflect on how we might experience a capitalist subjectivity in the context of alcohol and nightlife.

Pregaming with the sociological imagination

It's a Saturday afternoon, and you have plans to meet with friends before heading out to a popular nightlife area of the city nearest you. Upon entering the liquor store, you might notice various marketing and advertising displays, with promotional materials and thematic paraphernalia strategically placed about the store. Just like the seasonal section of the grocery store, there are summer spirits and winter whiskies that need to move off the shelves. The products are designed to convey particular feelings, themes, and motifs that should connect with some prototypical buyer, and there is something for virtually every person, mood, and budget. Some products look like vintage medicine bottles, others like liquid candy. Higher up on the shelves, or in locked displays behind the shopkeeper's counter are bottles that look like sophisticated elixirs – with price points to match. At the shelving's bottom we might find items that could be mistaken for windshield wiper fluid or an enzyme treatment product that belongs nowhere else but inside some part of your car, or a deviant relative in crises.

If we were attending some different social gathering (e.g., a tailgate, birthday party, game night), the purchase made at the liquor store might correlate with the specific theme, class location,[36] or symbolic marker we wish to communicate when we arrive. For a homemade sangria or booze-forward punch (triple sec is of importance here), the DeKuyper and Hiram Walker brands offer no frills options. This section of the liquor store is analogous to the ingredients section of your neighborhood food mart: Like allspice, bay leaves, and cinnamon sticks, there are only so many varieties that can compete with each other on the shelf. As such, you'll seldom find more than one or two brands of apple liqueur, blue curacao, butterscotch schnapps, etc., in the cordials section of the store.

Higher priced products might already come packaged in a box that needs no additional wrapping. If intended as a gift, the presentation value is part of the whole experience, making them perfect for special occasions. Flavored vodkas can be found in youthful and effeminate branding and marketing materials, named with target audiences in mind. *White Girl Rosé* and *Skinny Girl Vodka* stand in stark contrast to the *Ron de Jeremy* bottle design, but all of them were designed with demographic targets in mind. Aged scotch bottles are adorned with more distinguished, if not aristocratic-looking, symbols and fonts. Like the ubiquitous recognition of the Monopoly man, some readers might recall a logo featuring an old man, centered on the bottle and captured in confident mid-stride, with a top hat and walking cane for posterity.[37]

You're also correct if you think this thought experiment is too froufrou or superfluous. I mean, we're at the liquor store. It doesn't have to be that deep. Surely there is another customer there, in search of something utilitarian like a domestic light beer that they don't plan on enjoying for the taste. Its sole purpose is for tomorrow's tailgate games, like beer pong or flip cup. A different customer grabs whatever red wine is on sale just so they don't show up empty-handed to a family event. We could go on forever. The point is that, no matter what you're looking for or why you are there, there are teams of people – in offices far away and many of them generously compensated – that 1) design and manufacture the product and 2) make it readily available for purchase at countless locations across multiple continents. From Brussels to Bogotá, from Singapore to Santo Domingo, a crisp Heineken is available for purchase, and there are robust systems in place to make it so.

If you haven't already put this book down in disgust, you should know that we are not even at the halfway mark of this thought experiment (bear with me). Tonight's gathering is at a friend's pregame – or the social gathering where alcohol is consumed in a private residential space prior to collectively moving to some commercial or public space to presumably socialize (and perhaps drink) some more. Upon arrival, the host has music playing from a curated playlist on Spotify or some other major streaming service. Some tracks from this "weekend party hits" playlist will contain lyrical references to feelings, activities, and cultural associations related to the general state of inebriation, and others with direct reference to alcohol products and brands. The lyrics of these songs, much like the lyrics of many *Billboard* Top 100 tracks, are embedded not only with values and claims associated with material and interpersonal success (e.g., being wealthy, sexually desirable, and socially prolific), but also serve as effective adverts for some "make and model" of alcohol – or a type of spirit and a specific brand. Examples include cognac (e.g., Hennessy),[38] tequila (e.g., Patron),[39] wine (e.g., Moscato),[40] or brands of champagne (e.g., Moet, Ace of Spades,[41] Cristal).[42] Activities like popping bottles, making it rain, and whatever the vernacular of the day is for *getting f*cked up*[43] are part and parcel to these social and cultural value systems that may not be exclusively about alcohol itself, but where alcohol plays a supporting role for the protagonists of the story.

Human geographies of alcohol consumption

From the pregame area, we enter "the strip," or urban environment where bars and clubs are clustered around a small number of blocks or streets. Bars, pubs, and clubs are anticipating our arrival, with employees in their set positions for the night. Many of us are familiar with observing *others* when they've had too much to drink (never yourself, of course), and there are serious and irreversible harms associated when alcohol consumption goes too far or is paired with other high-risk activities (e.g., sexual assaults, DUI/DWI-related fatalities). As such, the nightlife arena might have a visible infrastructure for minimizing foreseeable harms associated with these practices, with a mixture of private and public institutions and agents serving in security-related roles.[44] Curb-space might be created and reserved for ride-share services to more efficiently (and safely) pick up and drop off passengers. Barricades, traffic cones, parking signs, and other subtle adjustments all underscore how nighttime mobilities differ from daytime rhythms, and there might be bicycle cops, police details, and other strategically placed objects that nudge people towards and away from certain actions and movements. Street vendors, food trucks, and performing artists are also in the mix, as everyone is using the sidewalks, streets, and public areas in slightly different ways and drawing from different customs and rituals.

Both time and space influence the rhythm of these environments, and the social world found in one nightlife area can be radically different if you are there at 11am versus 11pm. The human beings who regularly occupy one of these periods may never know who or what exists in the other. Those who are working through the night, for example, are not accountable for the same kinds of deliverables and performances that we'd expect from the randomly selected office-worker that moves through this same space during the daytime. Bounders, bartenders, and barbacks alike are not spending their first hours at work chipping away at e-mails that need attention. PowerPoint slides, Excel spreadsheets, and deliverables to/from direct reports are not central to the jobs that many nightlife workers do. The occupational culture is organized around different kinds of deliverables and productivity measures.[45]

If we are in a major metropolitan city, we might take notice of the diversity of options available for a range of lifestyles, cultures, and recreational preferences. Communities of all kinds have a chance of carving out their own niche for nightlife leisure and recreation. Sometimes they are wildly successful, with entire sections of an urban environment serving as a hub for a particular political or lifestyle location. After all, there are opportunities, when the sun goes down, to express different parts of oneself. The person who presents themselves in one way at 1pm might share lesser-known features of their personhood and personality at 1am. But we should not romanticize nightlife or treat it as a stable utopia. Nightlife surely offers safe spaces in some contexts and for some people, opening windows for transgressing and playfully subverting dominant social norms and conventions. But we can still find many of the dominant hegemonies similarly replicated at night.

Examples are found wherever we choose to look for them. Primarily white spaces don't have to advertise themselves as such, while "hip hop night" and "urban night" can serve as coded signals for demarcating a space socially organized as Black or non-white. Patriarchal capitalist values are also thoroughly on display.[46] Admission standards and nightclub marketing materials reinforce the notion that packs of dudes are undesirable patrons of the [straight] club. This heteronormative force manifests itself in policies and practices that seek to produce male–to–female ratios that cater to a patriarchal notion of courtship. Those who never set foot in this nightlife environment might nevertheless catch glimpses of these gendered projects on the radio: "*Ladies free before midnight*," "*Ladies drink free all night*," "*Ladies 18, Gentlemen 21 and up!*" Other gendered projects are far less subtle: You can order popular shooters by names like *buttery nipple*, *red headed slut*, *blow jobs*, *aborted fetus*, *slippery nipple*, or *screaming orgasm* – all of which simply underscore that we occupy a social world where one can say these words to another human being, prompting in turn the presentation of a purchasable product: The drink. Because I like to think of sociology as "the study of why things don't have to be this way"[47] it's worth mentioning here that it is possible to exist in some other social universe, similar to ours, where the names of the such products are gendered differently. Perhaps in some other time and place, we might ask the bartender for *the fuqboy*, *the dad-bod*, or the *one-minute wonder*. Since we are on the topic of phalluses and objectifications of the body, we might reflect on the symbolic meaning of all those plastic and inflatable penises that frequently accompany the stereotypical bachelorette party.[48]

The velvet rope and class consciousness

Unbeknownst to most, the velvet rope at the entrance of the modern nightclub can function as a sorting tool to create and administer class consciousness. At the entrance of the modern nightclub, you'll find that the pathways of entry correlate with the kinds of economic and social capital that you are prepared to exchange. Based on your presentation of either, you will be sorted accordingly, but to the untrained eye this can be easy to miss. To those that may have never been to a nightclub – or simply have no reference point or recollection for what the entrance of a busy nightclub might look like – worry not. You don't need to be a social scientist or a club goer to observe how lines metaphorically evoke class consciousness and then physically sort human beings into these subjective states. On various occasions, many of us will have experienced *some* iteration of what it means to have our mobility and physical environment regulated in this way. People are not being sorted at random, of course, but in a manner that corresponds to their material and political capital (e.g., how much they spend, or what kind of personhood is represented by their ID card, or their dress code, or their country of citizenship). Airports, theme parks, and hotel lobbies regularly do this.

Commodifying time and space

Recall, if you will, the ways in which lines (or queues, for my two British friends) are salient throughout the entire airport experience. You arrive at the airport and begin the check-in process. Those with more airline status (or an airline-affiliated credit card) might have one sort of line, and First-Class passengers may find themselves in another. The security theater of TSA soon follows.[49] At most airports in the United States you will be promptly directed to enter one of three types of security checkpoint lines. One is for regular passengers, another for the generally more efficient and faster-moving TSA Pre-Check, and a third for its *even faster*[50] private sector (and biometrically invasive) counterpart, CLEAR.[51] The two faster-moving lines have different access costs and membership requirements. What's more, there are different rules for different lines, with a clear rank-ordering between them.

While it can be useful to define power at the interpersonal level as the difference between who gives orders and who receives them, an additional way to define power as its systematically practiced is to see which groups are treated as though their time is more or less valuable. Time is a social and symbolic currency. After all, money can come and go, but time cannot be recuperated.[52] Prisoners *serve* time itself, whereas corporate executives have support staff who do everything they can to *make* time as productive and efficient as possible. We understand this at our social and cultural core, and it shows up in courtship rituals (e.g., being late to a date) and in angry online reviews concerning waiting times and delays. In other words, it is *better* and *more status-conferring* to spend less time waiting around. While the airport security experience can evoke class consciousness, a sense of equality momentarily returns as everyone is equally subject to either the millimeter wave scanner – where your genitalia barely escape the gaze of underpaid TSA performing artists[53] – all of which are part of the security theater.

Some of the well-traveled readers of this book might already claim TSA PreCheck or Global Entry as something they possess and enjoy. At some point, some readers might have felt something close to a sense of relief (*Thank goodness for PreCheck!*) or if not, a sense of wishful aspiration (*I really need to make time to apply for PreCheck!*). Depending on which group you're in, you might feel entitled to the benefits of your relatively privileged position, or you might feel hyper-conscious about how another group of people have it better than you. Alternatively, the entire airport experience might be so obnoxious that you may have never given this any thought whatsoever, and finding this entire section about lines and airports superfluous. The point is that whether in the nightlife setting or beyond, lines give order to different physical *and social* paths of entry into some regulated space. And whether it's airport security theater or the nightclub entrance, the line that you ultimately enter will often align with your class location, social capital, and material interests.

From the personal to the structural

From this perspective, we can more personally engage with big picture questions of criminogenic capital, or how our mode of economic organization, and our *social* economic practices manifest themselves in everyday life. This is a qualitatively different kind of approach than beginning with definitions concerning who owns the means of production, or how neoliberal governance results in the increased commodification of everyday life. The analysis that

I encourage you, the reader, to consider is one that takes the mundane and the relatable, and situates it within a sociological framework. It is here where I would like to begin bridging these reflections on lines and waiting times to major themes concerning economic structure. Of course, this book does not seek to reduce all social phenomena to class and economic structure, as it is "impossible to reduce the functioning of a society to a dominant type of procedures."[54] But we can at least hold constant that it takes a lot of energy to convince people to live the way that they do without questioning the fundamental premise of why things are configured in a particular way. In the nightlife setting, it takes a bit of work to convince people that spending money on a VIP table in a nightclub is a worthy use of their time and material resources. Perhaps more correctly stated, it takes a lot of energy to maintain an ideological, social, and cultural structure that cultivates the desire to participate in such practices, particularly when our time and resources could be directed towards an infinite number of alternatives.

Is this a byproduct or a defining feature?

Part of why capitalism is criminogenic is that it requires the production and maintenance of stratified human worth.

> The destructive passions by which the peace of society is interrupted is to be found in the luxury, the pageantry and magnificence with which enormous wealth is usually accompanied. Human beings are capable of navigating considerable hardships with cheerfulness, when those hardships are impartially shared (or equitably distributed) with the rest of the society, and they are not insulted with the spectacle of indolence and ease in others, no way deserving of greater advantages than themselves. But it is a bitter aggravation of their own calamity, to have the privileges of others forced on their observation, and, while they are perpetually and vainly endeavouring to secure for themselves and their families the poorest conveniences, to find others reveling in the fruits of their labours.[55]

The velvet rope at the entrance of the modern nightclub is a sorting tool for reinforcing class consciousness. Having people lined up at the entrance is something a nightclub *needs*. Having a slower moving line of "regular" people is something that a program like TSA PreCheck and CLEAR also fundamentally *require*. It is central to the business model. If space and time *couldn't* be commodified, this could all look very differently. But in the stratified society that we exist in, many people are used as means toward the ends of a relatively smaller and more privileged group. What good is the VIP or First Class experience if you can't differentiate yourself from the less privileged hoi polloi of the nightclub – or the airplane? Promoting and profiting from this ordering of class consciousness, the existence of many people waiting in longer and slower lines, or sitting in smaller and more cramped rows of seats, is a prerequisite for commodification, or cultivating "supply and demand." Outside of any popular nightclub, the entrance line will move slowly for many instrumental reasons. One of these is that the appearance, from the outside of the club, of this high demand is itself a generator of increased desirability for entering the nightclub. Those who are waiting in line outside are working for free as adverts for the business. After all, a crowded store (or restaurant) suggests that the experience is highly desired, and a long line at the front of the nightclub suggests that this is a good place to be on a night out.

Similar to paying for early boarding, there are recognized ways for skipping the line, like using your economic capital to improve your relative standing. In the same way that you can purchase TSA PreCheck and/or priority boarding, you can offer some cash to one of the doormen to skip the line. Unlike the airport setting, though, social capital is also valid payment: Name-drop the relevant name, and you're in. Unlike a rigidly configured caste society, it is possible to experience upward and downward mobility along those vertically organized class locations. Possibility and probability are two different things, but some individuals and groups have relative flexibility in placing themselves, as opposed to being placed, in their intended class location.

Like the suburban gated community, the VIP section has both physical and symbolic barriers. Once inside, VIP tables/sections have extra security who generally exercise favorable discretion towards those more esteemed (i.e., higher-ranked) patrons. The tables are prominently displayed, usually in a physical arrangement where the more resourced customers are *physically* elevated above their less-endowed counterparts, defining themselves and the recreational space they inhabit by using less-resourced people as a reference point.[56]

There are menus with Monopoly money prices, but not everyone is expected to actually pay the same amount for the same experience. The bottle list is more of a meritocratic instrument and a deterrent device, signaling that the transfer from hoi polloi to the nobility doesn't *require* that you be someone important, but that you be prepared to spend a certain minimum for the commodified space. In today's influencer culture, for instance, social capital is ever more important, to the point where nightclubs will not only offer comped (i.e., free) VIP tables to certain socialites, but even pay people to be there. The physical placement of tables, and which ones remain "reserved" more so than others, is also a way of commodifying social and physical space *among* the well-resourced clientele. Like a hotel that has *executive suites* and *premium executive suites*, physical space in the nightclub, like the price points for the alcohol products, can be further segmented into *premium* and *ultra-premium*. There are VIP tables and then there are ultra-VIP tables (e.g., adjacent to the DJ booth, or with the best view of the dance floor).

At some venues and on some nights, making it rain (i.e., throwing cash with frivolous abandon) can be another culturally acceptable and normative way of underscoring your class position for the night. It also signals your social and cultural background, because not everyone will know what this means or what it entails (ask older members of your family if they know what it means to make it rain – or make it clap). If you're in the VIP section in a heterosexual bar for the night, by now the cocktail waitress(es) will have identified the group's MVP: The person who is responsible for the bill. After mundane pleasantries establish shared norms and expectations for the VIP experience, the scripted spectacle advances, and the presentation of bottles begins.

Sparklers – or flashing strobe lights in cities with updated fire codes – are part of the ceremony. The sparklers and flashing lights aren't for their intrinsic visual display. This is neither a firework display nor a light-show. The purpose is to make sure everyone else in the club is aware of who is who and for you to have a 15-second video of status-conferring *fun*. If your party – or your tab – are large, you might have multiple cocktail waitresses deliver your products not in traditional religious robes, but in clothing that sexualizes the worker. This is a different kind of church. Metaphorically speaking, the sacrificial offering is not some Old Testament animal or kid, but a symbolic representation of your actual disposable income. A liquor bottle that could cost you $44.99 if purchased across the street when the sun is out is converted into a $300 or more, plus tax and gratuity, expenditure. Of course, the price is less about the alcohol than about the commodification of space and the ability to be part of the privileged few who are seen by the many.

Sometimes it just feels good . . . but why?

Examples of this culturally prescribed fixation with symbolic and actual material accumulation is everywhere you choose to look for it. Consider the lyrical content in *Billboard* Top 100 soundtracks that promote patterns of consumption and pre-packaged notions of what it means to be "successful." Consider the social practice of throwing money (e.g., making it rain) and popping bottles in the nightclub, and alcohol commercials for "ultra-premium" liquors that convey prestigious and discerning lifestyles. When we look around us and see how capitalism has conditioned our socio-cultural value systems, our class consciousness, and our recreational activities, it is reasonable to ask whether many of us *wish* we could be within the social networks of those people that are featured in documentaries and investigative reports concerning *crimes of the powerful*.

Intellectually defending the reasons for why people enjoy these kinds of experiences would be a fool's errand if we think we're above the simplest of explanations: It feels good. We can't possibly expect there to be intellectually sophisticated reasons for everything that we do. The desire to wait in long lines for the latest Apple products, the practice of collecting Birkin Bags, the popularity of Canada Goose jackets, and the fact that there is an actual market for clothing designed by Kanye West all underscore that perhaps the flaunting of one's wealth simply *feels* good. We've been conditioned for so long to view our sense of self and daily activities as being significantly tied to economic structure and material distinctions, that it should be intuitive that we would want to symbolically share that we're doing a decent job playing the game. The core logics of that game – the racial capitalist patriarchy found in what we call "the rat race" – have become internalized in psychological and sociological ways. If we lived in a society where our running speed was the most important status-conferring indicator, we would be unable to know how fast or slow we are unless we competed with others. Since we live in a society where money and capital are the primary status-conferring metrics, perhaps we can use a better word than *good* to describe what it feels like to flex our class position from time to time: It is status-affirming. It is validating. It is a self-soothing ritual for underscoring that we could be worse off than we actually are, and we are better off than we might have otherwise been.

Whether in the nightlife setting or in any social setting, drinking – like smoking – is done for no other reason other than the fact that it, indeed, elicits positive sensory and psychoactive experiences. (Some readers might identify with the idea that blowing smoke, literally, feels good.) Just as smoking culture has its micro-rituals and symbolic practices, drinking has been incorporated into all kinds of settings and ceremonies to fit the context. People drink in good times and in bad. There are drinks for the summer day-parties and winter nights; There are spirits – and glasses – for celebrating specific events, and all kinds of discreet containers for taking booze where the actual demand for alcohol is curtailed by legal and economic interests (e.g., under-age settings, large concert venues, cruise ships, the movie theater, the Amtrak train). Up until this point, those of us who wish to reduce or completely abstain from alcohol consumption might be hyper-conscious of the ways in which we are culturally and structurally nudged towards 1) consuming and 2) participating in these *rituals* of consumption. These rituals are so prevalent that alcohol-free products continue to proliferate, underscoring the embeddedness of these social rituals so that non-consuming individuals can still participate. All of this is to say that there are deeply intimate and *social* dimensions that belong in any academic writing about social science, and which must be included in book-length manuscripts on capitalism or political economy.

Conclusion

The state is fundamentally designed to promote and defend a capitalist mode of social, political, and economic organization. The state, therefore, cannot be a neutral arbiter or vessel that can be filled by whoever wins in a competition of free ideas, or in a truly democratic process. The state, and thus the law, are structurally configured to replicate a capitalist mode of social organization, or, as the writings of John Locke would have it: To promote and defend life, liberty, and property. The foundational contradiction here is that the law, and the state, cannot be value-neutral despite popular claims that it is.

The *racist capitalist patriarchal state* is not a coherent organism that wakes up in the morning and does things. Such terms, like *neoliberal hegemony* or *carceral regimes*, reflect patterns, systems, institutional arrangements, and habits that are enacted, experienced, and enabled by people. In this chapter I have outlined how I approach the study of state power and political economy. In unpacking other key concepts, I have disentangled the relationship between normative or moral standards and legalistic standards for conceptualizing *crime*, and that criminal laws are themselves reflective of particular configurations of power and political preferences.

Other configurations of power can be readily observed in the production, distribution, and consumption of alcohol. More so than a mere marketplace, the consumption of alcohol is a social and aesthetic practice that has context-specific rituals and cultural scripts. Through the use of a sociological imagination, we are better situated to connect our lived experiences to broader features of the political economy and make sense of our subjectivity in a criminological framework. Alcohol – both in the form of powerful systems and intimately personal practices – thus offers a novel platform for studying crimes of the powerful. In the next chapter, I focus more fully on the conceptual and theoretical underpinnings of crimes of the powerful scholarship before returning to the nightlife environment.

Notes

1 For a critique of how the penal state and carceral state are used in ambiguous and undefined ways, see Rubin, Ashley and Michelle S. Phelps. 2017. "Fracturing the Penal State: State Actors and the Role of Conflict in Penal Change." *Theoretical Criminology* 21(4):422–440.

2 See Cobb, Jelani. 2016. "Working-Class Heroes." *The New Yorker*, April 17 (www.newyorker.com/magazine/2016/04/25/learning-to-talk-about-class) and Shenker-Osorio, Anat. 2013. "Why Americans All Believe They Are 'Middle Class'." *The Atlantic*, August 1 (www.theatlantic.com/politics/archive/2013/08/why-americans-all-believe-they-are-middle-class/278240/).

3 Johnson, Kevin R. 1995. "An Essay on Immigration Politics, Popular Democracy, and California's Proposition 187: The Political Relevance and Legal Irrelevance of Race Symposium on Immigration Policy." *Washington Law Review* 70(3):629–674.

4 The U.S. Senate, like the Supreme Court of the United States, was originally envisioned to be shielded from democratic influence. While the direct election of senators was brought about through the 17th Amendment of 1912, the U.S. Senate remains largely consistent with what the Founders and Framers collectively intended. As of June 1, 2020, the U.S. Senate is 74% male and over 90% white. See Congressional Research Service. 2020. Membership of the 116th Congress: A Profile. *CRS Report R45583* (https://crsreports.congress.gov).

5 As featured in NPR, Greenblatt (2014) writes:

> The 17th Amendment was one of several innovations during the so-called Progressive Era meant to promote direct democracy, such as ballot initiatives, recall elections and party primaries. The idea was to circumvent the stranglehold that various monopolies and oligarchies had on state officials of the day. "The state legislatures were just a mess, especially with regard to this issue," says John Hibbing, a political scientist at the University of Nebraska who has studied the amendment. "People were just buying their way in. It was a real cesspool."
>
> (Greenblatt, Alan. 2014. "Rethinking the 17th Amendment: An Old Idea Gets Fresh Opposition." *NPR*, February 5 (www.npr.org/sections/itsallpolitics/2014/02/05/271937304/rethinking-the-17th-amendment-an-old-idea-gets-fresh-opposition)).

See also Bomboy, Scott. 2018. "What Would the Senate Look Like Today Without the 17th Amendment?" *National Constitution Center*, April 8 (https://constitutioncenter.org/blog/what-would-senate-look-like-without-the-17th-amendment).

6 Chomsky, Aviva. 2018. "Histories of Class and the Carceral State: A Response to Paul Durrenberger and Dimitra Doukas." *Dialectical Anthropology* 42(1):33–50; Collins, Patricia Hill. 2008. *Black Feminist Thought: Knowledge, Consciousness, and the Politics of Empowerment*. Routledge; Democracy Now! 2018. "Boots Riley on How His Hit Movie 'Sorry to Bother You' Slams Capitalism and Offers Solutions." *YouTube*. July 17 (https://www.youtube.com/watch?v=XdCPvMNKvhE); Harvey, David. 2014. *Seventeen Contradictions and the End of Capitalism*. Oxford University Press; Marx, Karl. [1867] 1977. *Capital*. Vintage Books.

7 As Osgood (1896) writes, both the London Company and the New England Council were corporate forms that developed from the English chartering system of 1606. However imperfect the taxonomy of corporate forms during the colonial era, charter governments were themselves civil corporations at a time when primitive accumulation, mercantilism, and colonialism (i.e., capitalism of the systematically coercive and dispossessive sort) were in full swing, allowing for the reasonable inference that the Founders and Framers were born into a world where this sort of economic order was dominant. See Osgood, Herbert L. 1896. "The Corporation as a Form of Colonial Government. I." *Political Science Quarterly* 11(2):259–277.

8 Carceral studies broadly refers to interdisciplinary research and theorizing on formal social control and the coercive powers of the state that include, but also extend beyond, traditional methods of incarceration. For an overview of carceral studies from a criminological vantage point, see Brown, Michelle and Judah Schept. 2017. "New Abolition, Criminology and a Critical Carceral Studies." *Punishment & Society* 19(4):440–462. See also Rubin, Ashley and Michelle S. Phelps. 2017. "Fracturing the Penal State: State Actors and the Role of Conflict in Penal Change." *Theoretical Criminology* 21(4):422–440.

9 E.g., the neoliberal state, the capitalist patriarchy, the McUniversity, the military-industrial-academic complex, the power elite, the ruling class.

10 See Chambliss, William and Robert Seidman. 1982. *Law, Order, & Power*. 2nd ed. Addison-Wesley Publishing Company, p. 171.

11 See de Certeau, Michael. 1984. *The Practice of Everyday Life*. Translated by Steven Randall. University of California Press, p. xiii.

12 See Bernard, Thomas J. 1981. "The Distinction between Conflict and Radical Criminology." *The Journal of Criminal Law and Criminology (1973–)* 72(1):362.

13 Prechel, H. 2016. "Organizational Political Economy of White-Collar Crime." In *The Oxford Handbook of White-Collar Crime*, edited by S. Van Slyke, M. Benson and F. Cullen. Oxford University Press, p. 299.

14 Poulantzas, Nicos. 1974. *Classes in Contemporary Capitalism*. London: Verso.

15 Oxenfeldt, Alfred R. 1951. *Industrial Pricing and Market Practices*. New York: Prentice-Hall, p. 478.

16 While I do think that most readers will not care very much about this difference, it is consistent with previous scholarship of nightlife contexts. Denzin (1977:906) and Hamilton et al. (1938:3–4) both write how the nightlife industry – as a term – can be misleading, since

> there is no such thing as an industry. . . . There is only a host of individuals . . . engaged in varied assortment of activities. . . . They are human beings who engage in human activities. . . . It is amid this babble of tongues, this confusion of purposes, this drama of divergence that industry is to be found. . . . Yet industry is a name of what is at best a loose aggregate of business units engaged in performing a shared service or producing an identifiable commodity. . . . An industry is like an individual. . . . It has a character, a structure, a system of habits of its own. Its pattern is out of accord with a normative design; its activities conform very imperfectly with a charted course of industrial events.

See Denzin, Norman K. 1977. "Notes on the Criminogenic Hypothesis: A Case Study of the American Liquor Industry." *American Sociological Review* 42(6):905–920. See also Hamilton, Walton, Mark Adams, Albert Abrahamson, Helen Everett Meiklejohn, Irene Till and George Marshall. 1938. *Price and Price Policies.* McGraw-Hill.

17 Hadfield, Phil, Stuart Lister and Peter Traynor. 2009. "'This Town's a Different Town Today': Policing and Regulating the Night-Time Economy." *Criminology & Criminal Justice* 9(4):465–85, p. 465.

18 Benson, J. Kenneth. 1975. "The Interorganizational Network as a Political Economy." *Administrative Science Quarterly* 20(2):229–249.

19 Marx, Karl. [1867] 1977. *Capital.* Vintage Books; Weber, Max. [1921] 1978. *Economy and Society*, edited by G. Roth and C. Wittich. University of California Press; Durkheim, Emile. [1893] 1933. *The Division of Labor in Society.* The Free Press; Mills, C. Wright. 1956. *The Power Elite.* Oxford University Press.

20 As Michael Lynch (2013:138) describes: Political economic research is an interdisciplinary explanatory framework employed across disciplines including economics, history, political science, anthropology, and geography to examine economic influences and effects within social systems. See Lynch, Michael J. 2013. "Political Economy and Crime: An Overview." *Journal of Crime and Justice* 36(2):137–147. See also Leighton, Paul and Donna Selman. 2012. "Private Prisons, the Criminal Justice – Industrial Complex and Bodies Destined for Profitable Punishment." Chapter 20 in *Routledge Handbook of Critical Criminology*, edited by Walter S. DeKeserredy and Molly Dragiewics. Routledge.

21 Hadfield et al. (2009:466).

22 Michalowksi, Raymond. 2016. "What is Crime?" *Critical Criminology* 24:181–199.

23 For an example of how this applies to food systems, see Leon, Kenneth S. and Ivy Ken. 2017. "Food Fraud and the Partnership for a 'Healthier' America: A Case Study in State-Corporate Crime." *Critical Criminology* 25:393–410. See also Leon, Kenneth Sebastian and Ivy Ken. 2019. "Legitimized Fraud and the State-Corporate Criminology of Food – A Spectrum-based Theory." *Crime, Law and Social Change* 71:25–46.

24 Hillyard, Paddy and Steve Tombs. 2007. "From 'Crime' to Social Harm?" *Crime, Law and Social Change* 48(1–2):9–25.

25 Chambliss, William J. 1988. *On the Take: From Petty Crooks to Presidents.* 2nd ed. Indiana University Press, p. 8.

26 Chambliss (1988:2).

27 Chambliss (1988:2).

28 Randall, David. 2008. "A Tonic for the Troops: The Spirit of the G&T Endures." *The Independent.* Retrieved October 21, 2019 (www.independent.co.uk/life-style/food-and-drink/news/a-tonic-for-the-troops-the-spirit-of-the-gt-endures-1003460.html). See also Raustiala, Kal. 2013. "Why the Gin and Tonic Was the British Empire's Secret Weapon." *Slate Magazine.* Retrieved October 21, 2019 (https://slate.com/technology/2013/08/gin-and-tonic-kept-the-british-empire-healthy-the-drinks-quinine-powder-was-vital-for-stopping-the-spread-of-malaria.html).

29 Ostrander, Gilman M. 1956. "The Colonial Molasses Trade." *Agricultural History* 30(2):77–84. See also Ostrander, Gilman M. 1973. "The Making of the Triangular Trade Myth." *The William and Mary Quarterly* 30(4):635–644.

30 Barrows, Susanna and Robin Room. 1991. "Introduction." In *Drinking – Behavior and Belief in Modern History*, edited by Susanna Barrows and Robin Room. University of California Press, p. 9.

31 Baer, Justin and William J. Chambliss. 1997. "Generating Fear: The Politics of Crime Reporting." *Crime, Law and Social Change* 27(2):87–107; León, Kenneth Sebastian. 2019. "The Colombian National Police and the Politics of Crime Control Evaluations." *International Journal for Crime, Justice and Social Democracy* 8(4):18–32 (www.crimejustice journal.com/article/view); Andres, Peter and Kelly M. Greenhill. 2010. *Sex, Drugs, and Body Counts – The Politics of Numbers in Global Crime and Conflict.* Cornell University Press.

32 Pianin, Eric. 1998. "Alcohol Lobby Fights Drunken Driving Bill." *Washington Post*, p. A01 (www.washingtonpost.com/wp-srv/politics/special/highway/stories/hwy032698.htm).

33 Pianin (1988).

34 Rabin, Roni Caryn. 2018a. "Federal Agency Courted Alcohol Industry to Fund Study on Benefits of Moderate Drinking." *The New York Times*, March 17. See also Rabin, Roni Caryn. 2018b. "Major Study of Drinking Will Be Shut Down." *The New York Times*, June 16.

35 Food and Water Watch. 2016. "70 Percent of U.S. Beer is Controlled by Two Companies that Want to Merge." January 8 (www.foodandwaterwatch.org/impact/70-percent-us-beer-controlled-two-companies-want-merge). See also Notte, Jason. 2015. "These 11 Brewers Make over 90% of all U.S. Beer." *Market Watch*, July 28 (www.marketwatch.com/story/these-11-brewers-make-over-90-of-all-us-beer-2015-07-27).

36 Class location refers to a more holistic way of defining class – or socioeconomic status. Unlike static indicators like annual income, net worth, residential zip code, or education level, class location is a fluid and context-specific definition that requires stratified relationships among a given social group. There are various class locations *among* millionaires, and there are various class locations *among* the working poor. Race, gender, and sexuality also function to demarcate class locations as they are experienced and reproduced in real-world settings, provided that such concepts (like race, gender, and sexuality) are experienced and communicated as *hierarchical* categories as opposed to horizontal options void of privilege, status, or stigma. Class location need not be an explicitly economic position, but it is always a position that can be rank ordered relative to other class locations. See Wright, Erik Olin. 1979. *Class Structure and Income Determination*. Academic Press; Ritzer, George. 2014. *Encyclopedia of Social Theory*. Sage.

37 I am referring to Johnnie Walker, the General Motors equivalent of blended whiskies. Black Label might be viewed as analogous to Chevrolet, and Blue Label as the ultra-premium trim Cadillac.

38 Holman, Bianca. 2016. "Hennessy's Popularity Is Not Due to Hip Hop. The Story is Much Deeper than That." *Vinepair* (https://vinepair.com/articles/hennessys-popularity-is-not-due-to-hip-hop-the-story-is-much-deeper-than-that/).

39 Johnson, Annie. 2013. "Four Alcohol Brands Dominate Popular Music Lyrics." *USA Today* (https://eu.usatoday.com/story/news/nation/2013/12/12/four-alcohol-brands-music/4000593/); Singh, Maanvi. 2014. "Pop stars Are Sippin' on Patron, and Teens are Binge ing." *National Public Radio* (www.npr.org/sections/health-shots/2014/04/09/300512450/pop-stars-are-sippin-on-patron-and-teens-are-binging).

40 Sanders, Sam. 2013. "Moscato Finds a Younger, Hipper – and Browner – Audience." *National Public Radio*, June 27 (www.npr.org/sections/codeswitch/2013/06/27/196210549/MOSCATO); Williams, David. 2012. "Why Moscato is the New Rappers' Delight." *The Guardian*, April 21 (www.theguardian.com/lifeandstyle/2012/apr/22/moscato-kanye-west-wine).

41 Osei, Anthony. 2011. "Did Jay-Z Make $50 Million Off Ace of Spades?" *Complex* (www.complex.com/music/2011/03/jay-z-ace-of-spades).

42 Shames, Jade. 2010. "Hennessy or Cristal? Top Ten Booze-Pimping Rap Lyrics." *LA Weekly* (www.laweekly.com/music/hennessy-or-cristal-top-ten-booze-pimping-rap-lyrics-2410520); Joseph, Ryan. 2014. "The History of Champagne in Hip-Hop." *First We Feast*, December 22 (https://firstwefeast.com/drink/2014/12/hip-hop-champagne-history).

43 As a random sampling of similar phrases (in alphabetical order), popular music and popular culture often make associations between nightlife environments and the act or state of being/getting *(cross)faded*; *crunk*; *drunk*; *faded*; *high*; *lit*; *smashed*; *tipsy*; *trashed*; *turnt*; *twisted*; *zooted*, or whatever the youth are saying these days on the Twitter and elsewhere.

44 See Hadfield, Phil. 2006. *Nightlife and Crime: Social Order and Governance in International Perspective*, edited by Phil Hadfield. Oxford University Press.

45 Surely, in many cases, the drudgery of sitting at a cubicle is traded for the drudgery of standing at a door, or behind a bar, or in a DJ booth. In Chapter 4 I unpack what it meant for me to experience this environment as both a researcher and a bartender.

46 Race and gender are inseparable from any comprehensive analysis of class structure. I will return to racialization and patriarchal configurations of power in Chapter 2. For a robust source of scholarship on race, class, gender, and alcohol, see Barrows, Susanna and Robin Room. 1991. *Drinking: Behavior and Belief in Modern History*, edited by Susanna Barrows and Robin Room. University of California Press.

47 This phrasing is attributable to Ivy Ken (https://sociology.columbian.gwu.edu/ivy-ken).

48 For a sociological analysis of bachelorette parties, see Montemurro, Beth. 2006. *Something Old, Something Bold: Bridal Showers and Bachelorette Parties*. Rutgers University Press.

49 Levenson, Eric. 2014. "The TSA Is in the Business of 'Security Theater,' Not Security." *The Atlantic*. Retrieved November 10, 2019 (www.theatlantic.com/national/archive/2014/01/tsa-business-security-theater-not-security/357599/).

50 At the time of writing, the website headline reads: "Move at the speed of life – with CLEAR, your eyes and fingertips get your through security faster at airports and stadiums nationwide" (www.clearme.com).

51 Ibid.

52 See Cole, J. 2011. "Mr. Nice Watch" Featuring Jay-Z. *Cole World: The Sideline Story*.

53 If these jobs were so serious so as to warrant the title of *officer*, then perhaps they shouldn't be paid near-poverty wages.

54 de Certeau (1984:48).

55 Godwin, William. [1798] 1976. *Enquiry Concerning Political Justice*, edited by Isaac Kramnick. Pelican Classics, pp. 90-91.

56 For a rich overview of the vacuous 'money economy' where "sham individualism" produces rituals of self-assertion, and the desire to be distinct from "the masses," see Dick Hobbs, Philip Hadfield, Stuart Lister and Simon Winlow. 2003. "Chapter 1." In *Bouncers: Violence and Governance in the Night-time Economy*. Oxford University Press, p. 20.

2 Science, politics, and imperial criminology

In criminology, like in all academic fields, intellectual inquiry is never value-neutral. Our academic discourses are not vacuum-sealed from the material, political, and socio-cultural features of the corresponding time and place. Criminal justice systems also do not exist in isolation. Neither do the processes of criminal law creation nor the general values embedded in the body of criminal law. Our social and legal approaches to defining crime, criminality, and criminalization are thus inseparable from broader features of the political economy – which are often beyond the purview of formal criminology and criminal justice (CCJ) inquiry.[1]

Political economy – revisited

Political economy can be a loaded term in the sense that it can reflect a wide range of meanings, which will vary by context and application.[2] Broadly defined, the term refers to the interaction between politics and economics, or the ways in which individuals and groups of people organize themselves around – and compete over – known material interests. Included in this framework is the relationship that individuals and groups have with the state and with the supply chain of material and nonmaterial resources. This includes questions of property rights, taxation, social welfare policies, and the legitimacy and authority that institutions have in deciding on these and other matters.

Before introducing any political economic explanation for crime, it is important to specify some of my background assumptions. We are all material beings. As social beings, but also as physiological beings, we cannot permanently transcend our bodies or elevate beyond our corporal selves. Prior to any higher-order thinking, long-term planning, or intellectual pursuit, we need basic material needs to be satisfied. These include food, water, shelter, and outlets for using the physical, mental, and emotional energy that we feel physiologically and psychologically necessary to expend. In other words, we do not exist in some transcendent state that is *above* these basic necessities, and unless we are ultra-privileged, we cannot spend our lives totally ignorant or oblivious to how we will meet these basic needs.

We do not all grow our own food, bottle our own water, build our own shelters, and take sole responsibility for educating any offspring we might have. Political economy is, at its core, the study of how human beings relate to these material and physical resources, and the social, cultural, political, and economic practices and belief systems that follow from such exchanges. We come to develop abstract concepts that reflect these configurations of trade and custom, and over time they come to be known by all kinds of names, like inalienable rights, human rights, civil rights, public utilities, private property, public commons, private enterprises, and more.

Some might recognize this as a historical materialist framework, where the presumption is that the material aspects of a society influence the nature and development of non-material features, at least more so than the reverse. This might sound vague and under-specified, but it becomes quite intuitive via examples. Raw material conditions – which include the topography and natural resources of the land, the water supply, the flora and fauna, the temperature and climate – shape the social, cultural, and political-economic features of that social order more so than the reverse. In other words, you have no sea-faring skills or myths without access to the sea, and you have no language or cultural reference points for snow if you exist in the tropics. As individuals and as groups, we organize ourselves in a way that takes into account our reliance on physical, tangible, material things. Fuel, water, transportation, housing, livestock, climate, weather, and soil quality are just some of the many examples of physical components that make complex human societies possible – or impossible.

Whereas discussions of capitalism or liberalism are often framed as ideological, intellectual, or political projects, they are ultimately anchored in material interests, and were guided by such interests at the time of their origination. Historical materialism reflects this analytic lens, emphasizing the logistical, tangible, material conditions of a society, and how such conditions evolve in a contingent process of negotiation throughout history.

Why should any reader care about this? Perhaps we can consider the common discourse about neoliberalism. Neoliberalism is an over-used and under-defined term, but it captures an umbrella of ideas, practices, and orientations. Neoliberal governance refers to "the policies and processes whereby a relative handful of private interests are permitted to control as much as possible of social life in order to maximize their personal profit."[3] This is not some abstract political location, but the ideological Kool-Aid for defending an economic world system that commodifies all elements of social and ecological life. In this arrangement, the state becomes less concerned with the public commons and is reconfigured to better facilitate the conversion of all institutional arrangements into an efficiency-maximizing, profitability-seeking, cost-benefit enterprise.

Neoliberalism is not merely a prescriptive set of economic and political arrangements. It is also, as David Whyte and Jörg Wiegratz argue, a moral project.[4] It is the justification for what is currently happening. Commodification has no limits, and spreads to marketize social relations, individual subjectivities, our relationships, and our everyday practices.[5] Not only is every *thing* for sale, but life itself is commodified, traded, and subject to market demands and cost-benefit discourse. Air, water, soil, genes, seeds, and living organisms are things to be patented and profiteered. Neoliberalism "reproduces particular forms of subjectivity, disciplining and incentivizing individuals into particular modes of thinking and acting" Whyte and Wiegratz (2016: 234).

You are not merely a consumer, but you're also being consumed. Your attention span, location, consumer habits, and even the songs you listen to are all in this Big Data soup of commercialization (it's offensive at this point that we even have to pay for our smart phones, given all the money we make for others by virtue of us simply using them!). What's more, the current neoliberal paradigm contains an assumption that global marketization will become "more open, competitive, and efficient," which will in turn increase "liberal forms of democracy, transparency, and accountability."[6] In other words, neoliberalism presumes that increases in capitalism will yield increases in democracy. How exciting!

It turns out that many of us are, in fact, not that excited. Zooming out for a second, if we think about it long enough, and talk about it publicly enough, and agree on the legitimacy of the evidence in front of us, it becomes easy to recognize that we are all taking part in a system that is, in countless ways, patently unfair, harmful, and hard to justify. From tenured professors to college dropouts, and from sex workers to senators, there appears to be a shared navigation of a particular form of cognitive dissonance; where we are hip to – and perhaps consciously disapproving of – select forms of systematic exploitation that our collective lifestyles and modes of capitalist social organization depend on. Whether we recycle or not, or donate to a progressive cause or not, or carpool, or try a vegan diet, etc. – we can't escape acting out the imperatives of this overarching system every day.[7]

This allows us to simultaneously identify with Netflix documentaries that speak "truth to power" while we change cars every three to five years and buy Apple Air Pods if we can afford them. This reflects, in part, a Mertonian form of *ritualism*, taking part in a decrepit consumer culture through our external behavior while retaining the false sense of moral righteousness by virtue of possessing an internal recognition that the system is morally incoherent and logistically unsustainable.[8]

This did not happen by accident.

Structural contradictions – the big picture

One of the primary issues with our political economic order is that there is a contradiction between prescriptive belief systems (ideas of how things ought to be) and descriptive practices (the way things actually are). These are not merely gaps or inconsistencies, but structural contradictions that anchor many of the social problems of our time. Like the deeply entrenched roots of a tree, structural contradictions are the base from which many visible manifestations of conflict branch outward. For audiences in the United States specifically and the Global North generally, structural contradictions are anchored in the inter-related ideas and practices respectively associated with liberalism and capitalism.

Prescriptively, every human being has equal worth (something something inalienable rights! Something something human rights!). Descriptively, though, our modern-day understandings of liberal statist personhood (i.e., having citizen-ship of a certain country) is predicated on controlling the membership roster. Citizenship only exists as a function of policing its boundaries and maintaining categories of non-citizenship. At international borders, millions of people, in your lifetime alone, will realize that claims or notions of international human rights or humanitarian law will lack any coherence whatsoever when the rights of sover-eign states are used to deny their entry into another country. When it comes to the idea that all humans are created equal, theory and practice differ significantly.

Capitalism is home to a parallel contradiction. Virtually every private enter-prise is organized around extracting surplus value from other human beings or, in simple terms: Paying people less than what their labor is actually worth, so you can keep that difference for yourself. Organizational hierarchies are conceptually and empirically reflective of this stratification, where the few at the top of the pyramid are situated there as a function of the work done by the many more who are below them. This necessarily requires that people be treated as though they have differential value, worth, and purpose.

We can look at this in less traditional ways, and my point is more than simply pointing out the old school contradictions between the bourgeoise and prole-tariat classes – or those who own the means of production and those who can only sell their labor. In political systems, there is this prescriptive "one person, one vote" expression. In the private, commercial sphere, shareholders are orga-nized around a different framework. The system is "one dollar, one vote," and those with more dollars have correspondingly more votes. Moreover, an elec-torate in the Global North is more-or-less free, at least nominally so, to choose their political representatives, but completely unfree to choose how the mate-rial features of their society are organized (we have zero say in how our food is systematically produced, how our energy systems are structured for both the short- and long-term, or what kinds of medicines and medical procedures will be developed – and for what purposes). In other words, our dominant politi-cal economic structure is one that is rife with structural contradictions, and it would be naïve to presume that these contradictions don't permeate across institutional contexts like criminal justice systems and legislative processes like criminal law creation. Structural contradictions theory informs how

> Acts become defined as criminal in an attempt to resolve conflicts and dilemmas produced by contradictions inherent in the structure of political, economic, and social relations of a particular historical era. . . . Criminal behavior is a response of people in different social classes and groups to structurally induced contradictions.
>
> (Chambliss 1988: 216)

In the process of responding to structural contradictions, Anglo-American law[9] developed with an ideological underpinning of a commitment to equality, justice, and universality.[10] These ideologies, however, sometimes contradict role expectations and the need to efficiently accomplish other goals expected of law enforcers, entrepreneurs, and government officials. Criminal networks "emerge as a solution to the conflicts generated by these contradictions."[11] These criminal networks, however, need not be bearded men with foreign accents. The network can be the process of influencing legislative outcomes through legitimized campaign financing or the shared understandings between public police officers and private security staff.

Our legal system is one that helps to superficially reconcile core contradictions in belief systems and systematic practices. Some examples include:

"Calling" slaves inhuman but relying on their human qualities, stigmatizing women as inferior but depending on them for survival and the maintenance of essential social relations, defining the talents of workers as less valuable than the talents of administrators but being unable to produce a nail without the workers' "labor".[12]

Institutions like police, courts, and corrections are used to operationalize bodies of criminal and civil law that hide these contradictions, or at least recast them as matters of "law and order." There is so much to be desired about CCJ scholarship and even more concerning the status of criminal justice systems in the United States. It is, however, not a mere coincidence or inadvertent outcome that the United States is home to people who think of themselves as the freest in the world, while also being the site of the most robust series of carceral controls the modern world has ever known. I am not interested in throwing rocks at the criminology bus, but in giving a clear account of *how* and *why* CCJ scholarship has largely failed to include a historical or political economic perspective.

Science, politics, and empire

In criminology, like in all academic fields, intellectual inquiry is never value-neutral. Our academic discourses are not vacuum-sealed from the material, political, and socio-cultural features of the corresponding time and place. Access to water, arable land, flora and fauna, and natural resources are some of the countless examples we can use to make clear that human civilizations are anchored around material needs and interests. Such interests will not only influence the culture, ideology, and social practices of that society, but they will also influence the discourses of science.

Of course, the scientific method is ostensibly value-free and objective, at least on paper. In reality, the person using it, and the problems to which scientific claims and methods are directed, reflect identifiable values, intellectual paradigms, and material concerns. The topography and climate of a place will present puzzles and opportunities for academic inquiry. An ocean prompts the development of certain navigational skills. The Wright Brothers will physically place themselves in an area where they can test their theories of flight. A military empire will recruit physicists and rocket scientists from around the world to make more effective weapons.

In critical terms, albeit overgeneralizing terms, the socio-legal translation is both simple and simplistic:

> type of society = type of law
> type of political economy = type of law

Or as Frédéric Bastiat put it: "When plunder becomes a way of life for a group of men living in society, they create for themselves, in the course of time, a legal system that authorizes it and a moral code that glorifies it."[13] The point here is that legal systems, moral codes, and the frameworks of knowledge creation will not exist in some transcendent state that is divorced from the physical and material world, but be conditioned by it.

With "modern" ways of studying and knowing things being of European orientation in the Global North, we cannot ignore how science has "been used as a justification to propose, project, and enact racist social policies" in service of colonial and imperial objectives.[14] Just as Euro-centric belief systems condition how Europeans quantify and qualify the world around them, racial capitalist systems and states have generally been home to intellectual power-brokers who advance racial capitalist projects.[15] Settler colonial states are home to settler colonial sciences (for criminologists, think about the proliferation of global police studies, which usually goes by other names like homeland security studies, international security studies, conflict studies, political violence studies, whatever).

Resistance to systems of oppression have always existed across time, place, and context.[16] However, the dominant ideological and intellectual landscape of the United States in particular, and former colonial powers generally, has been one where bodies of knowledge have aligned with liberal statist (i.e., capitalist) projects.[17] Criminology emerged as a pseudo-science for justifying the coercive and paternalistic control of "othered" subjects, and there is no shortage of literature from both the Global North and Global South that has documented the hegemonic and imperial underpinnings of criminology and its discourses. But why limit such critiques to criminology when they apply virtually every conventional mode of academic inquiry? Given the emphasis on positivism and empiricism in social science, and the fetishization of external validity and objectivity, we can subvert these words and use them to unpack the historical relationship between science, politics, and empire.

Empiricism and empire

While the word *empiricism* is not linguistically related to the word *empire*, there is an intimate colonial relationship. By way of example, the Spanish crown struggled immensely to "understand and control the far-flung realms" of the colonized Americas, given the difficulty "in discerning reliable facts from the cacophony of opinions reaching Madrid."[18] To better rationalize colonial control, there needed to be a better way of securing reliable information. Similar to the film *Avatar*, the colonizing group was far less effective in administering formal control of a faraway place that was geographically, culturally, and politically distant. Basic datapoints (i.e., research) on the colonial subjects and their environs were required for more effective administration and control.

Whether in this century or in previous ones, whichever nation, state, or society has the most advanced technology will also likely have the best weapons and the best material foundation. This is the relationship between science and empire, as economic prosperity, military might, and technological innovation all correlate with each other in the empires of past and present. For example, in the aftermath of the French Revolution, the Academy of Sciences sought to reconfigure standardized units of measurement.[19] The English colonies followed a similar process of rationalizing control, and "in the absence of modern disciplinary distinctions, colonial leaders adapted the techniques of first-hand observation, detailed description, and inductive interpretation from an emergent natural science in order to manage and effectively exploit New World novelty."[20] This history is coincidentally reflected in the United States' iterative adoption of the imperial measurement system, which both the British and now American empire have used to rationalize global supply chains, labor and supply inputs, and war-making technologies – all of which are proper scientific endeavors supported by powerful interests and institutions, making such sciences *imperial* in both name and function.[21]

Higher education itself is increasingly commodified to extract more surplus value from the academic workforce while more efficiently training and indoctrinating pliable and politically neutralized workers. Universities are primarily corporate entities, using their human, economic, and political capital to secure returns on investment, patent technologies, and secure grant monies for state-corporate projects. The relationship between imperial logics and scientific inquiry can be seen in all kinds of examples, including the contemporary geopolitical hysteria over Chinese spying and theft of intellectual property from research institutions in the U.S.[22] Universities are, after all, actual laboratories and intellectual hubs for the technologies that are used to advance the tripartite of state-corporate power: capital accumulation, military advantage, and the technological and scientific advancement needed for both.

Just as European powers relied on researchers and explorers to advance material interests in the colonial era, *today's* military-industrial-academic complex[23] advances the same imperative: Aligning knowledge systems with state-centric priorities. Colonial technologies were applied towards imperial objectives and can be found in the past and present funding structures for academic[24] and industrial research into war-related technologies, agricultural and industrial supply chains, and economic development.[25] (If you want funding for your wind tunnel research, connect its relevance to a weapons system or a space industry interest; if you want grant money to fall in your lap as a criminologist, put "research for, by, and with the police" in your Twitter bio and study something like handcuff design, stoppage power of firearm ammunition, or light/paint/decal schemes of first responder vehicles.)

Modernity as the normalization of war

The most harmful systematic forms of violence are things that are done to *others* or done in settings of war or coercive diplomacy, and are therefore beyond the scope of conventional police, courts, and corrections research (the curriculum in the United States is so U.S. focused that it comes as no surprise that correctional institutions like Guantanamo Bay have no obvious place in the formal study of justice institutions). Criminologists in the Global North are paradoxically unconcerned with some of these forms of violence that occur not necessarily *in* our society – but as a function of our social order.

It is uncommon to explicitly acknowledge precisely how and why the very freedoms we enjoy are predicated on systematic violence, dispossession, and extermination. War, liberalism, and capitalism are, nevertheless, intimate bedfellows. We could entertain contemporary world history as temporary and precarious periods of peace, which serve as intervals between the previous war and the forthcoming one.[26] But there's more to this claim. War is not merely *naturalized* in modernity, but omnipresent both in its material components and in its ideological projects.[27] War itself is often framed as something that is exceptional, or qualitatively distinctive from the normal order of things. In truth, what makes a state modern is the rationalization of both life and death. As Midgley (2006: 246) puts it: "*We* are more advanced than *they* because we can kill them faster than they can kill us."[28] (As a reader, which group do you think you belong to? Under what conditions would your membership in that group change?)

Much of Western culture is "infused with a keen sense of duality, of war as a terrible thing to happen but on occasion a noble and necessary thing to do"[29] and the War Eagle on the U.S. Seal symbolically reflects this duality of a sovereign that *prefers* peace, but is also designed around preparedness for violence. For scholars of law and power, there is a multidisciplinary focus on *states of exception*[30] or legal regimes that are simultaneously separate from the normal order of things, but also co-constitutive of that same order. Such literature shows how human beings have used fanciful legal abstractions to allow for places like Guantanamo Bay, practices like family separation, and dystopian methods of killing like unmanned drones dropping ordnance on civilians to exist not in any contradiction to our prescriptive values or way of life, but as a function of it.

Just as modernity and war are intimate pairings, so too are notions of slavery and freedom.[31] In discussions racial capitalism, this paradox of critiquing the very system by which our material basis is generated can be explored further: "The fundamental factor provoking rebellion against slavery was the social system itself, the degradation, exploitation, oppression, and brutality which it created, and with which, indeed it was synonymous."[32] The same can be said about capitalism, which was always intertwined with slavery in the Americas. Existing within the same paradigm, they are extensions – if not iterations – of each other. I do not mean to be flippant or reductionist here. For slavery to exist, there must be a coercive relationship between capital and labor, and an instrumental relationship towards both property and the stratification of personhood. Phrased differently, there must be some overarching material reason for why racialization and racial supremacist belief systems not only come about, but endure. For capitalism to exist, there must be a coercive method of retaining class divisions and forms of stratification among the labor force, along with prescriptive claims that would seek to render such an arrangement as obvious, necessary, and natural. Such claims can look like this one: "In all societies there must be a class to do the menial duties, to perform the drudgery of life. . . . Such a class you must have, or you would not have that other class which leads progress, civilization, and refinement."[33] Whether it's via unemployment rates, fiscal policy, penalties for the nonpayment of debts, or variations in types of citizenship and residency, humans – we are led to believe – must be divided up into class positions that are useful to the core logics of capitalism. Chattel slavery was the logical extension of taking that imperative to its extreme, just as eugenics and assimilationist policies are ways of taking racial superiority to an extreme.

Whereas the business school curriculum, like popular discourse, might replicate some definition of capitalism that has nothing to do with racism or racialization, we don't need to get caught up in conceptual debates about whether capitalism always and everywhere generates racism. *Actually existing* capitalism has racialized and gendered human beings into various stratified categories.[34] Because I am interested in the relationship between political economy and intellectual discourses, I will now turn to the concept of coloniality to reflect on the enduring and "long-standing patterns of power that emerged [from] colonialism [and] define culture, labor, intersubjective relations, and knowledge production well beyond the strict limits of colonial administrations."[35]

The role of imperial criminology[36]

The criminological community generally has failed to account for its role in supporting racist, classist, and colonial modes of social organization. Criminological theory is historically reflective of a coloniality of knowledge, as the field has largely served to reinforce colonial modes of hierarchical dominance. I am not alone in taking this orientation, as other have framed dominant criminological theory as epistemic violence[37] and cognitive injustice.[38] Right now, in 2020, racism remains deeply embedded within and across scientific disciplines, found everywhere, including medicine and the biological sciences,[39] theories of jurisprudence and political philosophy,[40] the social sciences generally,[41] and criminology specifically.[42] This did not happen at random. For European colonial rule to coexist with prescriptive political philosophy, ideologies and belief systems were needed to justify dispossession and differentiation along notions of power, privilege, and personhood.[43] Not much has changed, when you consider that the U.S. is often framed in the dominant culture as a beacon of freedom and democracy while simultaneously being home to the most robust systems of mass incarceration and surveillance that the modern world has ever known. Back then, European ethnocentrism and genuine beliefs in cultural and ethnic superiority (e.g., white supremacy) were part-and-parcel to European efforts to impose colonial and imperial rule.[44] While the Framers and Founders sought to part ways with certain modes of European governance, many colonial modes of domination – and corresponding ideological justifications – remained, foremost of these being race and the technologies and ideologies that make racialization an identifiable, socially constructed thing.[45]

Both "race and class oppression have been inextricably intertwined" since the U.S. was established as a settler colonial state.[46] Scientists have largely been disciplined to first internalize and then perpetuate modes of inquiry that reflect these same Euro-centric standpoints.[47] In criminology, the field has employed perspectives that legitimize discriminatory carceral logics like the repackaging of racial policing into spatial policing[48] or managerial evaluations of correctional programs.[49] These critiques are part of a broader historical process of converting racism into racialized social control that are omnipresent in U.S. legal, political, economic, and social institutions.

Criminology, like many social sciences, cut its teeth on its ability to justify and legitimize coercive powers of the state. It is important to note here that there was nothing self-evident or predetermined about how criminology would "emerge to become a discipline for disciplining and controlling the Other at a time when colonial administrations were imprisoning most regions of the world."[50] Just as there were competing views and robust disagreements among the major European thinkers of the Enlightenment Era, we cannot attribute coercion and hegemony to all of Western liberal philosophy (after all, as we often teach in our introductory courses, Classical School Criminology was quite progressive for its time, and not all of the European dudes who had their writings proliferate during this Enlightenment Era were adamant intellectual defenders of colonialism and racial superiority). In the genealogy of Western criminological thought, Cesare Beccaria and Jeremy Bentham – two intimate friends – centered the idea that humans have free will, and generally exercise it in order to maximize pleasures and minimize pains. This predictability of behavior made it controllable. Virtually all introductory criminal justice textbooks in the U.S. include the contributions of Classical School Criminology through the teaching of deterrence levers (i.e., swiftness, certainty, and proportionality) in disincentivizing criminal actions. The applications to state power and legal sanctions are obvious, but like any technology, these ideas concerning deterrence are value neutral, as the principles of deterrence can be applied to morally virtuous and reprehensible ends alike.

However, it is the Positivist (or Positive) School of Criminology that would eventually emerge as the dominant source of coercive modes of subjugation and formal social control. Whereas the Classical School perspective viewed all human beings as largely equal in their capacity for free will and utilitarian decision-making, the Positive School sought to identify traits that are *independent* from free will (e.g., individual control) but strongly "predictive" of behavioral outcomes. The study of criminal *actions* as rational behaviors (a Classical School orientation) changed to the positivist (or trait-based) study of criminal *actors*. Focusing on sociolegal and state-centric conceptualizations of *criminals* instead of crimes, the Positivist School could be more readily applied to justify Eurocentric notions of racial, ethnic, cultural, and Judeo-Christian supremacy, which included "[t]he needs of slavery and sustaining the dispossession of indigenous communities by colonial expansion westward."[51] By the late 1800s, the Italian School of Criminology (inseparable from and synonymous with the Positivist School) was widely hailed as the foremost body of knowledge concerning the study of crime and criminals.[52]

These ideas were tremendously influential in both the Global North and Global South. The official flag of Brazil is a testament to the transatlantic reach of European positivism in Latin America.[53] In 1885 Cesare Lombroso, Raffaele Garofolo, and Enrico Ferri, among other positivist intellectuals, participated in the Third International Penitentiary Congress in Rome.[54] Among the attendees was Argentinean penal lawyer Norberto Piñero, who two years would later claim that "The Positivist School will go around the world for humanity's benefit."[55] As an ideological justification for racialized economic subjugation:

> The ruling classes [in Latin America] were aware of the increasing gap between the economic efficiency of industrial nations and their own, but considered this to be an inevitable consequence of the racial composition of Latin America. The problem had to be attributed to innate characteristics, be they physical or mental. Auguste Comte and Herbert Spencer helped to assert this position, giving it a scientific context, but criminal anthropology was more useful since it helped to justify the presence of criminals in those countries. In this respect, Indians and Blacks were considered Latin America's first criminals, followed by immigrants.[56]

Similar processes occurred in Argentina, Brazil, Cuba, and Peru.[57] As a hemispheric phenomenon, contemporary positivist criminology remains *the* dominant paradigm insofar as it purports to discover objective, scientific, and stable causes of *crime* and *criminality* – often in a manner that de-prioritizes broader understandings of criminalization and intersecting influences of political power, state definitions of crime, and political economy.[58]

Neocolonial justice systems[59]

What should we make of actually existing criminal justice systems? The neocolonial features of U.S. criminal justice systems can be readily examined in descriptive terms, considering how "patterns of over-incarceration and police violence, which are especially concentrated on people of color, have actually gotten worse" at the same time that so much focus has been on criminal justice reforms Simon (2017: 1625). When situated in a historical context, these racial disparities are not aberrations from an otherwise legitimate system, but the consequences of targeted efforts to subjugate and exclude racialized subjects from the body politic (see Mody 2014). Such racialization processes are not random, or done in furtherance of some metaphysical or spiritual imperative, but in tandem with material and economic interests. It is here where racial capitalism – as a political location but also as an empirical subfield – becomes most relevant.

The U.S. criminal justice system is part of a broader social control apparatus that has racial capitalist functions. The framing of the U.S. criminal justice system as a neo-colonial enterprise is neither new nor novel, but such critiques come from *outside* CCJ scholarship. Allen (2005) for example, highlights internal colonialism in the United States as "a structure of social relations of domination and exploitation among heterogeneous cultural groups within a single state."[60] A system can be said to possess colonial functions and features on the basis of whether it

> racializes relations between colonizers and colonized groups, helps stabilize a market system dominated by those controlling capital, establishes Northern science as the ultimate body of knowledge, and allocates the control of formal and informal systems of social control to those human groups considered as superior.[61]

In both descriptive and analytic terms, our formal criminal justice systems serve to maintain "a colony in a nation."[62] Institutions of state control are reserved for "the nation" – or majority white (or white-like) segments of the population for whom the criminal justice system gives some measure of comfort, protection, and legitimate recourse (Hayes 2016). This ordering of safety, however, comes at the cost of vigorously maintained forms of subjugation, restriction, and coercion of internal colonial subjects residing in "the midst of police scrutiny, economic marginalization, and political disenfranchisement."[63] In other words, institutions of democracy fundamentally rest on carceral modes of exclusion and control,[64] just as Euro-centric notion of modernity rest on imperial modes of economic, political, and military force.[65] Measurably harmful practices are not only "systematically ignored, misperceived, non-criminalized, unreported, and unrecorded" but increasingly normalized and legitimized into *the way things are*.[66] This is not a critique of criminology, really, but of our dominant political and intellectual climate.

Given these inheritances, it becomes easier to understand *why* CCJ scholarship has obfuscated any direct explanatory insights into crimes of the powerful and existential questions of justice. But there are also more practical, less historically expansive reasons for why CCJ scholarship has long been ill-suited for addressing crimes of powerful systems.

The criminology and criminal justice research enterprise

As a labor force, academics share the same kinds of social dynamics found amongst any kind of coherent occupational group. There are fads, trends, taboos, networks of privilege and relative authority, gossip, internal politics, internal divisions, and tribalistic tendencies. No matter the discipline or field, arts and sciences are inherently political. Sometimes the politics are high stakes, and such instances arise when academics touch the third rail of a given political or ideological system, prompting serious backlash. In less dramatic applications, it is reasonable to understand why there are gatekeepers to having one's work supported, validated, and made visible, or rejected, stigmatized, and rendered not *invisible* but perhaps *deviant* and thus punishable. There are formal and informal norms for how to go about *doing* scientific inquiry, and there are methods that are more or less favored at any given time. Whereas higher education is romanticized as being committed to science and inquiry, such a process is not a neat and orderly march towards enlightenment, but a checkered dialectic process of regressive, reformist, and revolutionary attempts to push or constrain the boundaries of a given discipline. Keeping in mind that the most esteemed Western universities in the United States have their origins in religious instruction,[67] there are certain kinds of questions that get supported more so than others, no matter the time period, the discipline, or the identities of the researchers. Sometimes the academic discourse seeks to move in an unchartered direction, and sometimes it seeks to keep things exactly as they are.

Like virtually all academic fields, criminology is hierarchical and structurally conservative. Tenured faculty hold significant sway over the career trajectories of junior faculty. Tenured faculty have every incentive to *not* question the very foundation of their previous works, while untenured junior faculty have every reason to acquiesce to the canons and preferences of old masters. As Steve Hall and Simon Winlow write, "Alternative thinkers from the past and present have been rejected for reasons that are not discussed openly," encouraging the reproduction of antiquated ideas. "New ethnographic research conducted by younger academics is either ignored or forced into traditional theoretical frameworks . . . [t]hus, new thinking fit for purpose in the twenty-first century is discouraged" on a structural basis.[68]

As a research enterprise, social scientists replicate the unintended consequences found in any other bureaucratic industry, opting for the paths of least resistance for attaining organizational objectives. Like any large academic department, our jobs are not merely designed around advancing research into our topics of interest, but doing it in a way that is highly visible and commodified. Full-time faculty must situate their work into bureaucratic and disciplinary rubrics and metrics, but from our academic training we are socialized to value the pursuit of such metrics in the first place. Sure, institutions and job types vary, but they also are all largely the same. We are rewarded for how we contribute to identifiable rankings and ratings, which involve everything from extramural grant funds, to enrollment figures, the employment outcomes of our students, and the disciplinary and subfield politics of being represented in *the top-tier* outlets, venues, forums, and networks. Some of the more obnoxious forms of mentorship include conversations on things like: (What press did you publish your last book in? What is the impact factor of the journals on your C.V.? Are you transforming the nature of your discipline?).

What's more, the academic environment is *not* the romanticized occupation where tenured, free-thinking individuals pursue inquiry on matters of both basic and applied research. This is a big business, or an enterprise that in many ways has become politically pacified, hyper-competitive, and structurally disincentivized from asking meaningful questions about the inherently criminogenic features of our social order.[69] Given that the United States incarcerates a greater share of its residents than any other country on the planet, it seems intuitive that criminology and criminal justice is one of the most popular majors in colleges and universities throughout the country. Mass incarceration doesn't just materially benefit prison guard unions and surveillance technology companies. It provides the material and intellectual basis for our jobs. I literally have my current job because the robust systems of criminalizing and subjugating human beings provides a demand for experts who know can make these systems *less bad: better*, or *more efficient*, or *less distasteful*, or *more compliant with democratic values*. Additional reasons for why CCJ scholarship doesn't structurally incentivize crimes of the powerful research include the following.

Opportunity costs

There are few statistical sources that provide a high degree of confidence on who takes bribes and who gives them,[70] and accurate quantitative data are lacking for crimes of the powerful more generally.[71] Qualitative research methodologies can advance scientific inquiry when quantitative approaches are lacking in either quality or availability, but they are incredibly labor- and time-intensive, and academics are rewarded for quantity of publications. As such, academic researchers are not well represented among the publications that uncover hidden realities concerning white-collar crime, public corruption, or other crimes of the powerful. The reasons vary, and range from the logistical opportunity costs of conductive immersive qualitative research to the incentive structure of academe. When researching sensitive populations or matters of deviance, other practical obstacles include gaining and sustaining access to such research sites and ensuring the protection of research "subjects".

Theory testing > theory building

Contemporary CCJ training is heavily geared towards quantitative theory testing. Academe is conservative in this regard, since older generations of scholars are reluctant to abandon their "tried and true" ways of building their careers around an existing theoretical and methodological toolkit. This practical consideration presents issues for studying crimes of the powerful, because most criminological theory is incompatible with studying political economic relationships or criminogenic structures. This reluctance was on full display at the 2019 American Society of Criminology conference, where a large panel was held on the topic of Building a Black Criminology – which is the title of a book by the same name. The majority of the session was spent on one of the authors – a senior criminologist – collegially debating another senior sociologist of crime on the quantitative applicability of social disorganization theory.

Available data

Moreover, criminal justice data and conventional survey methods do not adequately capture the kinds of crimes of that would be of interest to white-collar, corporate crime, or state crime scholars. Such activities of interest are often omitted from the direct purview of criminal law, and even when included as felonies and misdemeanors, they are under-emphasized in the purview of formal criminal justice oversight and control. Police, courts, and corrections were designed to account for less powerful segments of society, thereby leaving out the activities and actors most relevant to crimes of the powerful.

Productivity demands

Case study methods and qualitative methods are time intensive, and risky in that they might offer insights that conflict with the established canon. Moreover, quantitative methods lend themselves to efficient scholarly output. It can take years to complete one qualitative project. It can take a month to crunch numbers and write a 5,000-word paper on how the data align with pre-existing ideas of how variables relate to each other. Logistically, being at my computer is a far easier mode of research than being out in the field. In the "publish or perish" world of academia, we are occupationally geared towards cranking out as many papers as possible. That incentive, paired with the relative lack of data relative to street-level crimes, lends itself to a practical obstacle in studying crimes of the powerful.

Following the money

Criminology is not a source of research-driven policy, but a production site of policy-driven research.[72] Private charities, governments, and public–private partnerships shape the kinds of research questions that criminologists ask. There is not only an insatiable quest for finding "what works" – but also an avoidance on recognizing that very few things about criminal justice systems are actually working. Criminologists, like other academic disciplines, are in the habit of following the money, and the U.S. Department of Justice is not equally interested in all kinds of crimes, from all kinds of perspectives.[73] If you're a rocket scientist, *both* your intellectual skills and your occupational incentives are most supported when your work aligns with capital accumulation projects (e.g., monetizing outer space) or war-making technologies (e.g., improving a weapons system). If you are a criminologist, the same logic applies, and we follow the money that flows towards different kinds of capital accumulation projects (e.g., getting current and former inmates pacified into precarious states of employment) and the increased efficiency of domestic forms of formal social control (e.g., policing tactics; surveillance; less-than-lethal technologies).

Criminology, then and now

There is a rich contemporary history of how criminology has evolved over time. Intellectual and political fractures of criminology are extensively documented in recent works.[74] As Koehler (2015) thoroughly describes, the history of "cop shop" criminal justice programs – or police science curricula – constituted a major segment of the field's development. In the aftermath of Civil Rights Era and Cold War Era ideological and political conflicts, the most radical perspectives on crime, violence, and social harm were neutralized in various ways. Koehler (2015) and Barak (2020) each speak to how former California Governor Ronald Reagan successfully neutralized the hub of Marxist criminological scholarship at the University of California – Berkeley, resulting in what Koehler (2015) dubs the fracturing of a discipline. As a result, criminological inquiry would be divided into administrative justice sciences, law and society, and radical (i.e., Marxist) criminology.[75]

Taken together, there are a series of contradictory forces that characterize the failure in centering crimes of the powerful and an analysis of the most robust forms of social harm. But a long list of scholarship has already been done on the harms perpetrated by powerful actors and institutions. Some of these benchmark studies have been referenced in the Preface of this text in Table 0.1. Beyond this subfield, there are plenty more that illuminate our understanding of crimes of the powerful, regardless of whether the authors would characterize their work as such. Critical race theory, critical legal studies, decolonial and postcolonial studies, ethnic studies, American studies, and Black feminist theory are all examples of scholarly fields or areas where the work is fundamentally about powerful systems and the harms they predictably and reliably generate. Edward Said's *Orientalism*, like Angela Y. Davis's *Freedom is Constant Struggle: Ferguson, Palestine, and the Foundations of a Movement* or Nelson Maldonado-Torres's *Against War: Views from the Underside of Modernity*, are fundamentally about criminogenic and powerful systems, and offer a far more compelling critique of legal order than, say, the race-blind nature of Quinney's 1974 thesis. Whether scholars outside of criminology and sociology view themselves or label their work as being situated within the penumbra of crimes of the powerful is a separate matter.

Structural contradictions, capitalism, and criminology

Structural contradictions theory provides criminologists with a compelling option for making sense of these historical processes and ongoing dilemmas. The law is inherently contradictory. Many claims exist at the same time and sit in contradiction to each other. Legal regimes privilege some groups and interests over others. These interests and groups are not relationally situated at random but configured along axes of capital-centric vectors. The existence of contradictions creates dilemmas and conflicts which the people in positions to influence and create law try to resolve. Since they generally limit their efforts to manipulating the symptoms of the contradictions (i.e., resolving conflicts and dilemmas) the resolutions generate further contradictions, conflicts, and dilemmas. Thus goes the process of law creation become ongoing and dialectical Chambliss and Seidman (1982: 203), allowing for the piecemeal gains and incremental reforms that come about not through benevolence or altruism, but through the agitation, resistance, and mobilization of groups that fight within that given system.

From this perspective, there is nothing deterministic or self-evident about capitalism. It just so happens to be the case, empirically speaking, that actually existing in capitalism is not merely a series of criteria concerning the structure of an economy and the existence of property rights and contract laws. It is a wholesale packaging of racializing patriarchy. These are not mere ideological claims or abstract interpretations, but a reference to specific systems that advance classism, racism, and sexism in a way that maintains privileged and oppressed classes.[76] Class exploitation has been robustly studied in both conceptual and empirical terms by academics generally, and both feminist and critical race scholars specifically. Yet some critical scholars of various disciplinary traditions appear to be hesitant in directly confronting the structural violence that is inherent to capitalism.[77]

One can engage in any manner of process tracing or historical analysis to show how colonial belief systems generated hierarchical "categories of conditions that *resulted from*, rather than drove, [colonial] social arrangements."[78] As a structural trend, academic disciplines of all kinds have laundered colonial (i.e., racist, gendered, capital-centric) paradigms of reasoning as *objective* science, regurgitating the same fundamental logic: Seeking evidence for pathological explanations to separate "criminal" from "non-criminal," "good" from "evil," "white" normativity from "black" otherness. By omitting these details from the primary curriculum, the canon of criminological theory is artificially cordoned off from centuries of Euro-centric supremacy on shaping 1) how criminal laws are defined and 2) the political economy of formal social control. To this day, structural relations of power and systemic modes of subjugation are predominately discussed in terms of cross-sectional *spatial variance* and group-specific traits or pathologies.

Evidence of how racism remains embedded in criminological discourse is plentiful.[79] Racism is a founding hallmark of the field. The colonial past, however, remains with us in the present. In a more contemporary article titled "Race and Criminology in the Age of Genomics," the authors write

> the sad history of racism from colonialism to the Holocaust, all of which is interesting, but it is history not science . . . thus it addresses racism, not race, and then conflates the two terms . . . there is no scientific justification for racism, but there is for race.[80]

In short, *scientific* attempts to further cast racial differences as naturally determined continue largely unimpeded, and with better intellectual and political cover.[81] To be clear, there is robust agitation for moving beyond frameworks that conflate racially disparate inequalities with essentialist understandings of genetics and biology.[82]

Just as patriarchy conditions knowledge claims of sex and gender; racism conditions knowledge claims on race. Thus, many empirical studies of crime fail to include the longstanding historical processes of criminalizing and policing both sexuality and Blackness.[83] Today, in the criminological canon, the bulk of our graduate students are instructed how to *test* outdated theories; a cursory review of top-tier journals in criminology underscore this bias, and research questions can be rather sterile, analogous to asking population management questions like: *Among those who are poor, non-white, in single parent households [etc.], what is the difference between those who offend and those who do not?* Surely, we should expect more from ourselves, particularly from the hubs of influence within the field (e.g., top CCJ programs).

Myths about our imperial society can be found in many places, from the military plane flyovers at domestic college football games, to the discourse about soldiers *fighting for our freedoms* abroad, as if our freedoms were forcibly imprisoned in the oil fields of the Middle East or in the arable fields of the Americas. As if our freedoms are mystically converted into Chiquita bananas or barrels of oil that must flow from these peripheral lands to the centers of consumption – or metropoles. Myths are necessary, since it doesn't sound all that great to tell military recruits that the real reason they are training for or going to war is so that we can never have a shortage of low-priced fruits and vegetables in places like Walmart and Costco. It would be a buzzkill to inform military recruiters that the gears of empire – the aircraft carriers, the fighter jets, the tanks, the Humvees, etc. – all rely on the petroleum, and until they don't, the supply chain of these raw materials must be under the control of "the good guys." There is something in it for us, as well. We can continue changing cars every three to five years while not realizing that the actual costs of gasoline, like many of our foods, is not at the pump or the checkout counter, but in taxpayer contributions to "defense" spending and the loss of life via endless proxy wars.

Myths are everywhere. They include the discourses and public memories of the "Cold" War, which itself was a shooting war in many countries and a genocidal endeavor based on dehumanizing those who entertained *ideas* that undermined capital's empire. Hearts and minds that were misaligned with capital were subversive and thus extinguishable. Even our folk devils align with these myths. Fidel Castro and Hugo Chavez, for example, are not critiqued for who they are or what they specifically did, but in wholesale political–ideological terms (e.g., look at what they represent and how they are brand ambassadors for *evil socialism*). The failures of political pariahs and under-performers of capitalist democracies, and the normalized corruption enabled by the Global North and the United States are not treated this way. No single Western leader is held up as a symbolic ambassador of the broader incoherencies and contradictions of capitalism itself (capital moves freely while labor is segmented and immobilized, but the discussion usually doesn't extend far beyond a tally count of which U.S. president has deported the most people, and President Obama, "deporter-in-chief," is not framed as a folk devil for the contradictions of "free trade").

Conclusion

To call something like Western liberalism or capitalism *criminogenic* is therefore to paint with too broad of a brush, and attribute structural harms to something that is generally far beyond the scope of how we conceptualize guilt, wrong-doing, and responsibility. Labeling capital or capitalism as criminogenic is like calling basketball or higher education or macroeconomics criminogenic, in that we are applying the language of criminal responsibility to various systems. These systems can refer to rules, principles, expectations, teams, and collec-tions of individuals who do not necessarily *intend* to produce the harmful out-comes in question, or who are conditioned to not understand such activities as ethically or morally problematic.

Given that the political dimensions of academic inquiry are not limited to criminology, there is no reason to dismiss criminology and criminal justice as irreparably hegemonic or imperial. All academics, particularly in the tenure-track, have been disciplined to contribute to a system-wide configuration of imperial science anyway, so the expectation that our work will be transformative on this matter is unjustified. Just because our concepts and definitions are dif-ficult does not mean that they are unusable. And just because criminology has historically reinforced logics of formal social control, that does not mean that we can dismiss the well-established findings that has emerged from CCJ research. In the next chapter, I synthesize dominant themes and trends in crimes of the powerful scholarship and how they help make sense of the nightlife economy.

Notes

1 Lynch, Michael J. 2013. "Political Economy and Crime: An Overview." *Journal of Crime and Justice* 36(2):137–147.
2 As Lynch (2013:138) defines it,

> the term political economy indicates the use of an explanation that establishes a connection between the economic system and the social sphere and highlights the

influence of economic relations on social relations and institutions. In this sense, political economic research is not itself considered a discipline but is rather seen as an interdisciplinary explanatory framework employed across disciplines including economics, history, political science, anthropology, and geography to examine economic influences and effects within social systems.

> (Lynch, Michael J. 2013. "Political Economy and Crime: An Overview." *Journal of Crime and Justice* 36(2):137–147)

See also Selman, Donna and Paul Leighton. 2010. *Punishment for Sale: Private Prisons, Big Business and the Incarceration Binge.* Rowman & Littlefield; Buist, Carrie L. and Paul Leighton. 2015. "Corporate Criminals Constructing White Collar Crime – Or Why There is No Corporate Crime on USA Network's *White Collar* Series." In *Routledge Handbook of Crimes of the Powerful*, edited by Gregg Barak. New York: Routledge.

3 McChesney, Robert W. 1999. "Introduction" in *Profit Over People: Neoliberalism and Global Order*, by Noam Chomsky. Penguin Randomhouse, p. 7.

4 Whyte, David and Jörg Wiegratz. 2016. "Neoliberalism, Moral Economy and Fraud." In *Neoliberalism and the Moral Economy of Fraud*, edited by David Whyte and Jörg Wiegratz. Routledge.

5 Whyte and Wiegratz (2016). See also Harrison, G. 2010 *Neoliberal Africa: The Impact of Global Social Engineering.* London: Zed Books.

6 Whyte and Wiegratz (2016:2).

7 Hall, Steve and Simon Winlow. 2017. "Ultra-Realism." In The Routledge Companion to Criminological Theory and Concepts, edited by Avi Brisman, Eamonn Carrabine and Nigel South. Routledge, p. 404.

8 Hall, Steve and Simon Winlow. 2015. Revitalizing Criminological Theory – Towards a New Ultra-Realism. New Directions in Critical Criminology. London and New York: Routledge.

9 The Romans struggled with similar contradictions. Promoting equality and democracy *without* risking the chance that the many would take away the privileges (and property) of the few was of central concern. Rather than disguise the contradiction with hegemonic ideology, different voices are increasingly recognizing that these contradictions are a natural feature of the human condition, both at the individual or small-group unit and in the all iterations of a body politic (see TED Radio Hour. 2016. "Is Capitalism Compatible with Democracy?" *Democracy on Trial.* TED Talk, November 4 (www.npr. org/2016/11/04/500126088/is-capitalism-compatible-with-democracy).

10 Chambliss, William J. 1988. *On the Take: From Petty Crooks to Presidents.* 2nd ed. Indiana University Press.

11 Chambliss (1988:216).

12 Chambliss, William J. and Robert Seidman. 1982. *Law, Order, and Power.* 2nd ed. Addison-Wesley Publishing Company, p. 70.

13 See Bastiat, Frederic. 1845. *Economic Sophisms.* G. P. Putnam's Sons (http://hdl.handle. net/2027/miua.4728225.0001.001).

14 Dennis, Rutledge M. 1995. "Social Darwinism, Scientific Racism, and the Metaphysics of Race." *The Journal of Negro Education* 64(3):243–252, p. 243; see also Boerhringer, Gill H. and Donna Giles. 1977. "Criminology and Neocolonialism: The Case of Papua New Guinea." *Crime and Social Justice* (8):58–63; Gilmartin, David. 1994. "Scientific Empire and Imperial Science: Colonialism and Irrigation Technology in the Indus Basin." *The Journal of Asian Studies* 53(4):1127–1149.

15 Jackson, Marissa. 2009. "Neo-Colonialism, Same Old Racism: A Critical Analysis of the United States' Shift toward Colorblindness as a Tool for the Protection of the American Colonial Empire and White Supremacy." *Berkeley Journal of African-American Law & Policy* 11(31):156–192; see also Allen, Robert L. 2005. "Reassessing the Internal (Neo) Colonialism Theory." *The Black Scholar* 35(1):2–11; King, Anthony D. 1977. "Exporting 'Planning': The Colonial and Neo-Colonial Experience." *Urbanism Past & Present*

(5):12–22; Pulido, Laura. 2018. "Geographies of Race and Ethnicity III." *Progress in Human Geography* 42(2):309–318.

16 Enlightenment Era intellectuals had intra-group disagreements on the extent to which liberalism could advance at the same time that the United Kingdom's social structure was predicated on imperial governance. See Sir James Fitzjames Stephen in Singh Mehta, Uday. 1999. *Liberalism and Empire – A Study in Nineteenth-Century British Liberal Thought.* University of Chicago Press, pp. 196–197; See also Criollo, Manuel. 2010. "Palestinian and Chicano Peoples Share a History of Resistance to Colonization, Racism, and Imperialism." *American Quarterly* 62(4):847–854; Dedetdale, Jennifer Nez. 2016. "'No Explanation, No Resolution, and No Answers': Border Town Violence and Navajo Resistance to Settler Colonialism." *Wicazo Sa Review* 31(1):111–131; Gonzalez-Cruz, Michael. 1998. "The U.S. Invasion of Puerto Rico: Occupation and Resistance to the Colonial State, 1898 to the Present." *Latin American Perspectives* 25(5):7–26; McGowan, Winston. 1990. "African Resistance to the Atlantic Slave Trade in West Africa." *Slavery & Abolition* 11(1):5–29; Missall, John and Mary Lou Missall. 2004. *The Seminole Wars: America's Longest Indian Conflict.* University of Florida Press; Peltras, James and Henry Veltmeyer. 2016. *Power and Resistance – US Imperialism in Latin America.* Brill; Walker, Isaiah Helekunihi. 2005. "Terrorism or Native Protest? The Hui 'O He'e Nalu and Hawaiian Resistance to Colonialism." *Pacific Historical Review* 74(4):575–602.

17 Nugent, David. 2010. "Knowledge and Empire: The Social Sciences and United States Imperial Expansion." *Identities* 17(1):2–44.

18 Rosenmüller, Christoph. 2018. "The Empirical Empire: Spanish Colonial Rule and the Politics of Knowledge." *Hispanic American Historical Review* 98(2):302–304, p. 303.

19 Ramani, Madhvi. 2018. "How France Created the Metric System." *BBC.* Retrieved April 28, 2019 (www.bbc.com/travel/story/20180923-how-france-created-the-metric-system); Smeaton, William A. 2000. "The Foundation of the Metric System in France in the 1790s." *Platinum Metals Review* 44(3) (www.technology.matthey.com/article/44/3/125-134/).

20 Mazzaferro, Alexander McLean. 2017. "'No Newe Enterprize': Empirical Political Science and the Problem of Innovation in the Colonial English Americas." Graduate Thesis. Rutgers University – School of Graduate Studies, p. 3; see also Cohn, Bernard S. 1996. *Colonialism and Its Forms of Knowledge: The British in India.* Princeton University Press.

21 Tyson, Neil deGrasse. 2018. *Accessory to War: The Unspoken Alliance Between Astrophysics and the Military.* W. W. Norton & Company; Gleiser, Marcelo. 2018. "'Accessory To War' An Uncomfortable Wake-Up Call For Some." *NPR.Org*, September 17 (www.npr.org/2018/09/17/648697495/accessory-to-war-an-uncomfortable-wake-up-call-for-some).

22 Feng, Emily. 2019. "FBI Urges Universities to Monitor some Chinese Students and Scholars in the U.S." *All Things Considered*, June 28 (www.npr.org/2019/06/28/728659124/fbi-urges-universities-to-monitor-some-chinese-students-and-scholars-in-the-u-s).

23 Giroux, Henry A. 2007. *The University In Chains: Confronting The Military-Industrial-Academic Complex.* Paradigm; Mills, Wright C. 1956. *The Power Elite.* Oxford University Press.

24 Leslie, Stuart W. 1994. *The Cold War and American Science: The Military-Industrial-Academic Complex at MIT and Stanford.* Columbia University Press.

25 Nugent, David. 2010. "Knowledge and Empire: The Social Sciences and United States Imperial Expansion." *Identities* 17(1):2–44, p. 8; Kelly, John D. 2006. *The American Game: Capitalism, Decolonization, Global Domination and Baseball.* Prickly Paradigm Press; Pels, Peter. 1997. "The Anthropology of Colonialism: Culture, History, and the Emergence of Western Governmentality." *Annual Review of Anthropology* 26:163–183; Steinmetz, George. 2006. "Imperialism or Colonialism? From Windhoek to Washington, by Way of Basra." Pp. 135–156 in *Lessons of Empire. Imperial Histories and American Power*, edited by Craig Calhoun, Frederick Cooper and Kevin W. Moore. The Free Press (coordinated

by the Social Science Research Council). In more practical terms, see the CIA World Factbook and its corresponding history or the correlation between empires of various epochs and the functional equivalent of zoological parks. See National Geographic Society Resource Library. 2011. "Zoo." *National Geographic Society* (www.nationalgeo graphic.org/encyclopedia/zoo/). Central Intelligence Agency. Web. "The World Factbook – Central Intelligence Agency." Retrieved March 10, 2018 (www.cia.gov/library/ Publications/the-world-factbook/geos/ho.html).

26 Sir Michael Howard. 2012. "Forward." In *The Oxford Handbook of War*, edited by Julian Lindley-French and Yves Boyer. Oxford University Press, p. vii.

27 Maldonado-Torres, Nelson. 2008. *Against War: Views from the Underside of Modernity*. Duke University Press.

28 Midgley, Mary. 2006. *Beast and Man: The Roots of Human Nature*. London: Routledge, p. 246, in Coker, Christopher. 2012. "The Collison of Modern and Post-Modern War." In *The Oxford Handbook of War*, edited by Julian Lindley-French and Yves Boyer. Oxford, Ch. 4.

29 Freedman, Lawrence. 2012. "Defining War." In *The Oxford Handbook of War*, edited by Julian Lindley-French and Yves Boyer. Oxford University Press, p. 18.

30 Agamben, Giorgio. 2005. *The State of Exception*. University of Chicago Press. See also Brophy, Susan Dianne. 2009. "Lawless Sovereignty: Challenging the State of Exception." *Social & Legal Studies* 18(2):199–220; Lloyd, David. 2012. "Settler Colonialism and the State of Exception: The Example of Palestine/Israel." *Settler Colonial Studies* 2(1):59–80.

31 Paquette, Robert L. and Mark M. Smith. 2016. "Introduction." In *Oxford Handbook of Slavery in the Americas*. Oxford University Press, p. 7.

32 Aptheker, Herbert. 1943. *American Negro Slave Revolts*. New York, p. 139. Doctoral Dissertation. Columbia University.

33 Genovese, Eugene D. and Douglas Ambrose. 2016. "Masters." Chapter 24 in *Oxford Handbook of Slavery*, edited by Robert L. Paquette and Mark M. Smith, p. 549. Oxford University Press.

34 Chomsky, Aviva. 2018. "Histories of Class and the Carceral State: A Response to Paul Durrenberger and Dimitra Doukas." *Dialectical Anthropology* 42(1):33–50.

35 Maldonado-Torres, Nelson. 2007. "On the Coloniality of Being." *Cultural Studies* 21(2–3):240–270, p. 243. See also Quijano, Aníbal. 2000. "Coloniality of Power and Eurocentrism in Latin America." *International Sociology* 15(2):215–232.

36 This section contains claims that appear in iterative form in León, Kenneth Sebastian. 2020. Latino Criminology: Unfucking Colonial Frameworks in 'Latinos and Crime' Scholarship. Accepted and forthcoming in Critical Criminology.

37 Ball, Matthew. 2019. "Unsettling Queer Criminology: Notes Towards Decolonization." *Critical Criminology* 27:145–161.

38 Carrington, Kerry, Bill Dixon, David Fonseca, David Rodríguez Goyes, Jianhong Liu and Diego Zysman. 2019. "Criminologies of the Global South: Critical Reflections." *Critical Criminology* 27(1):163–189; Carrington, Kerry, Russell Hogg, John Scott, Máximo Sozzo and Reece Walters. 2018. *Southern Criminology*. Routledge.

39 Feagin, Joe R. 2017. "Systemic Racism and 'Race' Categorization in U.S. Medical Research and Practice." *The American Journal of Bioethics* 17(9):54–56; Bhopal, Raj. 1998. "Spectre of Racism in Health and Health Care: Lessons from History and the United States." *BMJ* 316(7149):1970–1973; Gutin, Iliya. 2018. "Essential(Ist) Medicine: Promoting Social Explanations for Racial Variation in Biomedical Research." *Medical Humanities* 45(3):224–234.

40 Delgado, Richard and Jean Stefancic. 2017. *Critical Race Theory – An Introduction*. New York University Press; Yancy, George and Falguni A. Sheth. 2015. "How Liberalism and Racism Are Wed." *New York Times*. Retrieved March 10, 2019 (https://opinionator. blogs.nytimes.com/2015/02/27/how-liberalism-and-racism-are-wed/).

41 Elias, Sean and Joe R. Feagin. 2016. *Racial Theories in Social Science – A Systemic Racism Critique*. 1st ed. Routledge; Murji, Karim. 2018. "Racial Theories in Social Science:

A Systemic Racism Critique." *Ethnic and Racial Studies* 41(8):1519–1520; Ray, Victor. 2017. "Racial Theories in the Social Sciences: A Systemic Racism Critique." *Contemporary Sociology* 46(5):553–554.

42 Boerhringer and Giles (1977); Cook, Dee and Barbara Hudson, eds. 1994. *Racism & Criminology.* Sage; Kitossa, Tamari. 2012. "Criminology and Colonialism: Counter Colonial Criminology and the Canadian Context." *Journal of Pan African Studies* 4(9):204–226; Phillips, Coretta and Benjamin Bowling. 2003. "Racism, Ethnicity and Criminology. Developing Minority Perspectives." *The British Journal of Criminology* 43(2):269–290.

43 Quijano (2000).

44 Quijano (2000:541); see also Wallerstein, Immanuel. 1974. "The Rise and Future Demise of the World Capitalist System: Concepts for Comparative Analysis." *Comparative Studies in Society and History* 16(4):387–415.

45 Harris, Cheryl I. 1993. "Whiteness as Property." *Harvard Law Review* 106(8):1707.

46 Kienscherf, Markus. 2018. "Race, Class and Persistent Coloniality: US Policing as Liberal Pacification." *Capital & Class* 1–20, p. 3; Citing Wolfe (2006), Noura Erakat (2019) refers to settler-colonialism as a "structure of governance and indigenous elimination rather than a singular event of invasion and carnage" (p. 255). The United States is founded on a particular form of epistemic violence; one that includes a robust package of race, class, gender, religion, and capital-centric modes of social organization. The history of the Indian Wars alone, or the Seminole Tribe of Florida alone, underscores how indigenous elimination has never been a single process in the United States, but an all-encompassing paradigm. See Erakat, Noura. 2019. *Justice for Some – Law and the Question of Palestine.* Stanford University Press; Coates, Rodney D. 2003. "Law and the Cultural Production of Race and Racialized Systems of Oppression: Early American Court Cases." *American Behavioral Scientist* 47(3):329–351; Wolfe, Patrick. 2006. "Settler Colonialism and the Elimination of the Native." *Journal of Genocide Research* 8(4):387–409.

47 Search engine results for images of *manifest destiny* help visualize this point: A fair-skinned woman of European appearance majestically pointing westward serves as a symbolic representation for what would become a systematic dispossession and cultural genocide of native and indigenous peoples.

48 Bass, Sandra. 2001. "Policing Space, Policing Race: Social Control Imperatives and Police Discretionary Decisions." *Social Justice* 28(1):156–176; Bonner, Kideste Mariam Wilder. 2014. "Race, Space, and Being Policed: A Qualitative Analysis of Residents' Experiences with Southern Patrols." *Race and Justice* 4(2):124–151.

49 Brown, Michelle and Judah Schept. 2017. "New Abolition, Criminology and a Critical Carceral Studies." *Punishment & Society* 19(4):440–462; Ward, Geoff. 2015. "The Slow Violence of State Organized Race Crime." *Theoretical Criminology* 19(3):299–314.

50 Agozino, Biko and Stephen Pfohl. 2003. *Counter-Colonial Criminology: A Critique of Imperialist Reason.* Pluto Press, pp. 244, 246.

51 Simon, Jonathan. 2017. "Racing Abnormality, Normalizing Race: The Origins of America's Peculiar Carceral State and Its Prospects for Democratic Transformation Today." *Northwestern University Law Review* 111(6):1625–1654, p. 1637.

52 Olmo, Rosa del. 1999. "The Development of Criminology in Latin America." *Social Justice* 26(2):19–45; See also Wolfgang, Marvin E. 1961. "Pioneers in Criminology: Cesare Lombroso (1835–1909)." *The Journal of Criminal Law, Criminology, and Police Science* 52(4):361.

53 The popularity of Auguste Comte and European positivism would become formally integrated into Brazil's flag of 1889 with the phrase *Ordem e Progresso* (see Brown University Center for Digital Scholarship. n.d. "Positivism | Brazil: Five Centuries of Change." Retrieved March 10, 2019 (https://library.brown.edu/create/fivecenturiesof-change/chapters/chapter-4/positivism/); The Economist. 2018. "Jair Bolsonaro and the Perversion of Liberalism." *The Economist*, October 27 (www.economist.com/the-amer icas/2018/10/27/jair-bolsonaro-and-the-perversion-of-liberalism); Nachman (1977).

54 Olmo, Rosa del. 1999. "The Development of Criminology in Latin America." *Social Justice* 26(2):19–45.

55 Olmo (1999:25); see also Jimenez de Asua, L. 1957. *Tratado de Derecho Penal.* Buenos Aires: Losada, p. 1047.

56 Olmo (1999:25).

57 Aguirre, Carlos. 1998. "Crime, Race, and Morals: The Development of Criminology in Peru 1890–1930." *Crime, History & Societies* 2(2):73–90; Aliverti, Massimo. 2017. "On Two Italian Publications by the Cuban Anthropologist Fernando Ortiz (1881–1969)." *Acta Medica Mediterranea* 3:471–474; Carrington et al. (2019).

58 Chambliss, William J. 1975. "Toward a Political Economy of Crime." *Theory and Society* 2(2):149–170 (www.jstor.org/stable/656788); Young, Jock. 2011. *The Criminological Imagination.* Polity.

59 This section contains claims that appear in iterative form in León, Kenneth Sebastian. 2020. Latino Criminology: Unfucking Colonial Frameworks in 'Latinos and Crime' Scholarship. Accepted and forthcoming in *Critical Criminology.*

60 Mondaca, E. 2017. "The Archipelago of Chiloé and the Uncertain Contours of Its Future: Coloniality, New Extractivism and Political-Social Re-vindication of Existence." Pp. 31–55 in *Environmental Crime in Latin America: The Theft of Nature and the Poisoning of the Land,* edited by D.R. Goyes, H. Mol, A. Brisman and N. South. Palgrave Macmillan, p. 37; Allen, Robert L. 2005. "Reassessing The Internal (Neo) Colonialism Theory." *The Black Scholar* 35(1):2–11.

61 Mondaca (2017); cited in Carrington et al. (2019:15).

62 Hayes, Christopher. 2017. *A Colony in a Nation.* 1st ed. New York: W.W. Norton & Company.

63 Brewer, Rose M. and Nancy A. Heitzeg. 2008. "The Racialization of Crime and Punishment: Criminal Justice, Color-Blind Racism, and the Political Economy of the Prison Industrial Complex." *American Behavioral Scientist* 51(5):625–44, p. 625.

64 Agamben, Giorgio. 2005. *State of Exception.* Chicago, IL: University of Chicago Press; Simon, Jonathan. 2017. "Racing Abnormality, Normalizing Race: The Origins of America's Pecliar Carceral State and Its Prospects for Democratic Transformation Today." *Northwestern University Law Review* 111(6):1625–1654; McGovern, Mark. 2011. "The Dilemma of Democracy: Collusion and the State of Exception." *Studies in Social Justice* 5(2):213–230.

65 Giddens, Anthony. 1990. *The Consequences of Modernity.* Stanford University Press; Maldonado-Torres, Nelson. 2007. "On the Coloniality of Being." *Cultural Studies* 21(2–3):240–270.

66 Hall, Steve and Simon Winlow. 2015. *Revitalizing Criminological Theory – Towards a New Ultra-Realism. New Directions in Critical Criminology.* London and New York: Routledge, p. 1.

67 Kohlbrenner, Bernard J. 1961. "Religion and Higher Education: An Historical Perspective." *History of Education Quarterly* 1(2):45–56.

68 Hall, Steve and Simon Winlow. 2017. "Ultra-Realism." In *The Routledge Companion to Criminological Theory and Concepts,* edited by Avi Brisman, Eamonn Carrabine and Nigel South. Routledge, p. 402.

69 Hall, Steve. 2012. "Don't Look Up, Don't Look Down: Liberal Criminology's Fear of the Supreme and the Subterranean." *Crime, Media, Culture* 8(2):197–212. See also Nair, Yasmin. 2017. "The Dangerous Academic is an Extinct Species." *Current Affairs,* June 7 (www.currentaffairs.org/2017/04/the-dangerous-academic-is-an-extinct-species).

70 Noonan, Charles. 1987 *Bribes.* University of California Press, p. 693.

71 See Friedrichs, David. 2007. *Trusted Criminals: White Collar Crime in Contemporary Society.* 3rd ed. Thomas Wadsworth; Whyte, David. 2009. *Crimes of the Powerful: A Reader.* McGraw-Hill.

72 Hall and Winlow (2015:85).

73 Quinney, Richard. 1974. *Critique of Legal Order: Crime Control in a Capitalist Society.* Little, Brown & Co.

74 See Koehler, Johann. 2015. "Development and Fracture of a Discipline: Legacies of the School of Criminology at Berkeley." *Criminology* 53(4):513–544; Barak, Gregg. 2019. *Chronicles of a Radical Criminologist: Working the Margins of Law, Power, and Justice.* Rutgers University Press; Lea, John. 2017. "Book Review of 'Revitalizing Criminological Theory: Towards a New Ultra-Realism. By Steve Hall and Simon Winlow'." *The British Journal of Criminology* 57(5):1272–1275.

75 Koehler (2015).

76 hooks, bell. 2000. *Feminist Theory: From Margin to Center.* Pluto Press.

77 Golash-Boza, Tanya, Maria D. Duenas and Chia Xiong. 2019. "White Supremacy, Patriarchy, and Global Capitalism in Migration Studies." *American Behavioral Scientist* 1–19.

78 Ken, Ivy. 2010. *Digesting Race, Class, and Gender – Sugar as a Metaphor.* Palgrave. pp. 20–21.

79 Catoia, Cinthia Cassia. 2018. "The Discursive Production of Racism: From Slavery to Positivist Criminology." *Dilemas: Revista de Estudos de Conflito e Controle Social* 11(2):259–278; Rafter, Nicole. 2004. "Earnest A. Hooton and the Biological Tradition in American Criminology." *Criminology* 42(3):735–772.

80 Walsh, Anthony and Ilhong Yun. 2011. "Race and Criminology in the Age of Genomic Science." *Social Science Quarterly* 92(5):1279–1296, p. 1285.

81 Walsh and Yun's (2011) claim that "wherever the three major races coexist, the pattern of offending, particularly violent offending, is invariably black > white > Asian." Such claims are only defensible if one assumes that patterns of criminalization and the enforcement of criminal laws are either randomized or equitable (they are neither). Further evidence of intellectually cloaked racism can be found in the intellectual discourses and studies associated with the following studies: Rushton, Phillip J. and Glade Whitney. 2002. "Cross-National Variation in Violent Crime Rates: Race, r-K Theory, and Income." *Population and Environment* 23:501–511; Wright, John. 2009. "Inconvenient Truths: Science, Race and Crime." Pp. 137–153 in *Biosocial Criminology: New Directions in Theory and Research*, edited by A. Walsh and K. Beaver. Routledge; Eysenck, Hans J. and Gisli H. Gudjonsson. 1989. *The Causes and Cures of Criminality.* Plenum.

82 Fitzgerald, Kathleen J. 2014. "The Continuing Significance of Race: Racial Genomics in a Postracial Era." *Humanity & Society* 38(1):49–66; Kolbert. 2018. "There's No Scientific Basis for Race – It's a Made-Up Label." *National Geographic Magazine.* Retrieved April 26, 2019 (www.nationalgeographic.com/magazine/2018/04/race-genetics-science-africa/); Ogbunu, C. Brandon. 2019. "James Watson and the Insidiousness of Scientific Racism." *Wired*, January 29; Saini, Angela. 2018. "Racism Is Creeping Back into Mainstream Science – We Have to Stop It." *The Guardian*, January 22.

83 Fanon, Frantz. 1967. *Black Sin, White Masks.* Grove Press; Hansen, Laura L. 2017. "Crime, Race." Pp. 1–4 in *The Blackwell Encyclopedia of Sociology.* American Cancer Society; Muhammad, Khalil Gibran. 2011. *The Condemnation of Blackness – Race, Crime, and the Making of Modern Urban America.* Harvard University Press.

3 White-collar crime and corruption

Back to basics

Concerns over corruption have been a stable and universal feature in all recorded societies and civilizations.[1] Known as *mordida* in Mexico, *arreglo* in the Philippines, *baksheesh* in Egypt, *dash* in Kenya, *pot-de-vin* in France, and *propina* in Brazil, bribery and corruption are deeply embedded across time and place.[2] In a 2008 speech, Vladimir Putin referenced corruption as "the most weary-ing and difficult to resolve" of all Russia's problems.[3] In the course of the 2016 U.S. presidential election, an acolyte of Putin, then-candidate Donald Trump, evoked audiences with a campaign chant of "drain the swamp." Among other interpretations, this was designed to highlight populist perceptions of corrup-tion associated with Washington, D.C. – a place where "bribery and influence peddling have always been bipartisan affairs."[4] Such fixations, perceptions, and condemnations are far from new.[5]

Defining corruption is an elusive task, as it can be so context-specific that it reminds us of Justice Potter Stewart's attempt at describing pornography through the "I know it when I see it" standard.[6] Corruption, however, is inherently difficult to define, as formal or legalistic definitions are never power-neutral. Corruption discourses – or how people come to conceptu-alize and define something as corrupt – can be thought of as a putty-like substance that can be shaped, molded, and configured to meet instrumental needs. Claims of corruption have "a parasitic ability" to latch onto "different political projects," and the giver and receiver of any corruption-specific label are often engaged in a political or ideological project of one form or another.[7] In other words, corruption is not merely socially and historically constructed, but legally constructed in a manner that reflects the distribution of power in a given society.

Corruption – like crime – is an inherently political term. Politics refers to the ways that individuals and groups engage each other over the procedural and distributive outcomes of valued resources. If we view the law as a negotiated product and a valuable resource, then the spirit and letter of the law is contin-gent on how individuals and groups engage with each other, in both coopera-tion and conflict, to shape what laws and legal systems look like. The law in general, and the criminal law in particular, can be understood as a contingent form of discourse, or a language with its own rules, uses, and conventions. The law has game-like qualities that can be used, misused, applied, and mis-applied, molded to fit the needs, interests, and objectives of its users. This is consistent with the central tenets of critical legal studies, which emphasizes the inherently political nature of law and legality.[8] As such, the shape-shifting and inherently political nature of corruption makes it incredibly challenging to define, since corruption is ultimately whatever the courts say it is, and the courts are not in the habit of critiquing *legal* practices through such a crimi-nalistic lens. With these caveats in mind, there are identifiable patterns in how corruption is operationalized in legal and political settings, and we have devel-oped words and phrases to differentiate between different kinds of activities that might fall under the broad umbrella of "corruption." *Improper use of office, political horse trading, bribery, currying favor,* and *use of position for personal gain* are just some examples. In other words, there are clear definitions, however imper-fectly applied or limited in scope they might be.

As a research community,[9] criminology has empirically challenged con-ventional assumptions about crime and deviance while simultaneously rein-forcing state-centric belief systems and power structures.[10] Just as there has always been resistance, subversion, and incrementalistic reforms within all kinds of dominant systems, so too has the criminological discourse evolved. Scholarship on crimes of the powerful speaks to these ongoing projects and evolutions in how we engage with questions of power, order, governance, and social harm. Given the nature of this study, a brief overview of the scholarship trajectories of white-collar crime and public corruption is war-ranted here.

White-collar crime in context

The criminological research community is historically characterized by dis-agreements and open questions regarding the definition of crime.[11] This is particularly applicable to crimes that vary in their perceived acceptability, and where the identification of a victim is less obvious, and where the offender is perceived as non-threatening and/or has reputable social standing.[12]

Bribes and corruption have been present throughout all Western civiliza-tion, and have thus been of concern to many common people and elites alike. However, what *is* relatively new is the formalized study of white-collar crime and the concentrated focus on harms perpetrated by the economically and politically powerful by full-time researchers employed by institutions of higher education. In criminology proper, this type of scholarship is under-represented relative to the more conventional categories of crime, but it is gaining increased attention.[13]

Much of the historical insights into matters of white-collar crime, cor-ruption, and systematic social harms have been provided by investigative and watchdog journalists. The history of the term *muckrakers*[14] underscores this tradition of exposing actions and practices of commercial and governmental elites.[15] Writers like Lincoln Steffens and Upton Sinclair, through their respective works like *Shame of the Cities* (1904) and *The Jungle* (1906), raised awareness of the costs and consequences of private industry practices left unchecked and unrestrained.[16] Since the proliferation of the printing press, journalists continue to be at the forefront of identifying and describing phenomena that would qualify, and have qualified, as white-collar crimes and crimes of the powerful.

The history of academic inquiry is far more disperse. A conventional starting point for U.S. scholars might be 1898, when Louis Proal wrote a book about political crimes. In 1907, Edward Alsworth Ross warned of the *criminaloid*,[17] or businessmen who engage in harmful acts under the mask of respectability. Ross's criminaloid was "society's most dangerous foe, more [fearsome] by far than the plain criminal, because he sports the appearance of virtue and operates on a titanic scale."[18] Not long after, in 1926, the first manager of the Better Business Bureau, H. J. Kenner, published an article in *The Annals of the American Academy of Political and Social Science* describing a prototypical "white-collar bandit" responsible for "outstanding perils" that affected individuals and society.[19] Other notable works followed, including Matthew Josephson's 1934 book, *The Robber Barons – The Great American Capitalists*, which would give thorough treatment to practices that would later fall under the purview of antitrust laws. While these works were critiqued, in part, for being inflammatory, alarmist, or hyperbolic, these writers helped shed light on knowingly harmful – yet legal – features of the economy, and they did so decades before regulatory institutions were established to mitigate such harms.[20]

The crowned prince of white-collar crime scholarship, at least for criminologists, is Edwin Sutherland, whose last name is as familiar to many criminologists as Beccaria, Lombroso, and Volmer, among other white dudes. As president of the American Sociological Society, Sutherland delivered a 1939 keynote address that centered the importance of white-collar crime (WCC) as an empirical topic for social scientists.[21] The way he defined this subfield was of tremendous import for challenging the dominant ways of defining both crime and criminality. Sutherland was interested in crimes "committed by a person of respectability and high social status in the course of their occupation."[22]

Similar to E.A. Ross, Sutherland's definition was *agent*-based, not action-based. His focus was not on any specific offenses, but on the characteristics of the offenders.[23] Assuming the perpetrator was of respectable social status, Sutherland's criteria involved whether the act was 1) socially injurious and 2) punishable by criminal, civil, or administrative processes. He defined crime as a function of the "type of person" and not the "type of action" – and included activities that could be accounted for in civil or administrative and criminal law. Paul Tappan (1947) is among those who fundamentally disagreed with Sutherland's agent-based approach. Tappan found it problematic to use a legal word (i.e., crime) to describe phenomena not explicitly prohibited by – or found in – criminal law. Both a lawyer and sociologist, Tappan countered that Sutherland could only label phenomena as representing white-collar crime

if the act in question was legally defined as a misdemeanor or felony. What's
more, someone would have to be legally convicted or formally adjudicated
to qualify as a white-collar criminal, since all felons, like felonies, have to be
legally created before they can be said to *legally* exist.[24]

Why does this matter? In the wake of the Watergate scandal, investigators
found that President Nixon's re-election campaign sought to hide questionable –
if not illegal – campaign contributions. They also found an entire ecosystem
of private and public exchanges involving donation "cash slush funds in hundreds of U.S. corporations."[25] This was both a domestic and international
practice, as the Securities and Exchange Commission (SEC) found that over
400 U.S. companies had spent millions of dollars "bribing everyone from
prime ministers to police overseas" in furtherance of business interests.[26] Prior
to the introduction of FCPA, such practices could not have even been thought
of as illegal since there were no serious forms of regulatory oversight, reflecting the Western legal tradition of *nullum crimen sin lege*, or that there can be
no punishable crime unless the crime and the punishment are proscribed by
law. The Foreign Corrupt Practices Act (FCPA) of 1977 was a legislative
attempt to account for the bribery of public officials after this gap in the law
was understood as deeply consequential. With half a century of hindsight, the
Sutherland-Tappan debate better reflects the merits and drawbacks of assuming that laws are adequately geared towards regulating whatever we might
understand as *crime*.

Categories and definitions derive their utility from our manner of applying
them.[27] This explains in part why an encyclopedia of white-collar crime will
include everything from welfare fraud and insider trading to "crimes of trust"
like overcharging for services rendered. The following list[28] presents some of
the substantive categories that fall under this umbrella-like categorical term,
underscoring the variety of conceptual approaches and areas of emphasis sharing the WCC designation.

Corporate Crime: Legal violations and legitimized harms committed
by officers and representatives of corporate organizations, committed
to advance some combination of organizational and personal interests.[29]

Governmental Crime: The range of legal violations and harms that are
facilitated, inspired, or initiated by the state. This include large-scale
crimes of the state (e.g., genocide and war crimes) and lower-level forms
of political corruption (e.g., influence peddling or accepting bribes in
any official capacity as a public servant).[30]

Occupational Crime: Legal violations and legitimized harms committed
in the workplace.[31]

State-Corporate Crime: Crimes that are readily recognizable as symbiotic in function, involving some combination of public and private
actors and actions that operate with shared incentives. Examples include
crimes of global finance and the intentional failure of regulatory institutions to mitigate the known risks of an economic mode of production.[32]

Enterprise Crime: Cooperative enterprises that contain a syndicate element (i.e., organized crime function) that spans across legitimate and illegitimate market activities.[33]

Contrepreneurial Crime: Swindles, scams, and frauds that are presented as legitimate business functions, some of which escape formal designation as fraudulent, but nevertheless victimize the end-user/consumer/buyer.[34]

These categories are neither exhaustive nor mutually exclusive, and scholars at the individual and disciplinary level will vary in the degree to which they prioritize or ignore some of these categories or sub-components of another. Other categories are arguably redundant.

Articulating the nuances and caveats in defining WCC can seem like splitting hairs. Indeed, many criminologists find the longstanding discussions in how to best define and operationalize WCC as "tedious" and would rather devote time and intellectual energy on advancing theoretical and empirical questions. After all, conceptual and definitional questions can sustain debate for so long that they become repetitive and "interminable."[35] These nuances underscore the importance of clarity in what we mean when we use words like *crime* and *criminal*, and this book will be presenting activities that run the full gamut of licit and illicit, and prosocial and antisocial.

Choosing a coherent definition of white-collar crime is just the first hurdle. As social scientists, our work is fueled by data where – however imperfect the data generation process – the biases are generally known and accounted for. For instance, not all kinds of crimes are equally likely to be detected and, when when identified, not everyone is equally likely to be arrested, prosecuted, and subsequently convicted.

Virtually every introductory textbook in U.S. criminal justice courses references the hidden figure of crime,[36] or those legal transgressions that go undetected, unreported, or otherwise unaccounted for. Unlike violent or property crimes or crimes visible "in the street," WCC may often involve a diffuse form of harm and a less obvious process of victimization, which in turn partially explains its relative lack of formal criminal justice attention.[37] Relative to street crime, WCC receives less oversight and criminal law bandwidth, especially since criminal justice systems (i.e., police, courts, and corrections) historically developed around controlling the classes that were formally subject to purview of criminal law. Phrased differently, crime is often defined in such a way so as to appear that the wealthy in society have no desire to engage in it, and the enforcement of criminal law is primarily geared towards young, male, and non-white subjects. But for white-collar crime, there are some differences worth outlining here.

Theoretical perspectives for explaining white-collar crime

For the bulk of its existence as an academic field, criminology has been mostly concerned with the offender who "has arms, legs, most likely is young, male, and probably black."[38] The three major prongs of criminal justice (i.e., police, courts, and corrections) have also been designed around specific criteria and general assumptions concerning both criminal *acts* and criminal *actors*. In terms of criminal acts, the "bread and butter" felonies that are of most interest to criminal justice institutions include arson, assault, battery, burglary, homicide, larceny, motor vehicle theft, robbery, and sexual assault. The biased nature of criminal justice data is what allowed for the Yale Law Group to "empirically refute" that white-collar crimes are committed by powerful and respectable actors.[39] In short, data on white-collar crime do not adequately capture the powerful actor, or the *criminaloid* described by Edward A. Ross in 1907 as

> a buyer rather than a practitioner of sin, and his middlemen spare him unpleasant details. Secure in his quilted armor of lawyer-spun sophistries. . . . The wholesale fleecer of trusting, workaday people is a "Napoleon," a "superman."
>
> (Ross 1907:53)

Crimes of the powerful[40] and white-collar criminality have an understandably anemic role in the development, scope, and content of criminal law and criminal justice, despite knowing that the measurable harms of white-collar crime far exceed those of street-level crimes. Similar to how the medicalization of patriarchy and racialized subjugation was facilitated by pseudo-scientific concepts like *hysteria* or *drapetomania*, criminological theory has historically contributed to the intellectual laundering of self-serving ideologies onto the bodies of subjugated groups. As such, many theories in white-collar crime are not necessarily *explaining* what generates white-collar crime at a structural level, but merely offering descriptions of criteria that can be identified when comparing the legally compliant individual from the legally transgressive one. This is a very different question from asking: What makes such transgressions a rational choice to begin with?

Nevertheless, white-collar crime scholarship yields findings that are different from other crime categories.[41] For instance, whereas the image of the typical street offender – and the demographic representation of those under criminal justice supervision – is a young, relatively lower-income male of color; demographic trends in WCC scholarship are more diverse, especially with respect to income and socioeconomic status of the offender.[42] If we were using a Sutherland-style definition, of course, this would be tautological, or conceptually circular. (Defining crimes as offenses committed by powerful people would mean that the crimes would be, as the data would show, committed by powerful people!) But some of these important similarities and differences are worth summarizing, as follows.

Age: WCC offenders defy the age-crime curve. Ages 15–25 are not the "crime years," but, instead, the average WCC offender tends to be middle-aged or older.[43]

Sex: Similar to virtually all crime categories, male offenders are over-represented in corporate, governmental, and occupational environments.[44]

Race: WCC offenders tend to be white.[45]

Education: WCC offenders tend to have higher educational attainment levels.[46]

Employment: WCC offenders are more likely to have regular income and be employed, but this varies based on the type of WCC examined. Intuitively, employment rates for those convicted of welfare fraud will differ from those convicted of antitrust violations.[47]

Socioeconomic Status: By definition, some forms of white-collar crime are exclusively the domain of economic elites. Some studies have argued that white-collar crime is the domain of non-powerful offenders, but there are some tautological issues here.[48]

Marital Status: WCC offenders tend to be married, whereas in conventional crime, marriage is viewed as desistance factor.[49]

Criminal History: Those WCC offenders who are convicted of "high SES" offenses (e.g., antitrust or insider training) tend to have no prior convictions. Generally speaking, WCC offenders have fewer prior convictions and lower recidivism rates.[50]

Tautologies in criminological theory

Studies[51] that aim to explain white-collar crime across multiple categories and settings should be treated with suspicion.[52] If we don't have defensible theories for explaining prosocial or legal behavior, how could we have one for explaining antisocial or illegal behavior? If there are no integrated or comprehensive theories for what explains or predicts virtuous behavior, happiness, unfairness, passive-aggressive behavior, sarcasm, athleticism, public speaking charisma, or cringe worthiness, then attempting to do the same for a broad and permeable category like crime may be too tall of an order. Nevertheless, such approaches are well represented in the literature. The most obnoxious of these involve rational choice theory and techniques of neutralization – both of which focus exclusively on the individual offender.

The studies that successfully find empirical support for conventional criminological theories can be followed by reviews, critiques, and counter-publications with competing theoretical explanations. For example, Hirschi's social control theory has been tested,[53] as well as Hirschi and Gottfredson's self-control theory.[54] Gottfredson and Hirschi's ambitious "general theory of crime" (1990) has been challenged by many on both empirical and conceptual grounds.[55] Unlike the common inference that street criminals "lack self-control," Reed and Yeager (1996) – among others – assert that corporate offending is a product of "highly trained, properly ambitious, and conventionally socialized individuals who strain to manage ethical and legal dilemmas they regularly face and to find moral justification for their offenses."[56] Reed and Yeager (1996) highlight the problematic attempts to extend the general theory of crime since

Gottfredson and Hirschi "constrained the test of their theory by focusing on the white-collar offenses that most resemble conventional crime."[57]

These theories collectively represent a tautology. If the data do not lend support for one theoretical explanation, they surely lend themselves to another. Taken together, these theories thus represent a tautology, where no theory is truly falsifiable because there are always avenues for fitting the data to the theory. All the while, we know, in the back our minds, that the theories have little predictive value beyond correlational propensities or "risk factors" that explain some portion of the variance in a given measure of interest.

As Bill Chambliss writes:

> Everyone commits crime. And many, many people whether they are poor, rich or middling are involved in a way of life that is criminal; and furthermore, no one, not even the professional thief or racketeer or corrupt politician commits crime all the time. To be sure, it may be politically useful to say that people become criminal through association with "criminal behavior patterns," and thereby remove the tendency to look at criminals as pathological. But such a view has little scientific value, since it asks the wrong questions. It asks for a psychological cause of what is by its very nature a socio-political event. Criminality is simply not something that people have or don't have; crime is not something some people do and others don't. Crime is a matter of who can pin the label on whom, and underlying this socio-political process is the structure of social relations determined by the political economy.[58]

Rather than focus on the individual offender, why not opt for a theory of criminal justice detection? Or a theory of criminalization and formal social control? That is what would best account for how certain activities become 1) defined as being under the purview of criminal law and 2) acted upon by criminal justice agents and agencies. To be clear, arrest, prosecution, and sentencing data are not randomly generated but structurally biased towards less powerful groups.[59] The felon, like the felony, is *made*. Legal and social categories for criminals, deviants, outcasts, and so on are socially contingent and they ebb and flow. It is for this reason that my preferred starting point is political economic explanations, which can help us understand *how* acts and identities become criminalized.

Structural contradictions as an explanatory framework

As an analytic framework, structural contradictions theory views criminal acts as historically situated and contingent on the power dynamics and social order of a given time and place. Acts become defined as criminal in the attempt to resolve conflicts produced by contradictions embedded in the structure of political, economic, and social relations of a society. Under this theory, criminal behaviors are responses of people in different social classes and groups to the conditions stemming from structural contradictions.[60] Highly compatible with socio-legal scholarship, the gap between prescriptive (what should be) and descriptive legal orders and institutions is what produces conditions favorable to what becomes legally proscribed as criminal. "In the process of responding to structural contra-dictions, Anglo-American law developed with an ideological underpinning of a commitment to equality, justice, and universality. These ideologies, however, sometimes contradict role expectations and the need to efficiently accomplish other goals expected of law enforcers, entrepreneurs, and government officials. Criminal networks emerge as a solution to the conflicts generated by these contradictions.[61]

Shadow markets, or illicit economies, offer lucrative opportunities for com-modities, markets, and transactions that are prohibited by law but in which many people wish to participate. This not only applies to your bread-and-butter organized crime topics like firearms, prostitution, gambling, and drugs, but cur-rency itself. The state retains leverage over these markets by keeping them legally prohibited and thus subject to overt and explicit oversight. For this reason, and precisely for this reason, we end up in the situation where the efforts are always in the "supply-side" arena and seldom ever in the "demand-side" arena. Phrased differently, by making certain markets illegal, the state can selectively exercise discretion on when, where, and whom to prioritize in the *management* (not elimination) of illicit markets. Typically, enforcement is conducted against the most vulnerably or most politically unaffiliated members of the market. This is why wealthy and powerful actors can and have enjoyed relative impunity in vice markets. The rich and wealthy are not the focus of sex markets, drug markets, gambling markets, or others. Moreover, the *most* politically connected and pow-erful actors are actually shaping the very nature of enforcement, often co-opting the state's enforcement apparatus to serve their needs.

This framework is compatible with a wide array of criminological and soci-ological theories, and places them in a way that is consistent with a proper political economic analysis. For example, we could connect it to the classic Mertonian framework: There is a widespread cultural desire to consume and attain material advancement but everyone cannot possibly succeed or do so at the same pace. For crimes of powerful and non-powerful actors alike, those who do not "have enough money to live up to the minimum standard of consump-tion deemed acceptable by the culturally defined values" will be likely to find less-than-legal alternatives (i.e., Mertonian innovations) to acquire the money.[62]

We might also use institutional anomie theory, which posits that U.S. society is embedded with a cultural ethos that emphasizes material gains to such a large extent that those with limited resources or blocked opportunities innovate or find alternative means to achieve these culturally valued goals.[63]

According to Messner and Rosenfeld (1997), a society risks institutional anomie when:

1   Economic goals are assigned high priority in comparison with noneconomic goals (e.g., when students are advised to pick something "marketable" as opposed to something intellectually challenging or academically satisfying);

2   The claims of economic roles are typically honored at the expense of non-economic roles when conflicts occur (e.g., we are still debating maternity leave and paid sick days because it's "bad for business");

3   Social standing tends to be highly dependent on the performance of economic roles over noneconomic roles (e.g., the way we think about someone's attained "success" is often related to income or job title; and

4   The calculating, utilitarian logic of the marketplace penetrates other institutional realms (e.g., neoliberal market trends like Teach for America and Uber; or conceptions of healthcare that make illness and accident a basis for becoming a health insurance marketplace *consumer* of healthcare *product*).[64]

Structural contradictions theory is more than just an iterative fixation on the relationship between the opposing interests of the bourgeoise and the proletariat. It is a framework for understanding the myths that we tell ourselves all the time: That we can have an ecologically coherent future *with* our current capitalist modes of production. That we can have a liberal democracy where political decisions are subject to a vote, but economic decisions are not. That public health and wellness are compatible with our current mode of economic organization. That neoliberal governance and respect for the equal worth of all human life are compatible aims. And that liberalism can coexist with human rights. Rather than frame these and polemic, grand, overarching statements, there are ways that researchers can use structural contradictions theory in a manner that accounts for the specific nature of the place and context where they exist. To that end, I offer organizational sociology as a practical way forward.

Practical ways forward

Combining structure and agency into an organizational framework

For scholars interested in crimes of the powerful, organizational sociology offers a practical orientation. This perspective lends itself to formal and complex organizations as the unit of analysis, enabling one to examine individual agency within the context of their organizational setting.[65] Organizational offending is "any non-accidental behaviors committed for organizational gain within a non-criminal purpose organization that participates in, condones, or demonstrates willful ignorance of a governmentally punishable act within that organization that victimizes other persons or institutions."[66] Theories and concepts from organizational sociology can be usefully applied to substantive criminological problems. In earlier work, Diane Vaughan (1999) coined a term in studying what she described as "the dark side of organizations," or the adverse societal consequences stemming from the mistakes, misconducts, and disasters that are structural byproducts of the organizational form. "These harmful actions and the extensive social costs to the public . . . are not claimed as central to the domain of sociologists who define their specialization as organizations, occupations, and work" and at the time of writing, "only recently have text-books included harmful outcomes and organizational pathologies that adversely affect the public."[67]

Views from inside corporations consistently suggest that corporate offending is routine and a function of the social and cultural forces within the organization.[68] Anand et al. (2004) similarly found that this self-selection process in corporate settings helps "perpetuate corruption by weeding out those who are most averse to it," consistent with data from this study that suggest it is a liability to be too rule-abiding in orientation.[69] Anand et al. (2004) draw primarily from techniques of neutralization (rationalizations), along with elements of social learning theory (socialization processes), to analyze what they deem to be "the acceptance and perpetuation of corruption in organizations." Again, even when there are structural incentives to engage in acts that might be viewed by some as deviant (or are violations of criminal or civil law), not all individual agents will respond in similar ways.

Not only are there structural forces that influence individual behavioral outcomes, but the white-collar crimes of interest may be normatively embedded as unofficial customs of the workplace. "Indeed, surveys of corporate officials indicate that unethical and illegal practices are common,"[70] and previous research has found that unethical and illegal acts were connected to the culture established by management.[71] More contemporary citations and examples can be mined from major newspapers; whether the headline of the day is about Wells Fargo's unscrupulous account management practices,[72] intentionally deceptive emissions measurement scandals,[73] corporate tax evasion by top-rated companies,[74] or police manipulation of crime statistics,[75] the fundamental role of structural incentives and organizational pressures is what justifies an organizational unit of analysis.

In emphasizing the relationship between structure and agency, "bad apples can be the product of bad barrels."[76] Anand et al. argue that within the context of specific white-collar offenses, "fraud is taking place at virtually every organization," and when organizational wrongdoing is acknowledged, senior executives tend to scapegoat rogue individuals or isolated groups, arguing that these specific actors "do not represent the otherwise pristine organization."[77] Structural and individual factors complement each other, and the bulk of literature relating organizational sociology to questions of crime and deviance support the assertion that there needs to be more attention paid to the interaction between the two.

Data – however imperfect – do exist

Today, the most robust quantitative measures that we have of legally sanctioned white-collar offenses – as measured through arrest statistics – are found in the National Incident-Based Reporting System (NIBRS) and the Uniform Crime Report (UCR).[78] The Federal Bureau of Investigation (FBI) spearheads and facilitates both data collection programs, in partnership with other entities housed under the Department of Justice (e.g., Bureau of Justice Statistics). The UCR originated in the 1920s, whereas NIBRS was introduced in the 1980s to remedy some of the limitations of the UCR and encourage more reliable data-tracking practices. NIBRS data collection remains an imperfect process with approximately one-third of law enforcement agencies contributing the kind of data that NIBRS requires. Measurement issues and the hidden figures of crime remain sources of data insecurity, as white-collar offenses – particularly those that are sophisticated in nature or committed by/through elite actors or institutions – are the types of crimes most likely to evade detection by local law enforcement and formal adjudication through the criminal courts.

Crimes and harms perpetrated by powerful actors are not well represented in the bulk of criminal justice data sources, but a few U.S.-specific databases are available. The Department of Justice contains an office within its Criminal Division called the Public Integrity Section (PIS) to oversee specific opera-tionalizations of public corruption. PIS "oversees the federal effort to combat corruption through the prosecution of elected and appointed public officials at all levels of government."[79] In annual reports,[80] the DOJ's Public Integrity Section releases descriptive statistics and case narratives pertaining to federal prosecutions of corrupt public officials.[81] PIS data account for an array of fed-eral crimes, including accepting bribes, awarding government contracts with-out competitive bidding, accepting kickbacks from private entities engaged in or pursuing business with the government, overstating travel expenses or hours worked, selling information on criminal histories and law enforcement information to private companies, mail fraud, using government credit cards for personal purchases, sexual misconduct, falsifying official documents, theft of government computer equipment, and several forms of police misconduct.[82]

PIS data are used in quantitative analyses and are generally considered one of the most reliable sources of longitudinal data on domestic corruption.[83] Like other commonly cited criminal justice data (e.g., UCR, NIBRS, NCVS), PIS data are not without limitations. Prosecutorial and conviction data do not accu-rately reflect the scope of actual *prosecutable* corruption, and PIS data may be spuriously driven by extralegal or inconsistently detected factors (e.g., resource allocation across federal judicial districts). Corporate crimes are largely absent from these data.[84] Corporate offenses (no matter how "accidental" or "unantici-pated" in their presentation) are typically addressed via fines and other admin-istrative and civil proceedings where the organizational form bears symbolic financial costs but continues carrying out its business functions as usual. A poten-tial downfall of this bias in the data generation process is that those crimes that are captured in these data tend to correlate or represent the types of crimes that can be committed by people who may have low status or low social/economic capital (e.g., unemployed), which strays from the historical emphasis on the relative status and prestige of the offender.[85] Studies that rely on such data risk the possibility of drawing inferences from offenders who lack an occupation and lack relative "respectability" or "high social status" – as Edwin Sutherland origi-nally highlighted.[86] The biased nature of criminal justice data is what allowed for the Yale Law Group to "empirically refute" that white-collar crimes are committed by powerful and respectable actors.[87] Despite such imperfections, the PIS remain as the UCR- or NIBRS-equivalent of public corruption data, and while the "hidden figure of crime" (i.e., undetected crimes) still presents a challenge, they remain instructive for understanding baseline rates and longitudinal trends that can be triangulated with other modes of inquiry. These available data are valuable, but the laws that govern bribery and corruption law are, in their current form, structurally insufficient to account for the bulk of illegalities and legitimized forms of corruption that exist today.

Existing laws are insufficient

There are existing critiques of the shortcomings of bribery and corruption law, foremost of them being the scholarship of Zephyr Teachout.[88] I will only briefly mention one issue with existing laws. The legal criteria for establishing that a bribe took place versus the real practice of providing and accepting bribes are very different. The impeachment of Donald Trump speaks directly to this. Despite the insistence at the highest levels of judicial expertise that bribes be legally relevant *only* if there is an explicit *quid quo pro* exchange, rarely are bribes socially negotiated in such a clinical fashion. There are certain linguistic gaps that represent the incongruence between normative forms of expression and legally recognized (e.g., prosecutable) conduct, or the *linguistic legal gymnastics*[89] reflected in how political officeholders avoid prosecutable charges by using language that fails to meet the criteria for a *quid pro quo* exchange.

In the nightlife economy, phrases like "So how do you wanna handle this?" is a coded question that sets the stage for how two parties might navigate alternative arrangements that, for all intents and purposes, correspond to a bribe. When bribe-givers and bribe-takers are able to stay well below the criteria needed to legally claim a *quid pro quo* violation, it results in a rather anemic state of legal enforcement. Legal instrumentalism is a descriptive account of what many would find intuitive; law is used as a means to an end. The law and its operationalizations are instruments used to accomplish a range of functions and serve a range of values. It underscores the relevance of conflict theory, where the law is not some objective rubric assessing the validity of claims, but a putty that strong hands use to mold to their liking. As one interviewee put it:

> The rule structure is impossible to follow. . . . Regulators and the attorney general's office also send contradictory messages. When I'm given two sets of rules, I'm going to follow the one that is most beneficial to the business. We all have entertainment endorsements [the legal term used to allow for amplified sound and live music], but the liquor control board said that no enforcement occurs from 11am–6pm, because inspectors don't start their rounds until 6pm. The AG's office said this is incorrect, and that enforcement occurs at all times.
>
> (Party Bar Manager)

The previous excerpt transcends what conventional criminological theory would be unable to explain. Structural contradictions theory would be more appropriate for making sense of how legal and regulatory structures are contested arenas where different actors make sense of the dilemmas, conflicts, and contradictions that guide their occupational concerns and material incentives.

Conclusion

There is limited utility in applying conventional criminological theories to white-collar crime, corruption, and other crimes of the powerful. When offenses are regular in their occurrence; transcendent of any individual traits; legitimized as routine activities or "normal business practices"; and intellectually or politically defended, it becomes difficult to apply the traditional criminological perspectives to certain classes of harms. Despite these imperfections and open-textured debates in criminological theory, criminal justice systems are a separate arena where specific types of white-collar and corporate crime are operationalized and addressed. Data on crimes of the powerful are always challenging to reliably secure, and there are some databases that, however imperfect, nevertheless allow for empirical analysis.

As a partial remedy to this theoretical gap, structural contradiction theory offers an explanatory vehicle for making sense of the tensions and dilemmas between what we think criminal justice systems and criminological theory should explain, and what actually occurs. In many instances, activities that we call "crime" are rational responses to the structural contradictions that manifest themselves in political, economic, and interpersonal settings. Organizational sociology, or organizational perspectives, are highly compatible with structural contradictions theory, and center both structure and agency in how specific people navigate the incentives and dilemmas of their variously situated positions. With these theoretical and conceptual tools now introduced, the next chapter focuses on the auto-ethnographic portion of my research and takes us behind the bar in the nightlife economy of Metropolis East.

Notes

1 Noonan, Charles. 1984. *Bribes*. University of California Press; Ksenia, Gerasimova. 2008. "Can Corruption and Economic Crime Be Controlled in Developing Countries and If so, Is It Cost-Effective?" *Journal of Financial Crime* 15(2):223–233.

2 Buchan, Bruce and Lisa Hill. 2014. *An Intellectual History of Political Corruption*. Palgrave Macmillan. Noonan 1984; Carrillo, Juan D. 2000. "Graft, Bribes, and the Practice of Corruption." *Journal of Economics & Management Strategy* 9(2):257–288.

3 Holmes, Leslie. 2008. "Corruption and Organised Crime in Putin's Russia." *Europe-Asia Studies* 60(6):1011–1031.

4 Riordan, William L. 2015. The Plunkitt of Tammany Hall: A Series of Very Plain Talks on Very Practical Politics. Signet Classics, p. xi.

5 Teachout, Zephyr. 2014. *Corruption in America: From Benjamin Franklin's Snuff Box to Citizens United*. Harvard University Press; Steffens, Lincoln. 1957. *The Shame of the Cities*. Amereon.

6   378 U.S. 184 (1964).

7   Doshi, Sapana and Malini Ranganathan. 2018. "Towards a Critical Geography of Corruption and Power in Late Capitalism." *Progress in Human Geography* 43(3):436–457. https://doi.org/10.1177/0309132517753070.

8   Tushnet, Mark. 1991. "Critical Legal Studies: A Political History." *The Yale Law Journal* 100(5):1515.

9   Michalowski (2016) posits "that criminology is a subject matter more than an academic discipline" (p. 183), but also makes a case for criminology being a "topical field" in that it "relies primarily on general theories from core social science disciplines to create mid-range explanations for behaviors associated with the making, breaking, and enforcement of law" (p. 183). Another reason to avoid calling criminology a *discipline* involves a selective interpretation of Foucault's definition of the term: "The disciplines characterize, classify, specialize; they distribute along a scale, around a norm, hierarchize individuals in relation to one another and, if necessary, disqualify and invalidate" (Foucault, 1977/1995, p. 223). Michalowski argues that criminology has yet to be *disciplined* into coherent theoretical or methodological bounds, exemplified by the lack of agreement over its subject matter or "the overall purpose of the field" (p. 183). Michalowski, Raymond J. 2016. "What is Crime?" *Critical Criminology* 24:181–199.
    See also Friedrichs, David O. and Martin D. Schwartz. 2007. "Editor's Introduction: On Social Harm and a Twenty-First Century Criminology." *Crime Law and Social Change* 48:1–7; Schwartz, Martin. 1997. "Does Critical Criminology Have a Core? Or Just Splinters?" *Critical Criminologist* 3 (sun.soci.niu.edu/~critcrim).

10 Michalowski, Raymond J. 2016. "What is Crime?" *Critical Criminology* 24:181–199. Michalowski, Raymond J. and Ronald Kramer. 2006. *State-Corporate Crime: Wrongdoing at the Intersection of Business and Government.* Rutgers University Press.

11 Jeffrey, Clarence R. 1956. "The Structure of American Criminological Thinking." *Journal of Criminal Law and Criminology* 46(5):658–672; Young, Jock. 2011. *The Criminological Imagination.* Polity.

12 Green, Stuart P. 2004. "Moral Ambiguity in White Collar Criminal Law." *Notre Dame Journal of Law, Ethics and Public Policy* 18:501; Perri, Frank S. 2011. "White-Collar Criminals: The 'Kinder, Gentler' Offender?" *Journal of Investigative Psychology and Offender Profiling* 8:217–241; Cedric, Michel. 2015. "Violent Street Crime versus Harmful White-Collar Crime: A Comparison of Perceived Seriousness and Punitiveness." *Critical Criminology* 24(1):127–143.

13 Geis, Gilbert. 2016. *White-Collar and Corporate Crime.* Oxford University Press; see also Alalehto, Tage. 2015. "White Collar Criminals: The State of Knowledge." *The Open Criminology Journal* 8:28–35; McGurrin, D., M. Jarrell, A. Jahn and B. Cochrane. 2013. "White Collar Crime Representation in the Criminological Literature Revisited, 2001–2010." *Western Criminology Review* 14(2):3–19; Friedrichs, David O. 2015. "Crimes of the Powerful and the Definition of Crime." Pp. 39–49 in *The Routledge International Handbook of the Crimes of the Powerful,* edited by Gregg Barak. Routledge; Lynch, Michael J., Danielle McGurrin and Melissa Fenwick. 2004. "Disappearing Act: The Representation of Corporate Crime Research in Criminological Literature." *Journal of Criminal Justice* 32:389–398.

14 "The term 'muckrakers' was first applied to a group of American journalists, active around the turn of the century, who were committed to the exposure of business and industrial abuses and political corruption" (NYT Archives, 1985). "In modern use, the term has two related meanings. Used in the pejorative sense, 'muckraker' refers to a journalist who seeks out and publishes allegations of wrongdoing with the intention of creating a scandal. In the positive sense, the term implies diligence and a capacity to dig deep for the facts" (NYT Archives, 1985). Reflecting this paradox, Theodore Roosevelt is quoted as saying: "The men with the muckrakes are often indispensable to the well-being of society but only if they know when to stop raking the muck." *The New York Times* Archives. 1981. "Muckarker:2 Meanings." April 10, Section D: Page 27 (www.nytimes.com/1985/04/10/us/muchraker-2-meanings.html).

15 As Sullivan 2009 writes: Muckraking is the name given to the American investigative journalists who exposed the social injustices and political scandals of the early 20th century. The term *muckrakers* was first used by President Theodore Roosevelt in a 1906 speech to describe sensationalist-seeking journalists who were tarnishing the reputation of "honest men." The name is based on a character, the Man with Muckrake, in John Bunyan's *Pilgrim's Progress* (1678). For further reading, see Bunyan (1678), Sinclair (1906), and Steffens (1904/1957). Sullivan, Larry E. 2009. "Muckraking", in *The SAGE Glossary of the Social and Behavioral Sciences*, edited by Larry E. Sullivan. SAGE. Print page: 333. Online ISBN: 9781412972024. (http://dx.doi.org/10.4135/9781412972024.n1650).

16 *The Jungle* is appropriately categorized as a work of political fiction, yet it was empirically informed. By conventional standards, it would not qualify as an academic publication, but *The Jungle* nevertheless called attention to the real and systemic practice of sacrificing consumer and worker safety for private profit, and the serious (and preventable) harms occurring in the meatpacking industry of Chicago.

17 This term is originally attributed to the work of Cesare Lombroso, who in 1876 published *L'homme criminel* or *The Criminal Man*. Like many prominent sociologists of the time, E.A. Ross supported eugenicist frameworks for understanding social stratification, which coincidentally aligns with Lombroso's orientation to criminality: It was trait-based and specific to *kinds* of people. In Chapter 2 I address these and other racist underpinnings of social science theory.

18 Ross, Edward A. 1907. *Sin and Society: An Analysis of Latter-Day Iniquity*. Houghton Mifflin, p. 59.

19 Schoepfer, Andrea and Stephen G. Tibbetts. 2012. "From Early White-Collar Bandits and Robber Barons to Modern-Day White-Collar Criminals – A Review of the Conceptual and Theoretical Research." Pp. 63–83 in *Reflecting on White-Collar and Corporate Crime – Discerning Readings*, edited by D. Schichor, L. Gaines and A. Schoepfer. Waveland Press, Inc. pp. 64–65.

20 The US Occupational Safety and Health (OSHA) regulatory entity was created in 1971, and the Mine Safety and Health Administration (MSHA) was founded in 1977. See msha.gov for additional historical context.

21 Sutherland, Edwin. 1940. "White-Collar Criminality." *American Sociological Review* 5(1):1–12 (www.asanet.org/sites/default/files/savvy/images/asa/docs/pdf/1939%20Presidential%20Address%20(Edwin%20Sutherland).pdf), p. 9.

22 Sutherland, Edwin. 1949. *White Collar Crime*. Dryden Press, p. 9.

23 To be sure, homicides *can* be agent-specific if examining the characteristics of the victim, as is the case with killing a public official (e.g., law enforcement officer, public transit employee, assassinating a political figure, and other morbid scenarios). However, white-collar crime was introduced with an emphasis on the relative status or prestige of the offender (i.e., agent).

24 Hillyard, Paddy and Steve Tombs. 2007. "From 'Crime' to Social Harm?" *Crime, Law and Social Change* 48(1):9–25.

25 PBS Frontline. 2009. "The Business of Bribes." *PBS World* (www.pbs.org/frontlineworld/stories/bribe/history-of-anti-bribery-laws/).

26 PBS Frontline (2009).

27 For example, Edelhertz (1970) offered an action-based definition of WCC as "an illegal act or series of illegal acts committed by nonphysical means and by concealment or guile, to obtain money or property, to avoid the loss of money or property, or to obtain business or personal advantage" (p. 3), which avoids setting specific criteria about the relative status of the agent. Edelhertz, Hebert. 1970. "The Nature, Impact and Prosecution of White-Collar Crime." Report No. ICR 70–1. U.S. Department of Justice, May.

28 Adapted from Friedrichs, David. 2007. *Trusted Criminals: White Collar Crime in Contemporary Society*. 3rd ed. Thomas Wadsworth, p. 7.

29 Geis (2016).

30 Barak, Maya. 2015. "Collaborative State and Corporate Crime – Frauds, Unions and Elite Power in Mexico." Pp. 373–385 in *The Routledge International Handbook of the Crimes of the Powerful*, edited by Gregg Barak. Routledge.

31 Kennedy, Jay. 2016. "Employee Theft." Pp. 409–434 in *The Oxford Handbook of White-Collar Crime*, edited by Shanna R. Van Syke, Michael L. Benson and Francis T. Cullen. Oxford University Press.

32 Chambliss, William J., R. Michalowski and R.C. Kramer, eds. 2010. *State Crime in the Global Age*. Willan; Rothe, Dawn L. and Christopher W. Mullins. 2011. *State Crime – Current Perspectives*. Rutgers University Press; Ross, Jeffrey Ian, ed. 2000. *Controlling States Crime*. 2nd ed. Routledge.

33 Wainwright, Tom. 2016. *Narconomics: How to Run a Drug Cartel*. Public Affairs; Allum, Felia and Stan Gilmour, eds. 2011. *Routledge Handbook of Transnational Organized Crime*. Routledge.

34 See multi-level marketing businesses like Mona Vie and Mary Kay, or institutions that masquerade behind the label of "for-profit college," like Trump University.

35 Friedrichs, David. 2013. "Transcending the Conventional Definition of Crime: Toward a Twenty-First Century Criminology. Dedicated to the Memory of Gil Geis." A paper presented at Presidential Panel: Reconsidering the Definition of Crime Annual Meeting of the American Society of Criminology, Atlanta (www.asc41.com/Annual_Meeting/2013/Presidential%20Papers/Friedrichs,%20David.pdf), p. 3.

36 Problematically referenced as the "dark figure" of crime.

37 Green (2004).

38 Tombs, Steve and David Whyte. 2015. *The Corporate Criminal*. Routledge, p. 68.

39 Benson, Michael L., Shanna R. Van Slyke and Francis T. Cullen. 2016. "Core Themes in the Study of White-Collar Crime." Pp. 1–21 in *The Oxford Handbook of White-Collar Crime*, edited by S.R. Van Slyke, M.L. Benson and F.T. Cullen. Oxford University Press; Weisburd, D., S. Wheeler, E. Waring and N. Bode. 1991. *Crimes of the Middle-Classes: White Collar Offenders in the Federal Courts*. Yale University Press.

40 *The powerful* refers to economic and political elites. C. Wright Mills (1956) defined this term in his seminal text, *The Power Elite,* and referred to those individuals who occupy the most empowered positions within government, private industry, and the military. Any definition for power and those who possess or represent it is imperfect, and the elasticity of the term is discussed at length in Friedrichs (2015). Friedrichs, David O. 2015. "Crimes of the Powerful and the Definition of Crime." Pp. 39–49 in *The Routledge International Handbook of the Crimes of the Powerful*, edited by Gregg Barak. Routledge.

41 Alalehto (2015); Soothill, K., L. Humphreys and B. Francis. 2012. "Middle-Class Offenders: A 35-Year Follow-Up." *British Journal of Criminology* 52(4):765–785; Poortinga, E., C. Lemmen and M.D. Jibson. 2006. "A Case Control Study: White-Collar Defendants Compared with Defendants Charged with Other Nonviolent Theft." *Journal of the American Academy of Psychiatry and the Law* 34(1):82–89.

42 Benson, Michael L. and Elizabeth Moore. 1992. "Are White-Collar and Common Offenders the Same? An Empirical and Theoretical Critique of a Recently Proposed General Theory of Crime." *Journal of Research in Crime and Delinquency* 29:251–272; Johnson, David T. and Richard A. Leo. 1993. "Review: The Yale White-Collar Crime Project: A Review and Critique." *Law & Social Inquiry* 18(1):63–99.

43 Weisburd, David, Stanton Wheeler, Elin Waring and Nancy Bode. 1991. *Crimes of the Middle-Classes: White-Collar Offenders in the Federal Courts*. Yale University Press; Holtfreter, Kristy. 2005. "Is Occupational Fraud 'Typical' White-Collar Crime? A Comparison of Individual and Organizational Characteristics." *Journal of Criminal Justice* 33:353–365; Piquero, Nicole Leeper and Michael L. Benson. 2004. "White-Collar Crime and Criminal Careers: Specifying a Trajectory of Punctuated Situational Offending." *Journal of Contemporary Criminal Justice* 20(2):148–165.

44 Robb, George. 2006. "Women and White-Collar Crime Debates on Gender, Fraud and the Corporate Economy in England and America, 1850–1930." *The British*

Journal of Criminology 46(6):1058–1072; Morin, Rich. 2013. "Even in White Collar Crime, Female Crooks Face a Glass Ceiling." *Pew Research Center.* August 16 (https://www.pewresearch.org/fact-tank/2013/08/05/even-in-white-collar-crime-female-crooks-face-a-glass-ceiling/).

45 Sohoni, Tracy and Melissa Rorie. 2019. "The Whiteness of White-Collar Crime in the United States: Examining the Role of Race in a Culture of Elite White-Collar Offending." *Theoretical Criminology.* https://doi.org/10.1177/1362480619864312.

46 Wheeler, Stanton, David Weisburd, Elin Waring, and Nancy Bode. 1988. "White-Collar Crime and Criminals." *American Criminal Law Review* 25(3):331-357; Moore, Michael L. and Elizabeth Moore. 2016. "Are White-Collar and Common Offenders the Same? An Empirical and Theoretical Critique of a Recently Proposed General Theory of Crime." *Journal of Research in Crime and Delinquency* 29(3):251-272.

47 Kerley, Kent R. and Heith Copes. 2004. "The Effects of Criminal Justice Contact on Employment Stability for White-Collar and *Street*-Level Offenders." *International Journal of Offender Therapy and Comparative Criminology* 48(1):65–84. http://doi.org/10.1177/0306624X03256660; van Onna, Joost H. R., Victor R. van der Geest, Wim Huisman, and Adriaan J. M. Denkers. 2014. "Criminal Trajectories of White-Collar Offenders." *Journal of Research in Crime and Delinquency* 51(6):759–784.

48 See Geis (2016).

49 Klenowski, Paul M., Heith Copes and Christopher W. Mullins 2010. "Gender, Identity, and Accounts: How White Collar Offenders Do *Gender* When Making Sense of Their Crimes." *Justice Quarterly* 28(1):46–69.

50 Ragatz, Laurie L. and William Fremouw. 2012. "The Psychological Profile of White-Collar Offenders: Demographics, Criminal Thinking, Psychopathic Traits, and Psychopathology." *Criminal Justice and Behavior* 39(7):978–997; Holtfreter, Kristy, Shanna Van Slyke, Jason Bratton and Marc Gertz. 2008. "Public Perceptions of White-Collar Crime and Punishment." *Journal of Criminal Justice* 36(1):50–60.

51 Menard, Scott and Robert G. Morris. 2012. "Integrated Theory and Crimes of Trust." *Journal of Quantitative Criminology* 28:365–387; Braithwaite, John. 1989. "Criminological Theory and Organizational Crime." *Justice Quarterly* 6:333–338; Coleman, James. 1987. "Toward an Integrated Theory of White-Collar Crime." *American Journal of Sociology* 93(2):406–439.

52 Goode, Erich. 2008. *Out of Control: Assessing the General Theory of Crime.* Stanford University Press; Geis (2016).

53 Lasley, James R. 1988. "Toward a Control Theory of White-Collar Offending." *Journal of Quantitative Criminology* 4:347–362.

54 Gottfredson, Michael R. and Travis Hirschi 1990. *A General Theory of Crime.* Stanford University Press, Stanford, CA. Evaluated by Holtfreter, Kristy, Kevin M. Beaver, Michael D. Reisig and Travis C. Pratt. 2010. "Low Self-control and Fraud Offending." *Journal of Financial Crime* 17(3):295–307.

55 See Goode (2008); Geis (2016).

56 Reed, Gary E. and Peter C. Yeager. 1996. "Organizational Offending, and Neoclassical Criminology: Challenging the Reach of a General Theory of Crime." *Criminology* 34:357–377.

57 Reed and Yeager (1996:357).

58 Chambliss, William J. 1975. "Toward a Political Economy of Crime." *Theory and Society* 2(2):149–70, p. 165.

59 See Whyte, David. 2009. *Crimes of the Powerful: A Reader.* McGraw-Hill.

60 Chambliss, William J. 1988. *On the Take: From Petty Crooks to Presidents.* 2nd ed. Indiana University Press, p. 216.

61 Chambliss (1988:216).

62 Chambliss (1988:210).

63 Messner, Steven F. and Richard Rosenfeld. 2001. *Crime and the American Dream.* 3rd ed. Wadsworth; Schoepfer, Andrea and Nicole Leeper Piquero. 2006. "Exploring

White-Collar Crime and the American Dream: A Partial Test of Institutional Anomie Theory." *Journal of Criminal Justice* 34(3):227–235.

64 Messner, Steven F. and Richard Rosenfeld. 1997. "Political Restrain of the Market and Levels of Criminal Homicide: A Cross-National Application of Institutional-Anomie Theory." *Social Forces* 75:1393–1416; Rosenthal, Elisabeth. 2017. *An American Sickness: How Healthcare Became Big Business and How You Can Take it Back*. Penguin Press.

65 Vaughan, Diane. 2002. "Criminology and the Sociology of Organizations." *Crime, Law and Social Change* 37:117–136.

66 Green, Gary S. and Huisheng Shou. 2016. "Operationalizing Organizational Violence." Pp. 50–61 in *The Routledge International Handbook of the Crimes of the Powerful*, edited by Gregg Barak. Routledge, p. 51.

67 Vaughan, Diane. 1999. "The Dark Side of Organizations: Mistake, Misconduct, and Disaster." *Annual Review of Sociology* 25:271–305, p. 272; Perrow, Charles. 1984. *Normal Accidents: Living with High Risk Technologies*. Basic Books. Hall, Richard. 1996. *Organizations*. Prentice Hall.

68 Reed and Yeager (1996).

69 Anand, Vikas, Blake E. Ashforth and Mahendra Joshi. 2005. "Business as Usual: The Acceptance and Perpetuation of Corruption in Organizations." *The Academy of Management Executive* 19(4):9–23.

70 Reed and Yeager (1996:370).

71 Coleman, James William. 1987. "Toward an Integrated Theory of White-Collar Crime." *American Journal of Sociology* 93(2):406–439; Silk, Howard L. and David Vogel. 1976. *Ethics and Profits: The Crisis of Confidence in American Business*. Simon & Schuster.

72 Levine, Matt. 2016. "Wells Fargo Opened a Couple Million Fake Accounts." *Bloomberg View*, September 9 (www.bloomberg.com/view/articles/2016-09-09/wells-fargo-opened-a-couple-million-fake-accounts).

73 Hotten, Russell. 2015. "Volkswagen: The Scandal Explained." *BBC News*, December 10 (www.bbc.com/news/business-34324772).

74 Ip, Greg. 2016. "Apple's Tax Avoidance Illustrates Gap Between Law and Economics." *Wall Street Journal*, September 7 (www.wsj.com/articles/apples-tax-avoidance-illustrates-gap-between-law-and-economics-1473264984).

75 Francescani, Chris. 2012. "NYPD Report Confirms Manipulation of Crime Stats." *Reuters*, March 9 (www.reuters.com/article/us-crime-newyork-statistics-idUSBRE82818620120309).

76 Anand, Vikas, Blake E. Ashforth and Mahendra Joshi. 2004. "Business as Usual: The Acceptance and Perpetuation of Corruption in Organizations." *Academy of Management Executive* 18(2):39–53, p. 50.

77 Anand et al. (2004:39, 50).

78 Public Integrity Section (PIS) data is also relevant for specific forms of white-collar crime (e.g., governmental corruption), and this will be discussed in the forthcoming section on public corruption.

79 Department of Justice. 2016. "Public Integrity Section" (www.justice.gov/criminal/pin).

80 The Ethics in Government Act of 1978 requires the Attorney General to report annually to Congress on the operations and activities of the Justice Department's Public Integrity Section. The Report describes the activities of the Public Integrity Section during 2015. It also provides statistics on the nationwide federal effort against public corruption during 2015 and over the previous two decades. The Public Integrity Section was created in 1976 in order to consolidate in one unit of the Criminal Division the Department's oversight responsibilities for the prosecution of criminal abuses of the public trust by government officials. Section attorneys prosecute selected cases involving federal, state, or local officials, and also provide advice and assistance to prosecutors and agents in the field regarding the handling of public corruption cases. In addition, the Section serves as the Justice Department's center for handling various issues that arise regarding public corruption statutes and cases.

81 See Department of Justice (2016).

82 See Department of Justice (2016).

83 Dincer, Oguzhan C. and Burak Gunalp. 2012. "Corruption and Income Inequality in the United States." *Contemporary Economic Policy* 30(2):283–292; Glaeser, Edward L. and Raven E. Saks. 2006. "Corruption in America." *Journal of Public Economics* 90(6–7):1053–1072.

84 Simpson, Sally S. 2019. "Reimagining Sutherland 80 Years after White-Collar Crime." *Criminology* 57(2):189–207.

85 Ross, Edward A. 1907. *Sin and Society: An Analysis of Latter-Day Iniquity.* Houghton Mifflin; Sutherland, Edwin. 1949. *White Collar Crime.* Dryden Press.

86 Sutherland, Edwin. 1940. "White-Collar Criminality." *American Sociological Review* 5(1):1–12 (www.asanet.org/sites/default/files/savvy/images/asa/docs/pdf/1939%20 Presidential%20Address%20(Edwin%20Sutherland).pdf).

87 Benson et al. (2016); Weisburd et al. (1991).

88 Teachout (2014).

89 For purposes of this study, I am selectively using the term *linguistic legal gymnastics* to represent the careful attention to word choice that individuals exercise to mitigate against legal liability while simultaneously attempting to generate plausible deniability in the event of any legal action, allegation, or perceived misconduct. Within sociolegal studies, *linguistic gymnastics* has been used to account for a wide range of phenomena. These include 1) courts' attempt to reconcile gaps between statutes written in English and their interpretation and use in Spanish-speaking jurisdictions like Puerto Rico (see Freeman 2011), 2) critiques of judicial reasoning when there is robust intellectual disagreement with the ruling of a given case (see Moore 2014), and 3) debates about Constitutional interpretations (see Eisen et al. 2016). Eisen, Norman L., Richard Painter and Laurence H. Tribe. 2016. "The Emoluments Clause: Its Text, Meaning, and Application to Donald J. Trump." Memorandum published by Governance Studies at Brookings (www. brookings.edu/wp-content/uploads/2016/12/gs_121616_emoluments-clause1.pdf); Freeman, Andrea. 2011. "Linguistic Colonialism: Law, Independence, and Language Rights in Puerto Rico." *Temple Political and Civil Rights Law Review* 20:179 (http:// scholarlycommons.law.cwsl.edu/fs/82/); Moore, Schuyler M. 2014. "Garcia v. Google: Hard Cases Make Bad Law." *Huffington Post*, March 5 (www.huffingtonpost.com/schuy ler-m-moore/garcia-v-google-hard-case_b_4900376.html).

4   Getting behind the bar . . . and staying there[1] – on studying the nightlife economy

Part I

Defining the insider's account

This research is made possible through five years of occupational experience in the nightlife economy. My first four months working in this setting were in the capacity of a bouncer,[2] followed by an immediate transition into bartending. I would end up working for a total of five venues. Whereas some ethnographies are framed as "deployments" into a separate social world and are conditional on gaining access to a distinct environment, I was an insider prior to the start of this research. For academic inquiry, the status of being an "insider" does not inherently confer advantages or disadvantages relative to having the more conventional status of a neutral, detached, impartial observer – or "outsider."[3] Given the general inclination towards *objectivity* and *neutrality* in conventional social science, the use of the term *insider* comes with reasonable forms of baggage.

Being an insider can signal authority and expertise but can also inadvertently launder the uniqueness of one's experience into generalizable claims.[4] In other words, framing my authority as a writer as a direct function of my authentic insider status does not give me any additional credentials to make claims about other in-group members. An auto-ethnography by one truck driver or one university president tells us a lot about that one individual person and not necessarily anything about other truck drivers or university presidents. Intuitively, insiders vary in how they connect with the group to which they claim membership; you can be *in* a group but not *of* it, and you can be the most celebrated or most ostracized member *within* a given group. In short, merely being an insider does not automatically confer any special authority or legitimacy for making claims about other human beings. However, being an insider does give the author an ability to witness processes that might not be observable to outsiders.

A reflexive approach allows for fieldwork to be shared with its merits and limitations best accounted for. By acknowledging one's own biography and positionality and freeing oneself from the straitjacket of quantitatively oriented notions of objectivity and generalizability, a qualitative research design and analytic approach actually *gains* both legitimacy and understanding. In my case, I am using the phrase *insider's perspective* to simply denote that I worked in the nightlife sector prior to beginning my doctoral research, and I originally did not imagine a scenario where I would combine the ideas, topics, conflicts, and curiosities that were specific to my night job with something that I would connect to my day job. My occupational role in the nightlife setting *predated* my role as an independent researcher.

In this way, I am not claiming that my insider's perspective is inherently more or less authoritative, but probabilistically different from what it might have been if I had approached this environment without any prior experience in navigating these social and physical spaces. My approach is not through the lens of a social scientist exploring hitherto uncharted territory, but through that of a wage-laborer who sought to make the most sense of the social world in front of me. In the next section, I briefly unpack what it means to conduct an auto-ethnographic case study – which is the research design for this work.

The methodological as political: the auto-ethnography

When situating one's own experiences and subjectivity in broader cultural, social and political structures, it is the sociological imagination at work. Like wine and cheese, auto-ethnography and the sociological imagination are natural pairings, as it explicitly involves situating oneself (and others) into a broader sociological framework.[5] Whereas ethnography[6] is the systematic recording and analysis of a culture or society,[7] the prefix *auto* indicates that I am a member of the community being studied, and my membership is not predicated on the existence of the research.[8] Being both present in the text and represented in the subject matter, it is not only a tool in the methodological toolbox, but a political location for interacting with – and then writing about – other human beings.

As criminologists, our careers are built upon the claims we make about those who are generally far less powerful, resourced, and privileged compared to our peers and the audiences whom we engage. The things that take place in police, courts, and corrections, for instance, provide us with the data points that we need to do our work. In the case of alcohol and crimes of the powerful, mobsters and folk devils might serve as the popular face of Prohibition, just as the literature on drinking culture tends to "gaze downward" at less powerful groups.[9] As opposed to treating others as a means to an end, or a place where qualitative data are like gold to be mined and extracted, there is a more intimate relationship between the researcher and the researched.[10] Auto-ethnographic writing lends itself to a more intimate treatment of the subject being studied, since attributions made about *them* are also explicitly and implicitly guiding how others make sense of *you*.

The case study

Similar to auto-ethnography, the case study method – on paper – is not a prescriptive set of steps, but an orientation.[11] There are narrowly defined and consistent rules for conducting various kinds of regression analyses. There are virtually infinite ways to properly construct a case study. Case studies can involve a variety of methodological instruments and modes of inquiry, ranging from small-sample quantitative analyses of a bounded phenomenon to a mixed method analysis of some historical event. The cases themselves can be theoretical constructs (e.g., state-corporate hegemony in a particular setting) and empirical units (e.g., a quantified map of human feces in San Francisco).[12] Empirical units, in turn, can be operationalized at multiple scales, such as individuals, organizations, or broad and multifaceted social structures.[13]

My approach was informed by the best practices in conventional case study research,[14] adapted to fit my research questions and environment of study. In summarized form, this project was an in-depth, author-centric study of a relatively bounded phenomenon: The nightlife economy of Metropolis East, where my aim was to empirically document manifestations of white-collar crime, organizational deviance, and public corruption that might speak to processes found in other nightlife economies. I specifically focused on the complexity of white-collar crime and public corruption-related phenomena as it could be observed and documented in this setting, with a strong emphasis on how white-collar crime and corruption is generated and socially practiced by various participants. In what follows, I provide additional details on the major components of the research design.

Field interviews

Ethnographic interviewing involves both immersive observation and structured one-on-one interviews.[15] Unlike the sampling strategies in less compromising research designs, high-risk qualitative research is incompatible with probability sampling methods. It turns out that illegal or stigmatized acts are things that people generally try to keep secret. What's more, for such phenomena there is seldom – if ever – a coherent sampling population from which one could reliably identify ideal "study participants." I therefore relied on convenience (or availability) sampling, followed by a snowball sampling method to generate additional leads, in-roads, and participants.[16] An important consideration of snowball sampling is that it produces an ethnography of a particular social network, as opposed to an entire community.[17]

This is consistent with research where representative samples are either unfeasible or nonexistent.[18] Starting first with my personal networks and then extending beyond them through trusted referrals, my analysis extended through hub-and-spoke networks of venue-specific actors and social groups (e.g., bartenders who socialized together and were part of a core group of friends and business owners who managed several venues), allowing me to generate different independent leads. Respondents that felt comfortable with me usually were readily willing to suggest people, places, or news stories that I should consider for my research. Table 4.1 is a summary of the kinds of occupational positions included in this study:

Table 4.1 Occupational roles included in the study

Barbacks	6
Bartenders	18
Cocktail Waitresses	5
DJs	4
Managers	11
Owners	3
Police	4
Promoters	4
Security	13
Total	68

My formal protocols were informed by practices found in high-risk field research,[19] adapted to fit the idiosyncrasies of my research environment. All participants who provided in-depth narratives of white-collar crime and corruption were interviewed using IRB-approved instruments. However, many informal conversations provided generative material and broader context. I approached acquaintances, friends, and extended network contacts (i.e., people that I know of, but don't know personally) with a discrete but non-offensive solicitation. My introductory pitch involved tailored iterations of the following message: "I'm conducting a study on nightlife trends and I am interested in learning from your perspective. A major part of the project is especially sensitive and requires that we communicate in person. This is a funded study and you would be compensated for your time. Please let me know if you'd be able to have a 10–15-minute meeting or a 5-minute phone call if you're interested in learning more."

When meeting with high-priority interviewees, I presented two versions of my IRB informed consent document. One was a detailed and comprehensive form outlining the nature of the study and the corresponding risks, both actual and potential. The second version of the document – which is the one that respondents could keep – was a "safe copy," with all references to white-collar crime, organizational deviance, and public corruption removed and replaced with a different sociological subject matter. Participants could thus retain a printed copy of their rights, their liabilities, and the risks associated with human subject research, along with the contact information for the Institutional Review Board (IRB) and my Dissertation Committee Chair. Importantly, I informed each interviewee that the safe copy helps account for the possibility that even if a third party were to find this document, they would not be able to infer the crime-related focus of my research. Instead, they would have the IRB contact information for a study of the "sociological dimensions of courtship" in nightlife spaces.

My research protocol required that I *not* collect signatures. Instead, I used a series of checkboxes that each respondent would read and account for by simply checking each box and writing the date of our interview. Respondents who agreed to participate were provided with one of the following forms of compensation: a $40 Amazon gift card, $40 in cash, or $40 in the form of a personal check.[20] The informed consent document and my verbal instructions emphasized that they should *never* implicate themselves in any kind of illegality or liability, nor should there ever be a written record (e.g., text, e-mail, document) specifying the exact focus of the study with any personally identifiable information. One way that I communicated this former point was that if they wanted to say that they have been involved in or participated in any kind of white-collar crime or corruption-related activity, they should be sure to phrase it in a vague statement such as "I am completely certain that this practice exists" or "this is something that is 100% true from my experience."

Some respondents felt at ease discussing topics that might present legal or professional liabilities to themselves and others. The following excerpt illustrates this point and speaks to some of the reasons for why I opted to not record my interviews.

> I do two things routinely that could be criminal violations, but are certainly civil liabilities. I edit the clock in/clock out times to save the company money and I edit reported tips. One of these actions hurts the employees but the other one reduces their tax liability. That's the tradeoff.
>
> (Party Bar Manager)

The decision to forgo audio-recorded interviews was challenging. There is no way to know whether my respondents would have spoken in the same way had there been a recording device present. But as a separate matter, whether an interview is recorded or otherwise, one critically important consideration in field interviews involves credibility of the respondents. In short, regardless of the subject matter and the person being interviewed, it's not self-evident that we should believe what we are told, especially on sensitive topics related to white-collar crime and corruption. However, the working assumption is that respondents would be most likely to under-disclose information as opposed to fabricating information that might be a liability for the respondent. This assumption has limits. In the nightlife economy, there are intra- and inter-group forms of competition and conflict. As such, I scrutinized and sought to triangulate all claims that were made about organizations or individuals that did not have an immediate personal connection to the respondent. In terms of being critical of all claims made through my interview data, only the claims that could be independently corroborated or triangulated are included. In the next section, I briefly outline what this process entailed.

Triangulation, secondary data, and content analyses

Academic discourse on triangulation can appear unnecessarily dense.[21] Triangulation – as a verb – has more applied value than triangulation as a noun and subject of formalized study. Triangulation involves applying multiple approaches – both theoretical and methodological – for studying a given topic.[22] It is analogous to establishing a more defensible burden of proof for the validity of one's qualitative data. After all, just because someone tells you something does not mean that it should be reported. "This is what my respondent said" thus has to pass through the filter of "is it misleading or irresponsible to include what my respondent said?"

In practice, this sometimes felt like I was playing the role of a wannabe detective. For example, if someone made a claim that a certain venue engages in questionable practices related to auto-gratuity (e.g., manually changing the tip amount that is written on a credit card slip), I would check customer reviews on websites like Yelp to see if any customers had made complaints about such a practice, and checked for uploaded receipts that would identify the name associated with the bartender or cocktail waitress. I would review filed complaints on consumer websites like the Better Business Bureau and Google Reviews. Similarly, if someone made a claim that a group of nightlife business owners made contributions to a specific mayor's re-election campaign, then I would not only comb through the publicly available campaign contribution data, but also conduct research into the social networks of these industry actors to find out which fundraising organization can be identified as having a direct link to the participant's business network.

Other triangulation methods included reviewing the online comments sections of local newspaper articles, and examining publicly available social media accounts. Occasionally there would be a qualitative gem in the form of corroborating information, but such materials were also critical for developing new leads. Minutes (or the public records) from city agency meetings, purposive sampling of historic newspaper archives, and public records of Metropolis East were also studied extensively in order to fact-check data that emerged in conversations and interviews. Taken together, these steps are consistent with qualitative methodological practices in the social sciences, and triangulation is invaluable when conducting research into topics that involve hidden or problematic activities.[23] What's more, people are not as good as they think when it comes to recalling specific events and narrating previous experiences.[24] Evaluating interview data through these standards of corroboration ensure that the most important claims of this research do not hinge on what others have said in an unrecorded setting.

Taken together, my methods of triangulation result in a conservative orientation for making claims about the nightlife economy. There are tradeoffs. One drawback involves the qualitative equivalent of Type II errors, or "false negatives," where a researcher fails to claim empirical support for a theory when the evidence is actually there.[25] In practical terms, some findings are intentionally excluded from this study because they are based on information that I could not independently corroborate and that did not correspond to my own direct observation or experience.[26]

Qualitative data management

For digital field notes and data management, I relied on the *Evernote* software application, which synchronizes notes, recordings, and multimedia files across all registered devices. This was in addition to contemporaneous field notes, which I composed by hand on a pocket-sized notepad. Sensitive materials were written in shorthand but, as an added layer of security, I obtained a portable lockbox to keep sensitive documents pertaining to the study (e.g., interview notes and meeting schedules). Two-factor authentication was used for my digital files (maintained on Dropbox) and an automatic encryption feature was activated for my primary work computer. I used Atlas.ti to systematically code and analyze various data sources, which included interview notes, photos, budget reports, and all available newspapers on my topics of interest, among other sources.[27]

Pros and cons of research design

There are few reliable sources of data on crimes of the powerful and on topics of corruption and white-collar crime. While qualitative research designs are most advantageous, qualitative researchers often have their work evaluated by quantitatively oriented scholars. This has arguably contributed to a slow normalization of a defensive posture on the part of the qualitative researcher.[28] While the false dichotomy of quantitative "versus" qualitative methods is best dissected early in any given doctoral curriculum, there are inherent tradeoffs to consider when conducting qualitative social science inquiry. Some of these areas of dialogue are on fundamental topics like 1) internal and external validity, 2) replicability, 3) ethics of covert fieldwork, and 4) getting too close to the people, places, and social practices of the study. I will briefly speak to each of these.

On internal and external validity

Internal validity is consistent with the idea that we can study a social group (or a general process) for the purpose of understanding it *as it actually is*. Studying a social group (or some process) for the sake of understanding what it reveals about other groups or processes is more reflective of external validity. Phrased differently, external validity is about whether the data-driven findings extend beyond the confines of the research design. The case study method, by definition, does not seek to generalize beyond the boundaries of the specified case; the findings from a case study represent only the time, place, and observations specific to the research design.[29] However, case studies and related qualitative methodologies can provide inductive in-roads to phenomena that have yet to be empirically studied or theoretically understood at a large enough scale[30] – like crimes of the powerful.

For under-studied or undertheorized topics, the proliferation of inductive leads (e.g., multiple case studies) can provide the scaffolding for theory development, which in turn can allow for the testing of such theories and the continued refinement of how we understand that topic. An example that comes to mind is the general collection of studies on police corruption and police misconduct. Taken together, the "bad apple theory" for explaining such events becomes problematic when there is a large enough mass of studies that speak to something greater. If it were the case that only large metropolitan police departments experienced issues with "rogue units" or "excessive force" complaints, it might make sense to seek explanations tailored the characteristics of those individuals. When such issues are present across time (e.g., decades), across geographic settings (e.g., both large and small departments), and across actors (e.g., involving various types of officers), then the unit of analysis must move from "bad apples" to something resembling "bad barrels." Case studies are what can provide an empirical foundation for this kind of interpretation.

In crimes-of-the-powerful literature, the same can be said about white-collar offenses and corporate harms. It would be virtually impossible to study, in rich detail, bribery across multiple decades, continents, and organizational settings. Gaining access to privileged materials and informants on high-profile cover-ups would also be most appropriately tackled at the level of the case study. Through an accumulation of such studies, we come to better understand that there is nothing pathological that explains both exceptional and mundane instances of white-collar and corporate crime. The designers of the Ford Pinto, or the executives at Carnival, or Bernie Madoff himself are not solely responsible, in individualistic terms, for the criminal or harmful phenomena attributed to them. But it takes the accumulation of case studies on a given subject to provide an empirical foundation for a more comprehensive political economic explanation.

Replicability

From the positivist framework, ethnography and field studies are sometimes viewed as "untrustworthy" "in that researchers may arrive at different characterizations of the same or presumably similar phenomena under study."[31] This replicability concern is a false dilemma, as it is a substantive issue for all forms of inquiry, for all disciplines, and for all methodological approaches.[32] The virtue of the approach taken in this book is that many people who work both inside and outside the nightlife economy can reflect on whether my claims are consistent with what readers might observe in the nightlife environment nearest you.

Ethics and getting too close

Covert ethnographies on deviance *and* nightlife, both together and separately, produce a series of ethical challenges and concerns – resulting in the general stigmatization of covert ethnographies across scholarship silos.[33] Conducting ethnographic research on people who are unaware of your study is considered a form of covert ethnography. If it is the only available way to study a phenomenon of interest, then there are basic tradeoffs to consider. An ethically and logistically challenging study is – for some – at least better than no study at all. And the arbiters of whether a study was "worth the trouble" should be those who stand to gain or lose the most from the interpretation of the research, as opposed to the academy and its understandably canonical preferences.

If it is the task of a field researcher "to get as close to some set of individuals as possible"[34] and immerse themselves in the "bowels of the city,"[35] is it possible to get *too* close for comfort? Ethnography, after all, inherently carries the risk of "over-rapport" or "going native."[36] The dangers of identifying with "the others" is a theme found in popular culture and films, like *Avatar, The Last Samurai,* and so on. Social scientists can be uncomfortable about the instances where the disinterested and neutral data collector cannot simply act as an observant fly on the wall, and becomes instead an emotionally invested and empathetic "convert" of the social group.[37] There is an inherently social part of social science.

This concern is of both legal and professional consequence when the topic of study involves illicit or deviant activities. There have been sharp critiques of prominent researchers for their proximity to crime during their period of study.[38] Critiquing scholarship is always easier than doing it yourself, so the high-risk fieldwork of people like Sudhir Venkatesh and Alice Goffman – however voracious some of the critiques of their works have been – still offered novel contributions on empirics, theory, and methods. Ultimately, the fact that a research design is ethically challenging is insufficient for claiming that it should not be attempted.

With these points in mind, being too close is not a concern for an auto-ethnography. Being *implicated* is. Some of the activities that I have observed have constituted potential felonies, breaches of public trust, and predatory behaviors. In addition to direct observations, there were compelling allegations and rumors that, if true, might present severe liabilities for whoever exposed them. Nightlife is both a time and place where many secrets are out in the open, and where discretion, trust, and cultures of silence are problematically embedded. It is for these reasons that I only provide references to things that 1) can be corroborated using multiple methods and sources and 2) do not present threats to the safety or legal standing of myself or anyone involved in the research. Readers should know that there were no violent crimes that were enabled or influenced by my presence, actions, or inactions associated with my research.

Part II

The occupational environment of bartenders

Nightlife workers can often enjoy "a solidarity encouraged by the sense of sharing an unconventional timetable" and "having a different life-style from day workers."[39] As Melbin (1978) articulates, "[W]e refer to an island people or a desert people, or the people of arctic lands as a means of pointing out salient features of their habitats."[40] What might unite nightlife economy (or service industry) people? Those who have worked in nightlife might intuitively understand the relationship between their social experiences and industry culture and have vastly different social worlds compared to non-nightlife laborers.

Both within and beyond the U.S., studies examining the ways that nightlife industry employees navigate their work from an occupational or risk management perspective have been conducted. These studies include specific populations like bartenders,[41] bouncers,[42] and patrons.[43] Participating in night-life is a cultural activity,[44] and socio-cultural approaches are also present in the extant literature, with one study examining how youth drinking contributes to the creation of urban space, and how normative views on alcohol consumption vary by generation.[45] "Cultures of intoxication" and the ways in which identity is exercised and navigated are also represented.[46]

For criminology readers, opportunistic explanations (e.g., routine activi-ties theory) are prevalent in the empirical literature exploring the relation-ship between nightlife places and street crime.[47] Routine activities theory has been used to account for micro geographic and micro-temporal variations in various forms of crime and victimization,[48] in addition to the familiar trend of observing spatial concentrations of crime. There is a focus on substance use patterns and the physiological and victimization risks associated with alcohol consumption.[49] For example, among nightlife participants, those who com-bined alcohol with other controlled substances experienced "increased risk of involvement in physical aggression and demonstrated greater signs of visible intoxication."[50] Other studies examine workplace policies and regulatory struc-tures to better calibrate them in furtherance of risk management and crime prevention. For example, one study examined the integrity of the identifica-tion check practices of nightlife venues,[51] whereas others focused on the ways in which private and public entities collaborate to minimize risks and liabilities to public safety.[52] Some of these studies are rather specific, with one study examining the effect of "pre-gaming" and dynamic pricing on total alcohol consumption and observable disorder.[53] Other nuts-and-bolts studies include a risk-management study that concluded with practitioner-oriented recommen-dations, such as prohibiting glass containers. Victimology is also represented in the nightlife economy (NLE) literature.[54] Additionally, a handful of studies focus on barroom aggression and the ways in which bouncers and patrons alike navigate masculinity.[55] Except for three publications[56] referenced in this chap-ter, all of the studies are either qualitative or mixed in research design. Within the qualitative approaches, there is ethnography,[57] physical observation,[58] inter-views,[59] and the case study method.[60]

Bar culture

Working in nightlife comes with some lifestyle demands. Some of them have prosocial and healthy applications. Others, not so much. Your lower back, glutes, and hamstrings change in the direction of being more prone to soreness, stiffness, and low-intensity strains. Depending on how you care for yourself, your shoulders and elbows, particularly your dominant elbow, begin to hurt after enough shifts. Evidence of how you hold your tools and equipment can be found on the markings of your hand. Below your pinky finger, on the bridge between the palm and back of your dominant hand, or on specific knuckles, or on the cuticles of select fingers, you can find where the lime wedges and lime juice are most likely to make contact. The texture and appearance of your hands can reveal how you hold a bleached rag, or whether you use gloves when handling industrial cleaning solutions. One's class location is often marked on the body, and certainly on one's physiology.

We use our bodies intentionally, but different people are also used, commodified, and objectified (against their will) in ways that typically align with the business model. There is a double-edged sword of knowing what we're doing with our physical presentation of self, while knowing what others might be doing or might want to be doing in turn. (While I cannot personally attest to what it feels like to occupy a body other than my own, I've seen enough to feel comfortable making this claim.) As emotional laborers and corporal forms of advertisement, bar and nightclub staff use their own subjectivities to sell packages of feelings and experiences that align with certain configurations of class, sexuality, and strategic intimacy. Cocktail waitresses and bartenders alike understand that they are not selling *just* the professional services related to consuming alcohol. In plain English, bar staff are generally expected to *look* and *dress* and *act* a certain way.

Bartending is both a romanticized and a stigmatized occupation. In the former sense, there are common media portrayals of the saloon barkeep who knows a little bit of everything and a lot about people's drinking patterns and rituals. The ethnographic and qualitative literature on bars and bartending is diverse and rich with insights. While many segments of the bartending profession are culturally framed as a low-status form of manual labor,[61] many bartenders in less precarious states of employment can and do have "autonomy over the cultural knowledge and forms of professionalization that represent and impart" certain values.[62] As a class location, the presumption is that bartending is not what the person *wants* to be doing, but what they *need* to be doing as a means toward an end. This is a gross over-generalization, but it is also an empirical question. Jordan, a career bartender, made it a point to differentiate between the transient 20-somethings that would last a semester or two while they serve their friends during senior year of undergrad, and the career "lifers" that made bartending their primary occupational role, building a defensible form of financial security and professional identity around what many would denigrate as manual shiftwork.[63] Indeed, there were occasions where people around my same age, or slightly older, would seem to almost envy the fact that my job appeared to be inherently fun or enjoyable, whereas many white-collar professionals may not be as quick to make those claims about their own jobs. Without essentializing or over-generalizing a robust and incredibly diverse community of employees and laborers, it is safe to say that, for some, working in the nightlife scene is something that is chosen and enjoyed. For some, it's a temporary job that has its pros and cons, and for others it is a long-term career with another set of pros and cons.

There appeared to be an anecdotal cutoff point for differentiating between the transient and career bartenders. The age of 25 was a rough cut-point for separating the college startenders[64] from the blue-collar career workers. If you were working while in college, by 25 you'd likely be done with that lifestyle. If you're over 25 and working four-plus shifts behind the bar each week, it might correlate with not seeking employment in the standard nine-to-five office format. In truth, bartenders are a diverse bunch, and the methods for this research do not lend themselves to making generalizable claims as to what the prototypical or quintessential bartender identity consists of.

Bartenders, just like non-bartenders, have specific relationships with alcohol. Not every bartender actually drinks. Drinking "on the job" varies by location, employee, and context. Day shifts at your chain restaurant will obviously have different cultural norms relative to nightclubs that open only on two to four nights per week. There can be some potentially compromising situations in settings where drinking on the job (e.g., taking shots with co-workers or regulars) is a normative or expected practice. It can be an implicit part of the business model, where bartenders "throw the party" and encourage the purchasing of shots. If a bartender is ever offering you a free drink, and this is the kind of place that has loud music and draws large crowds, you can be fairly confident that it's part of the unofficial business model.

When you're physically moving for hours at a time, you can metabolize alcohol faster. As a diuretic, however, alcohol directly contributes to dehydration, making the consumption of water an important imperative when balancing one's professional and physiological needs. Jordan, a career bartender with decades of experience, emphasized the properties of coconut water as being "better than water for getting you hydrated." In the ice well of bars and clubs, or in the bar refrigerators, it is not uncommon to find a sports drink or other non-alcoholic beverage. Sometimes you might find a protein shake, other times you just might see some coconut water.

Tips and tipping culture

It is a precarious position to be in when your wages depend on the optional generosity of others. The history of gratuities – or tipping – is a story of class stratification. Tipping is something that implies an unequal power dynamic between the giver and receiver, whereby the person who is working for tips is at the relative mercy of the other party. While the topic of the racial, gendered, and classist biases of tipping is well covered by historians and journalists alike, there are important distinctions in the nightlife economy that can be useful to understanding various viewpoints concerning service wages and laws governing tipping practices.

Bartending is all about tips, and wages vary considerably. Within a single venue, the earnings for someone working a slow shift can be a quarter or sometimes even a tenth of someone working the most popular shift. The following data represent extremes, but the lowest paying shifts can yield around $100 whereas the highest paying regularly occurring shift was typically earning anywhere between $900–$1,100 dollars. At nightclubs, cocktail waitresses also stand to secure high wages, ranging from $250–600 on an average party night in Metropolis East nightclubs. Given the amount of money to be made, there is considerable competition for these optimal bartending shifts, and important subtleties to the practices surrounding shift scheduling.

There is a lot of money to be made, as evidenced by one local regulator in another major city calling nightlife "the goose that lays the golden egg."[65] Individuals who contributed to this study were associated with venues that were all economically prosperous. All venues, except for one, have remained in operation at the time of writing.[66] To underscore the profitability of shift-work in a tip-intensive economy, one doorman (i.e., bouncer) told a *Metropolis East* reporter that he can make more money standing outside enforcing entry policies than he would with an master's in business administration. On regular weekend nights, cocktail waitresses can expect to earn anywhere from $300 to $800.

Estimating one's monthly or annual wages in this kind of shiftwork can be surprisingly difficult, given the idiosyncrasies of each individual venue, the ebb and flow of consumer habits and unforeseen issues that affect the operation of any given business (e.g., snowstorm, regulatory shutdown). College bars have more predictable boom and bust fluctuations that coincide with the academic calendar. Nightclubs are generally never open every night. Windfalls and droughts are affected by the details large and small, like the booking of private parties by a non-profit or professional association, or the inclusion or exclusion of a venue as part of holiday pub crawl, or a whole ass pandemic.

Happy hour shifts that extend into the late night involve food and those shifts average $400 or more on a busy weekend. However, one particular venue that had no happy hour or food options – because it was an upscale nightclub with no kitchen – was a more attractive place to work at if one prioritizes hourly wages and not net income. For being on your feet all day in a physically taxing position,[67] someone who prioritizes their time above their wages will likely view a 12-hour shift (e.g., 4pm–4am) as less appealing than a nightclub shift. Those who work exclusively late-night shifts start serving at around 10pm, not getting busy until about midnight and closing out by 4am without ever handling food.

There is a lot of competition between, and high expectations of, bartending colleagues in venues where there are lucrative cash wages to be acquired in such a short period. Bartenders pooled their tips for every venue included in this study and, at the end of the night, each bartender would account for the tips that they generated. All three of these co-workers would pool their total amounts. It is expected that there will be an unequal distribution of tip totals, conditioned significantly by the layout of the venue. Each person plays an important role in keeping the bar functioning, and regardless of whether one's colleague brought in more tips on a given night, the money was always reported to be pooled and shared equally. I did find that if the difference is significantly large, and if it happens continuously, the underperforming bartender will not have a prosocial reputation in the venue, and risks being ostracized by colleagues or managers.

For larger venues that have multiple bars and employees, there can be a political dimension to shift-scheduling. In the venues studied, some of the intra-venue bars[68] were busier and more popular than others, producing variations in earnings. If you were new, less experienced, or did not perform according to some set of expectations, then you might be scheduled for a timeslot that doesn't have the same customer base for earning tips. Shift scheduling is inherently political because scheduling managers will often have competing pressures in making the schedule (e.g., balancing the needs of the bar with seniority, complaints about unfair shift distributions, employee preferences and biases). The schedule can also be used strategically by management to nudge someone off the job, which was observed at every venue that I studied. Employees who are scheduled in less profitable shifts, or scheduled haphazardly (e.g., scheduled for the less busy Friday night but not for the Saturday night or the holiday pub crawl), will be more likely to seek work elsewhere.

Tipping out the barbacks (i.e., those employees who do everything related to the operation of the bar *except* serve customers directly) from the bartender-generated tips is a uniform practice. In the venues included in this study, barbacks received 20% of the total tip pool. Barbacks are the true MVPs of any bar or nightclub, as they affect everything that bartenders do. They not only work longer hours, being among the first to prepare for the day/night and among the last to leave, but are responsible for both stylistic and functional elements of the bar experience. Properly sliced citrus, clean glassware, appropriate carbonation in the draft beer delivery system(s), and overall support of all bar-related functions are what make barbacks invaluable, and yet they are often marginalized in the workplace and treated as secondary in status to bartenders and cocktail waitresses. Some participants noted that one privilege of being a barback is not having to "deal" or communicate with customers. The aforementioned 20% never went *directly* to the barback(s) in the venues studied. The cash would either go to the general manager, the barback manager, or their functional equivalent. In the venues represented in the study, this accomplished two functions:

1   It allows for management to keep records of how much money is being allocated to barbacks from the cash tips; and
2   It results in a cash pool that can be split amongst all barbacks in a large venue.

Given the importance of barbacks and the ways in which they can "make or break" the customer experience and the bartender's working conditions, there are subtleties in the relationship between bartenders, cocktail waitresses, and barbacks. Barbacks can and do get shorted – or underpaid – and respondents for this study differed in their justification for why they might occasionally fail to provide the full percentage of monies owed. Some of these rationalizations include the notion of barbacks underperforming, prompting bartenders or cocktail waitresses to do 'extra' work. While *intra-group* wage theft occurs, virtually every experienced bartender understands that barbacks are critical to the success of a venue.

Respondents differed in their justification for shorting barbacks (i.e., not allocating the standard 20% payout from the total tip pool) for poor performance. When a barback is absent or perceived to not be meeting the normative expectations of that workplace, the bar can quite literally fall apart. Respondents noted random quirks at their venue, from a sink faucet that only works if the knobs are turned at certain angles, to the way that industrial dish-washers are reset, to small pegs or plastic caps that affect the operation of the soda-gun. All interviewees reported, to various degrees, how barbacks were the underappreciated core of the nightlife industry. They are often found outperforming bartending staff on almost every metric, including customer service. Their work contributes to the customer's experience (clean countertops, cold beers, rotating kegs, properly carbonated sodas from the beverage gun, etc.). A few respondents noted that if/when a barback underperforms and causes a bartender to do extra work, they may only tip out 18%, or even as low as 15%. Sometimes a bartender will round down, so if a 20% tip-out is $214, they might allocate $200. Conversely, adding extra money to the barback tip-out was found to be a common practice, particularly on busy nights and/or if their barback colleague was extra supportive. These occupational practices are shared only to contextualize the amount of discretion that any single blue-collar employee has in determining where cash flows travel and to demonstrate how the nightlife economy is cash-intensive and competitive.

On the snobbery of mixology

In terms of bar culture, the type of venue will often help clarify how someone's job is referenced. Barkeep, barman, barmaid, and bartender are all iterative references to the same job. In more contemporary settings, a new term has proliferated: Mixologist.[69] The proliferation of this term is in part a reflection of how some have sought to differentiate themselves from the lowly status of being *mere* bartenders and an implicit attempt to professionalize the practice of making drinks. Bartenders sling drinks and give their customers what they want. Mixologists treat drinks as things that shouldn't be slinged and help customers realize what they *should* want. Mixologists are the more pretentious of the two. Some segments of the industry "consider mixology's basic principles to be superior to those that became standard practice in American bars, such as soda guns and ice from basic ice machines."[70] As you might be able to infer, mixologists tend to work at venues that have higher price points and lower volume. They also tend to be associated with the more pretentious or "foodie" elements of food and cocktail culture, where phrases like "booze forward," "small batch concoction," "subtle expressions on the palate," and "velvet mouth-feel" are things you might say to your customer.

In short, mixologists are the bartenders who don't get invited to the party. A mixologist plays with syrups and tests the pH level of their ice cubes; a bartender plays on their phone. A mixologist is someone who serves drinks, whereas bartenders serve people.[71]

Getting behind the bar . . . and staying there[72]

Just like any other industry, there are multiple forces that influence who ends up working in the nightlife economy, and where.[73] Nightlife venues generally aim to provide a thematic ambience that is consistent with the general type of venue and its target customer base. All things equal, certain *looks* and presentations of self among bartenders can influence their place of employment, conditioning whether one works at a posh nightclub versus a party bar versus a waterfront bar and so on. Bartenders are both cultural intermediaries and Disneyfied versions of their place of employment.[74] Bartenders of certain venues are often expected to know, be, and enact or embody certain values that are consistent with their venue type. Think of the emotional labor that a waitress at places like Twin Peaks or Hooters is expected to perform as a routine part of their job, relative to the disposition you might expect from a bartender on a cruise ship or a high-end Vegas casino. Unsurprisingly, these performances are raced, gendered, and classed. To put it bluntly, I was never told to "smile more," whereas my female counterparts were.

Across all five venues that I worked at, however, there was an emphasis on the following kinds of attributes that hiring managers prioritized. In a 2015 e-mail, a bar manager wrote:

> When [John Doe] was the GM here he had a staff meeting where he said you have to be 2 of these 3 things:
>
> 1   Be a banger (sell a lot of drinks really fast and have high sales)
> 2   Throw the party (Dance behind the bar, participate in skits, do shots with people, smile, and make sure every guest is having fun)
> 3   Be a promoter (Have a lot of people say your name at the door and drive bodies to the bar)
>
> I want you to do a self-assessment of yourself and tell me what you think you are.

"Throwing the party" refers to the emotional labor and strategic intimacy[75] that comes with bartending at a high-volume party bar. One way that I would "throw a party" is to make strategic use of comped drinks. If I observed a bachelorette party or a birthday celebration, I would offer free or reduced-price drinks to incentivize a feeling of positive affect towards me, which would be one step in the direction of securing higher tips. Other ways of throwing the party include celebratory rounds of shooters for fans who are watching their team on television. A shot of whisky or a beer on the house is an easy way to make someone feel special, increase the probability of securing higher tips, and build your pool of regulars.

"Being a promoter" partially refers to the coveted yet simultaneously precarious reputation of "being a startender". In both college bars and upscale nightclubs, social capital is critically important for giving a business a competitive advantage. In the age of social media live stories and geotagged "check-ins," the ability to funnel friends and extended networks into the venue is a critically important consideration when making hiring decisions. As such, many bartenders are expected to be able to promote their shifts, bring in their customer networks, and generate a following of their own.

One e-mail record sent to a bar staff reads as follows:

> I want to know how you plan on promoting your shifts moving forward. Whether that is a theme night, or coming up with your own signature drink that you get the college girls hooked on, if you want to use more VIP cards, or you are going to pump Facebook all the time to make people realize they should come see you. Be creative . . . because these responses lead to better shifts. For example: [Jane and John] have both had busses of kids brought to [the bar].

In practice, this might look like a customer arriving at a nightclub and announcing to the doormen that they are there to see "Bartender So-and-So." Some venues will keep track of how many people ask for your name at the door, which is in turn a proxy for how effective a bartender is at bringing people to the business. In theory, the startender and the business where they work have a mutually beneficial relationship, insofar as the worker successfully builds a reliable customer that regularly patronizes the business.

In cases where social clout is an *expectation* of the job, it can become a liability for retaining shifts in the long term. In the college town where I lived and studied during my undergraduate years, this would be evidenced by a strategic hiring of one socially prolific member from each top-tier fraternity and sorority. Just as specific tailgate parties were associated with specific social groups and networks, so, too, were the nightlife hiring trends. In a roster of ten bartenders who simultaneously worked at a large nightclub, for example, it would be rare to have two bartenders from the same fraternity or sorority, but virtually all of the bar staff would be from a specific fraternity, sorority, or major student group. In Metropolis East, venues would offer competitions between their bar staff for "staff invite" counts. At the more upscale nightclubs, any personal contacts that one had could be added to a guest list that would include expedited entry and the waiving of any cover charge. Both of these benefits are substantial and encourage the generation of industry contacts and lists of regulars.

Generally speaking, startender types were presumed to be valuable only insofar as they could continue securing high numbers of patrons at the bar. As many people quickly learn, the older one gets, and the more removed from college one is, the more challenging it becomes to get large crowds of people to visit the same type of place week in and week out. As a result, promoter-type bartenders typically did not last too long, and this was mutually benefi-cial in cases where undergraduate and graduate students are bartending on a semester or academic year schedule, knowing that this is just a temporary job. To cycle promoters, the college bars I observed would often have a "guest bar-tender" program that would allow socially prolific people (e.g., 'influencers') to demonstrate their social capital and serve their friends at the bar. Usually they simply provided additional clout among a certain demographic (college kids), providing free and discounted drinks to their circle. The bar benefits not so much from the sales of the guest bartender, but from the social clout and new customers that they would presumably bring.

While bartenders are surely selling an experience and an aesthetic, it is even more important that they sell product. "Being a banger" refers to the most important trait of all: Generating sales numbers and racking up transac-tions. At the end of the day, the only way that physical appearance, emotional intelligence, and bartending skill can translate into real value is if the busi-ness is economically viable. In high-volume, high-speed bartending settings, being proficient with sales processing is critically important, and "banging out drinks" (making multiple drinks at an efficient speed) and being physically proficient in "having your head in the well" (i.e., scooping ice into cups) must also be met with technological proficiency. If you've ever been at a busy bar, you might have observed how the point-of-sale can slow down if not cripple an entire bar. If there are too few registers, or only one terminal for processing credit cards, or if an employee simply takes too long to navigate the point-of-sale software, your overall customer experience might suffer, but the venue is also losing time and money.

This notion that there are three categories of bartenders, is, of course, highly subjective and specific to the opinion of one general manager. These are not mutually exclusive categories, either. In reality, the most successful bartenders were those that could demonstrate competency in all three of these arenas, but we could add many more general traits, dispositions, or skill sets that we think makes for an effective bartender. For some, the prototypical bartender is some-one who is might be physically attractive, who possesses excellent interpersonal communication skills, and who can make and sell drinks efficiently but with-out making the customer feel any less important. In my experience, however, bartenders came from all walks of life and with all kinds of traits, skills, talents, and ways of communicating with others. What's more, customers treat service-sector employees in various ways, but a general pattern was this expectation that service workers were either in some college-related phase of their lives (e.g., the bartender as a student) or that they were under-educated blue-collar workers. I can't tell you how many times people would say, "You speak so well; why are you working here?" or "What do you want to do with your life?"

For some context as to what my own experiences entailed, at one point in my short bartending career I worked at four different venues throughout the week, and had a customer base that included people who would visit me at these various bars and clubs. I would spend Tuesday afternoons and evenings working happy hour and the late-night program for an upscale restaurant and lounge, Thursday nights at a party bar, Friday nights at a separate college bar, and Saturdays at an upscale megaclub. For each of these nights, the bar roster was hand chosen to meet the specific needs of the venue. For example, less experienced bartenders who were affiliated with a major student organization would be chosen to work college nights, and the most experienced bartenders would be chosen to work the busy happy hour where the customers were mostly business professionals from the downtown area. Over time, I would come to work primarily at the megaclub on Thursdays, Fridays, and Saturdays, and occasionally cover a shift – as needed – at other venues that were open throughout the week.

Because bartending is a form of shift-work, the time passed faster when I was busier. The physical and mental demands of being in a crowded, high-volume, high-transaction bar is unlike any other occupational experience. When the bar is slammed and you have two full rows of people jockeying for the ability to make eye contact with you and hand you their credit card or cash notes, you need physical dexterity, emotional intelligence, and communication skills. Staying cool under pressure, keeping your movements fluid but efficient, and being aware of your colleagues are all part of the art, science, and performative nature of bartending.

Prototypical layout

The following layout is conventionally found in various kinds of venues. Picture a wide bar with three bartenders and two barbacks. Names might differ, of course, but for the sake of example, the bartender *closest* to incoming flows of customers (e.g., the front entrance) will be working *point*. The person furthest away from this high-traffic area will often be the *service bar* that coordinates most directly with cocktail waitresses, barbacks, and, if applicable, busboys or waiters/waitresses that are running food and drink orders to tables throughout the venue. Intuitively, the bartender in between these two positions is working *center* or *middle*. Bartenders who work these slots on busy nights are typically the most proficient and well balanced in terms of their skill set, dexterity, and working knowledge of the customer base.

In terms of tipping culture, all three of these bartenders would typically be expected to pool their tips. This is critically important, because the layout of the bar is never designed in such a way where the customer is equally likely to visit any of the three bartenders. If tips were *not* pooled, then the result would be three employees jockeying for prime position to get the most traffic and thus the most tips. Bartenders generally stay in their assigned slots, so that the service bar employee is not making eye contact with waiting customers on the busier point-side of the bar. Customers go to open areas of the bar, not the other way around. Within the industry, however, the pooling of tips means that there can be animosity that develops when one employee generates impressive tip amounts while their counterpart generates very little. Some bartenders prefer working alone for this reason. If you consistently bring in $200+ in tips on a given shift, and your counterpart only brought in $50, it would be reasonable for you to *not* seek to work with this person on a regular basis.

The racialized and gendered workplace

Making discriminatory hiring decisions was reported as a norm by industry veterans, with one hiring manager sharing that "Facebook stalking" aids them in their decision on whether to interview someone for a potential job, regardless of their previous experience or referrals. One venue had a de facto policy of only hiring female bartenders who share similar physical traits, whereas another venue never had two of the same phenotypes or ethnic presentation at any bar. No two physical types (i.e., perceived presentation of race, class, gender, sex) could work next to each other, so if you were a prospective employee, it would be a liability for you to have similar skin, hair, and/or ethnic appearance as someone who already works there. Coincidentally, Latin nights and urban nights[76] (coded language for demarcating a social space as non-white) would be respectively staffed with a higher proportion of Spanish-speaking and Black bartenders.

Whether explicitly or implicitly, presentations of identity were always accounted for. At upscale nightclubs in this metropolitan city, there was a professional recognition of promoting diversity at the front door. According to one security manager, having different ethnic appearances and skin tones at the nightclub entrance signaled a more welcoming environment to potential customers. "People want to see other people who look like them," they claimed, and having female bouncers further aided in not only signaling a more welcoming environment, but in having more social and cultural capital available to negotiate any potential interpersonal conflicts.

Bars and the consumption society

The relationship between consumption, neoliberal commodification, and state harms is of increasing interest for criminologists.[77] Much of mainstream criminology has remained tethered to the "empirical realm of one-dimensional legally constructed definitions or crime that ignore a huge [hidden] figure of ill-defined, systematically ignored, misperceived, non-criminalized, underreported and recorded harms" that are "becoming increasingly normalized in everyday life."[78] Ultra-realism is one of these emergent perspectives that centers these relationships, albeit with its own merits and limitations.[79] As scholars in this area have underscored, many harms are becoming normalized and embedded within circuits of consumption.[80]

Fraud, corruption, and a flippant "that's just the way of the world" mentality has become increasingly commonplace in formal business settings. Framed differently, we have become increasingly desensitized to the harmful effects of Western states and their transnational corporations, and rather than addressing their harmful effects, the system on which they depend has become normalized as not merely the *only* way to do business, but the right way.[81]

In the wake of deindustrialization and the decline of manufacturing, nightlife commerce has helped to fill the physical and financial vacuum by further commodifying the social consumption of alcohol, and this can be observed across cities and settings in the Global North.[82] The meaning of consumption, however, varies in in different contexts but is of extreme relevance for studies of nightlife.[83]

Aesthetic consumption

Tutenges and Bøhling – among others – have studied how nightlife employees facilitate an environment that encourages drinking. Of course, some bars serve as multipurpose venues, markets, and places for the exchange of information. But in the abstract, certain nightclubs can be understood as venues for *aesthetic consumption*, where one goes to see and be seen.[84] It's not merely about who is beautiful enough, affluent enough, or best dressed in a space where intoxicating beverages are bought and consumed. Aesthetic consumption includes the markers of inclusivity and status that are available for sale and through differing modes of payment. You can use cash, credit, or debit, or use other forms of social, cultural, or political capital. "Aesthetic consumption" highlights how we pay for items that have no obvious utilitarian function, but promise to deliver a particular mood, or configuration of symbols for the purpose of outwardly projecting some lifestyle aesthetic. From posh and upscale nightclubs to biker dive bars, the entire premise of a venue often involves a social ordering that requires some method of sorting among its members, often beginning with the formal and informal rules and codes about who is encouraged and discouraged (or prohibited entirely) from entering in the first place. Whether at attempting to go to the LAVO Marina Sands Bay Rooftop Bar or the randomly chosen nightclub in a city near you, those who attempt to wear shorts, athletic clothes, baggy clothing, or headgear will often be prohibited as part of a venue's dress code, for instance.

Aesthetic consumption extends beyond drinking a purchased product, but being *seen* with a specific drink, and that experience being a form of consumption in itself. Martini glasses, like neat drams of whisky, are objects that we hold in certain ways, consume with a specific posture, and symbolically convey to others as part of our general presentation of self. Bartenders have a special occupational niche in serving as cultural intermediaries and enablers of these symbolic representations.[85] As bartenders, we rely on social and cultural markers to engage with a customer and provide a social environment that might yield a mutually beneficial relationship. For the customer, the "right drink" and the right "vibe" is of interest. For the bartender, the priorities are aligned with securing a favorable tip and the customer's desire to continue spending money or to return at another time. But the drink itself reveals other symbolic markers. Depending on the venue, context, and persons involved, sometimes people want a round of light bottled beers as fast as they can get it so they can return to their friends at a nearby booth. Other times, customers are open to being convinced as to what they might try, and how they might try it. An unfamiliar draft beer poured in a goblet or imperial stout glass provides the customer with an opportunity to engage with the experience of drinking.

Customers who have no idea what they want might offer pieces of information concerning whether they want something "fruity" or "sour"; "strong" or "not too strong"; "dark" or "light." Drinks with fruit as garnishes are interpreted differently than drams of whisky, poured neat. Drinks are raced and racialized, with prosocial and bigoted associations commonly made between customers of color and Hennessy – among other cognacs – and Hipnotic – among other cordials. Drinks like Jäger and cinnamon whisky like Fireball is classed, raced, and gendered in various ways.

The regulators and the regulated

I am certainly not the first to take interest in the "subtle organizational and interpersonal power-plays"[86] of the nightlife sector, and how these interorganizational network[s] engage with each other over the distribution of capital and authority."[87] Similar and previous research on political economies of nightlife settings can be found across scholarship silos. Hobbs et al. (2003) provide a model for writing immersive qualitative analyses that retains an incisive political economic framework. Hobbs et al. find that nightlife governance is "driven by a complex mix of licit and illicit opportunities that exist" at the nexus between profit-seeking enterprises and structured intoxication of alcohol.[88] Importantly, the authors emphasize the symbiotic relationships and entanglements that characterize the governance institutions and market actors, and how they are organized around ensuring commercial prosperity (Ibid.). Several studies examine the political economy of the nightlife industry, and the ways in which the NLE interacts, shapes, and is shaped by larger economic and social structures.[89] For example, there are studies of the macro-level forces that are noticeable in the nightlife economy,[90] such as the effect of increased corporate ownership and homogenization processes in nightlife hubs.[91]

Hadfield et al. (2009) conducted 50 in-depth interviews and found that licensing authorities and regulatory entities used whatever leverage was available under their authority to influence private sector actors. Whereas the authors articulate hard (coercive) and soft (co-optive) elements of "smart power" – we will find that in Metropolis East, some of these methods can be further dichotomized along the axes of legal and illegal.[92]

Conclusion

Major public corruption scandals or elite corporate offenses are often discovered through the work of investigative journalists, high-profile press releases following extensive investigations, or controversial leaks that bring the matter to light. For those readers who might be trained in social science research methods, by now you should know that this is *not* an exploratory text, or a mere qualitative case study that serves as "foreplay to the desired big statistical climax" that I won't be providing.[93] This book is an auto-ethnographic case study of a specific time and place, and my claims are based on observable phenomena that are interpreted through my own subjective lens. The claims and findings from this book might be of interest to lay readers and specialized researchers alike, and I encourage researchers to evaluate whether the phenomena described in this book can be observed in nightlife and other organizational settings. By the end of the book, I hope that you find yourself either more prepared or motivated to apply a sociological imagination not merely to things that you can experience in the nightlife setting, but anywhere that you fix your gaze.

Notes

1   This title is inspired by Calvey, David. 2000. "Getting on the Door and Staying There: A Covert Participant Observational Study of Bouncers." In *Danger in the Field: Risks and Ethics in Social Research*, edited by Geraldine Lee-Treweek and Stephanie Linkogle. Routledge.
2   Bouncers are security staff members who are responsible for the general physical safety of a private venue's patrons. A primary focus of their job is ensuring a modicum of order for entering a commercial space and ejecting unruly or noncompliant patrons from that space. Depending on the size of the venue, a bouncer might be the equivalent of a doorman – but bouncers in larger venues may work in specifically assigned areas. For more about bouncers, see Hobbs, Dick, Philip Hadfield, Stuart Lister, and Simon Winlow. 2003. *Bouncers: Violence and Governance in the Night-time Economy*. Oxford University Press.
3   Labaree, Robert V. 2002. "The Risk of 'Going Observationalist': Negotiating the Hidden Dilemmas of Being an Insider Participant Observer." *Qualitative Research* 2(1):97–122.
4   See Hodkinson, Paul. 2005. "'Insider Research' in the Study of Youth Cultures." *Journal of Youth Studies* 8(2):131–149.
5   Hodkinson (2005).
6   Ethnography has colonial (i.e., racist, capitalist) origins in the same way that criminology, like anthropology – as taught in the Global North – have colonial origins. See also Alonso Bejarano, Carolina. 2019. *Decolonizing Ethnography: Undocumented Immigrants and New Directions in Social Science*. Duke University Press.
7   Generally driven by participant-observation, extensive interpersonal interaction, and various degrees of immersion on behalf of the researcher.
8   Ellis, Carolyn and Tony E. Adams. 2014. "The Purposes, Practices, and Principles of Autoethnographic Research." In *The Oxford Handbook of Qualitative Research*, edited by Patricia Leavy. Oxford University Press, p. 260.
9   "Precious little work has been done on the drinking habits of dominant groups in any past culture. Our ignorance partly reflects where contemporary observers turned their gaze – downward – but it also reflects the concerns of modern social historians, who have scrutinized the populace far more closely than the well-to-do. As the historian Peter Gay has noted, the bourgeoise has remained virtually unstudied, in comparison with the working classes, the indigent, or the peasantry." Susanna Barrows and Robin

Room. 1991. "Introduction." In *Drinking – Behavior and Belief in Modern History*, edited by Susanna Barrows and Robin Room. University of California Press, p. 10.

10 Barrows, Susanna and Robin Room. 1991. *Drinking – Behavior and Belief in Modern History*, edited by Susanna Barrows and Robin Room. University of California Press, p. 260.

11 Schwandt, Thomas A. and Emily F. Gates. 2018. "Case Study Methodology." In *The SAGE Handbook of Qualitative Research*. 5th ed., edited by Norman K. Denzin and Yvonna S. Lincoln. Sage.

12 See Schwandt and Gates (2018) for a thorough discussion of the way a case can serve both as a theoretical construct and an empirical unit, along with an applied example from the literature: Diane Vaughan (1996) – who studied organizational wrongdoing – conducted a case study of the *Challenger* space shuttle explosion, but that alone does not clearly articulate *the case* as a unit of study. For Vaughan (1996), the case was NASA, and the study was focused on normal organizational deviance within the space agency. Vaughan, Diane. 1996. *The Challenger Launch Decision: Risky Technology, Culture, and Deviance at NASA*. University of Chicago Press.

13 Swanborn, Peter. 2010. *Case Study Research: What, Why, and How?* Sage.

14 Swanborn (2010:13); Simons, Helen. 2009. *Case Study Research in Practice*. Sage; Yin, Robert K. 1984. *Case Study Research: Design and Methods*. Sage; Gerring, John. 2004. "What Is a Case Study and What Is It Good For?" *American Political Science Review* 98:341–354.

15 Anderson, Elijah. 1998. "The Social Ecology of Youth Violence." *Crime and Justice* 24:65–104.

16 Heckathorn, Douglas D. 1997. "Respondent-Driven Sampling: A New Approach to the Study of Hidden Populations." *Social Problems* 44(2):174–199.

17 Garcia, Luis-Manuel. 2013. "Editor's Introduction: Doing Nightlife and EDMC Fieldwork." *Dancecult* 5(1):3–17.

18 Babbie, Earl. 2007. *The Practice of Social Research*. 11th ed. Cengage.

19 See Calvey, David. 2018. "Covert Ethnography in Criminal Justice and Criminology: The Controversial Tradition of Doing Undercover Fieldwork." In *Oxford Research Encyclopedia of Criminology and Criminal Justice*. Oxford University Press; Jameson, Janet. 2000. "Negotiating Danger in Fieldwork on Crime: A Researcher's Tale." In *Danger in the Field: Risks and Ethics in Social Research*, edited by Geraldine Lee-Treweek and Stephanie Linkogle. Routledge; Monaghan, Lee F. 2004. "Doorwork and Legal Risk: Observations from an Embodied Ethnography." *Social & Legal Studies* 13(4):453–480; Rigakos, George. 2008. *Bouncers, Risk, and the Spectacle of Consumption*. McGill-Queen's University Press.

20 Some respondents never used Amazon or did not care to create a new account. Others tried to reject the incentive, claiming that they were happy to share their views without need for compensation. I always ensured they would take possession of the compensation regardless, with the most discreet and anonymous form being the provision of $40 in cash.

21 The introduction of triangulation as a formalized empirical approach stems from the 1950s, and its prevalence has gained increased traction in recent years as younger generations of researchers consider mixed or multimethod approaches to their social science questions. See Lincoln, Yvonna S. and Egon G. Guba. 1985. *Naturalistic Inquiry*. Sage; Denzin, Norman K. 2012. "Triangulation 2.0." *Journal of Mixed Methods Research* 6(2):80–88.

22 Denzin, Norman K. and Yvonna S. Lincoln, ed. 2018. *The Sage Handbook of Qualitative Research*. 5th ed. Sage, p. 318.

23 See Lasslett, Kristian. 2017. *Uncovering the Crimes of Urbanisation: Researching Corruption, Violence and Urban Conflict*. Series on Crimes of the Powerful. Routledge.

24 Howe, Mark L. and Lauren M. Knott. 2015. "The Fallibility of Memory in Judicial Processes: Lessons from the Past and their Modern Consequences." *Memory* 23(5):633–656. http://doi.org/10.1080/09658211.2015.1010709.

25 For a general primer on Type I and Type II errors in crime and justice research, see Forst, Brian. 2004. *Errors of Justice: Nature, Sources, and Remedies.* Cambridge University Press.

26 For example, when one business owner claimed that another competing business owner engaged in payoffs and bribes, such data were excluded if no secondary respondent or third-party data source that could corroborate the claim.

27 I received no material incentives or benefits from Atlas.ti, Dropbox, or Evernote for 1) using their platforms during my research or 2) specifying them in this book.

28 Corbin, Juliet and Anselm Strauss. 2008. *Basics of Qualitative Research: Techniques and Procedures for Developing Grounded Theory.* 3rd ed. Sage, p. 418.

29 Byrne, David S. and Gillian Callaghan. 2014. *Complexity Theory and the Social Sciences.* Routledge.

30 Clarke, Adele. 2005. *Situational Analysis: Grounded Theory After the Postmodern Turn.* Sage; Corbin and Strauss (2008).

31 Becker, Howard S. 1970. *Sociological Work: Method and Substance.* Transaction, p. 40.

32 See Aguinis, Herman, Wayne F. Cascio and Ravi S. Ramani. 2017. "Science's Reproducibility and Replicability Crisis: International Business is Not Immune." *Journal of International Business Studies* 48(6):653–663. https://doi.org/10.1057/s41267-017-0081-0; Feilden, Tom. 2017. "Most Scientists 'Can't Replicate Studies by their Peers'." *BBC News*, February 22. Retrieved June 1, 2017 (www.bbc.com/news/science-environment-39054778); Resnick, Brian. 2018. "More Social Science Studies Just Failed to Replicate. Here's Why This is Good." *Vox* (www.vox.com/science-and-health/2018/8/27/17761466/psychology-replication-crisis-nature-social-science); Yong, Ed. 2018. "Psychology's Replication Crisis is Running Out of Excuses." *The Atlantic*, November 19 (www.the atlantic.com/science/archive/2018/11/psychologys-replication-crisis-real/576223/).

33 See Calvey (2018).

34 Goffman, Erving. 1989. "On Fieldwork (Transcribed and Edited by Lyn H. Lofland)." *Journal of Contemporary Ethnography* 18(2):123–132, p. 129.

35 Chambliss, William J. 1971. "Vice, Corruption, Bureaucracy, and Power." *Wisconsin Law Review* 4:1150–1173.

36 The phrase "going native" is a vestige of the power dynamics (and embedded racism and classism) found in traditional field methods.

37 See Ellis, Carolyn and Tony E. Adams. 2014. "The Purposes, Practices, and Principles of Autoethnographic Research." In *The Oxford Handbook of Qualitative Research*, edited by Patricia Leavy. Oxford University Press, p. 262.

38 See Lewis-Kraus, Gideon. 2016. "The Trials of Alice Goffman." *The New York Times*, January 12 (www.nytimes.com/2016/01/17/magazine/the-trials-of-alice-goffman.html?_r=0); Parry, Marc. 2015. "Conflict Over Sociologist's Narrative Puts Spotlight on Ethnography." *The Chronicle of Higher Education*, June 12 (http://chronicle.com/article/Conflict-Over-Sociologists/230883); Venkatesh, Sudhir. 2009. "Gang Leader for a Day: A Response to the Critics." *Sociological Forum* 24(1):215–19 (www.jstor.org/stable/40210346).

39 Melbin, Murray. 1978. "Night as Frontier." *American Sociological Review* 43(1):3–22.

40 Melbin (1978:5).

41 Geoffrion, Steve, Josette Sader, Frederic Ouellet and Remi Boivin. 2015. "Aggressive Incidents Inside a Montreal Barroom Involving Patrons, Barmaids and Bouncers: A Micro Level Examination of Routine Activity Theory." *Crime Science* 4(1):1–10; Tutenges, Sébastien, Trine Bøgkjær, Maj Witte and Morten Hesse. 2013. "Drunken Environments: A Survey of Bartenders Working in Pubs, Bars and Nightclubs." *International Journal of Environmental Research and Public Health* 10(10):4896–4906.

42 Tomsen, Stephen. 2005. "'Boozers and Bouncers': Masculine Conflict, Disengagement and the Contemporary Governance of Drinking-related Violence and Disorder." *Australian and New Zealand Journal of Criminology* 38(3):283–297. https://doi.org/10.1375/acri.38.3.283; Tomsen, Stephen. 1997. "A Top Night: Social Protest, Masculinity and the Culture of Drinking Violence." *British Journal of Criminology* 37(1):90–102.

43 Moss, Gloria A., Scott Parfitt and Heather Skinner. 2009. "Men and Women: Do They Value the Same Things in Mainstream Nightclubs and Bars?" *Tourism and Hospitality Research* 9(1):61–79; Franquez, Juan J., Jennifer Hagala, Steven Lim and Gisela Bichler. 2013. "'We be Drinkin': A Study of Place Management and Premise Notoriety among Risky Bars and Nightclubs." *Western Criminology Review* 14(3):34–52.

44 Amador, Calafat, Juan Montse and Duch Maria Angels. 2009. "Preventive Interventions in Nightlife: A Review." *Adicciones* 21(4).

45 Demant, Jakob and Sara Landolt. 2014. "Youth Drinking in Public Places: The Production of Drinking Spaces in and Outside Nightlife Areas." *Urban Studies* 51(1):170–184.

46 Measham, Fiona and Kevin Brain. 2005. "'Binge' Drinking, British Alcohol Policy and the New Culture of Intoxication." *Crime, Media, Culture* 1(3):262–283.

47 See Murray, Rebecca K. and Dennis W. Roncek. 2008. "Measuring Diffusion of Assaults Around Bars Through Radius and Adjacency Techniques." *Criminal Justice Review* 33:199–220; Roncek, Dennis W. and Pamela A. Masier. 1991. "Bars, Blocks, and Crimes Revisited: Linking the Theory of Routine Activities to the Empiricism of 'Hot Spots'." *Criminology* 29(4):725–753.

48 Geoffrion, Steve, Josette Sader, Frederic Ouellet, and Remi Boivin. 2015. "Aggressive Incidents Inside a Montreal Barroom Involving Patrons, Barmaids and Bouncers: A Micro Level Examination of Routine Activity Theory." *Crime Science* 4(1):1–10.

49 Hobbs et al. (2003); Bolier, Linda, Lotte Voorham, Karin Monshouwer, Ninette van Hasselt and Mark Bellis. 2011. "Alcohol and Drug Prevention in Nightlife Settings: A Review of Experimental Studies." *Substance Use & Misuse* 46(13):1569–1591.

50 Miller, Peter, Ashlee Curtis, Rebecca Jenkinson, Nicolas Droste, Steven J. Bowe and Amy Pennay. 2015. "Drug Use in Australian Nightlife Settings: Estimation of Prevalence and Validity of Self-Report." *Addiction* 110(11):1803–1810, p. 1810.

51 Monk-Turner, Elizabeth, John Allen, John Casten, Catherine Cowling, Charles Gray, David Guhr, Kara Hoofnagle, Jessica Huffman, Moises Mina and Brian Moore. 2011. "Mandatory Identification Bar Checks: How Bouncers Are Doing Their Job." *The Qualitative Report* 16(1):180–191.

52 Søgaard, Thomas Friis. 2014. "Bouncers, Policing and the (In)Visibility of Ethnicity in Nightlife Security Governance." *Social Inclusion* 2(3); Liempt, van Ilse. 2015. "Safe Nightlife Collaborations: Multiple Actors, Conflicting Interests and Different Power Distributions." *Urban Studies* 52(3):486–500. https://doi.org/10.1177/0042098013504010.

53 Hughes, Karen, Zara Anderson, Michela Morleo and Mark A. Bellis. 2008. "Alcohol, Nightlife and Violence: The Relative Contributions of Drinking Before and During Nights Out to Negative Health and Criminal Justice Outcomes." *Addiction* 103(1):60–65.

54 Kavanaugh, Philip R. and Tammy L. Anderson. 2009. "Managing Physical and Sexual Assault Risk in Urban Nightlife: Individual- and Environmental-Level Influences." *Deviant Behavior* 30(8):680–714. https://doi.org/10.1080/01639620902854639

55 Tomkins, Kevin. 2005. "Bouncers and Occupational Masculinity Contemporary Comments." *Current Issues in Criminal Justice* 17:154–161; Anderson, Tammy, Kevin Daly and Laura Rapp. 2009. "Clubbing Masculinities and Crime: A Qualitative Study of Philadelphia Nightclub Scenes." *Feminist Criminology* 4(4):302–332.

56 Tutenges, Sébastien, Thomas Friis Søgaard, Lea Trier Krøll, Kim Bloomfield and Morten Hesse. 2015. "Violent Work Environments: A Survey of Bouncers and Their Experiences of Violence, Stress and Other Work-Related Problems." *International Journal of Workplace Health Management* 8(2):129–141.

57 Geoffrion et al. (2015); Tomsen (2005); Tomkins (2005); Anderson et al. (2009); Monk-Turner et al. (2011).

58 Tomkins (2005); Kavanaugh and Anderson (2009).

59 Kavanaugh and Anderson (2009); Liempt (2015).

60 Søgaard, Thomas Friis. 2014. "Bouncers, Policing and the (In)Visibility of Ethnicity in Nightlife Security Governance." *Social Inclusion* 2(3):n/a.

61   Ocejo, Richard E. 2012. "At Your Service: The Meanings and Practices of Contemporary Bartenders." *European Journal of Cultural Studies* 15(5):642–658, p. 644; see also Sennett R and Cobb J. 1972. *The Hidden Injuries of Class.* London: Faber & Faber.
62   Ocejo (2012:656).
63   Ocejo (2012:644).
64   *Startender* can be defined in various ways, but refers to socially prolific bartenders that have their own customer base, which follows them through their shifts at different venues. See Lloyd, Richard. 2013. "Chapter 3: The Celebrity Neighborhood." In *Ethnography and the City: Readings on Doing Urban Fieldwork*, edited by Richard Ocejo. Taylor & Francis Group, p. 49.
65   Alcohol Beverage Control Board Meeting. 2015. "Fact-Finding Hearing in the Matter of: [Redacted.]" September 16.
66   A popular college bar was closed due to an incident where five people were stabbed in one night. See Hermann, Peter. 2015. "New Video Shows Three Men Being Sought in Stabbings at McFadden's Bar in Northwest." *The Washington Post*, January 14 (www. washingtonpost.com/local/crime/new-video-shows-three-men-being-sought-in-stabbings-at-mcfaddens-bar-in-northwest/2015/01/14/c4174ae4-9be1-11e4-96cc-e858eba91ced_story.html).
67   See Simonson, Robert. 2010. "The Bartender Appears to Be Shaken Up." *The New York Times*, November 30 (www.nytimes.com/2010/12/01/dining/01shake.html).
68   All venues studied had at least two bars within the business. These bars are differentiated with terms like "main bar" versus "back bar" or differentiated by the name/theme of the floor, if it was a multi-level venue.
69   See Ocejo, Richard E. 2012. "At Your Service: The Meanings and Practices of Contemporary Bartenders." *European Journal of Cultural Studies* 15(5):642–658.
70   Ocejo (2012:649).
71   Spiegel, Alison. 2014. "Don't Even Think About Calling Your Bartender A Mixologist. Here's Why." *HuffPost*, October 23 (www.huffpost.com/entry/bartenders-vs-mixologists_n_6014724).
72   This sub-heading is adapted from Calvey, David. 2000. "Getting on the Door and Staying There: A Covert Participant Observational Study of Bouncers." In *Danger in the Field: Risks and Ethics in Social Research*, edited by Geraldine Lee-Treweek and Stephanie Linkogle. Routledge.
73   See Lloyd (2013:49).
74   Ocejo (2012).
75   Hochschild, Arlie R. 1983. *The Managed Heart: Commercialization of Human Feeling.* University of California Press; Tutenges, Sébastien and Frederik Bøhling. 2019. "Designing Drunkenness: How Pubs, Bars and Nightclubs Increase Alcohol Sales." *International Journal of Drug Policy* 70:15–21.
76   *Urban night* functioned as a racially coded phrase, where Black patrons would not be the numerical minority in the venue, but the majority.
77   Rothe, Dawn L. and Victoria E. Collins. 2018. "Consent and Consumption of Spectacle Power and Violence." *Critical Sociology* 44(1):15–28.
78   Hall, Steve and Simon Winlow. 2015. *Revitalizing Criminological Theory – Towards a New Ultra-Realism.* New Directions in Critical Criminology. London and New York: Routledge, p. 1.
79   See Lea, John. 2017. "Revitalizing Criminological Theory: Towards a New Ultra-Realism. By Steve Hall and Simon Winlow (Routledge, 2015)." *The British Journal of Criminology* 57(5):1272–1275.
80   Smith, Oliver and Thomas Raymen. 2018. "Deviant Leisure: A Criminological Perspective." *Theoretical Criminology* 22(1):63–82, p. 65; see also Smith O. 2014. *Contemporary Adulthood and the Night-Time Economy.* Palgrave.
81   Whyte, David and Jörg Wiegratz. 2017. *Neoliberalism and the Moral Economy of Fraud.* Routledge.

82 Liempt, Van and Van Aalst. 2015. "Whose Responsibility? The Role of Bouncers in Policing the Public Spaces of Nightlife Districts." *International Journal of Urban and Regional Research* 39(6):1251–1262. https://doi.org/10.1111/1468-2427.12320; Roberts, James C. 2009. "Bouncers and Barroom Aggression: A Review of the Research." *Aggression and Violent Behavior* 14(1):59–68; Hobbs et al. (2003).

83 See Smith, Oliver 2014. *Contemporary Adulthood and the Night-Time Economy.* Palgrave.

84 Rigakos, George. 2008. *Nightclub: Bouncers, Risk, and the Spectacle of Consumption.* McGill-Queen's University Press, p. 42.

85 Ocejo, Richard E. 2012. "At Your Service: The Meanings and Practices of Contemporary Bartenders." *European Journal of Cultural Studies* 15(5):642–658.

86 Hadfield, Phil, Stuart Lister and Peter Traynor. 2009. "This Town's a Different Town Today: Policing and Regulating the Night-Time Economy." *Criminology and Criminal Justice* 9(4):465–485, 465.

87 Benson, Kenneth J. 1975. "The Interorganizational Network as a Political Economy." *Administrative Science Quarterly* 20(2):229–249.

88 Lily, Robert J. 2005. "Book Review: Bouncers: Violence and Governance in the Night-Time Economy." *Punishment & Society* 7(1):96–97.

89 See Liempt and Aalst (2015); Carah, Nicholas. 2014. "Watching Nightlife Affective Labor, Social Media, and Surveillance." *Television & New Media* 15(3):250–265; Chatterton, Paul and Robert Hollands. 2002. "Theorising Urban Playscapes: Producing, Regulating and Consuming Youthful Nightlife City Spaces." *Urban Studies* 39(1):95–116; Farrer, James. 2008. "Play and Power in Chinese Nightlife Spaces." *China: An International Journal* 6(1):1–17; Talbot, Deborah. 2004. "Regulation and Racial Differentiation in the Construction of Night-Time Economies: A London Case Study." *Urban Studies* 41(4):887–901; Hadfield, Phil. 2009. "Nightlife Horizons." In *Nightlife and Crime: Social Order and Governance in International Perspective*, edited by Phil Hadfield. Oxford University Press; Ocejo, Richard E. 2014. *Upscaling Downtown: From Bowery Saloons to Cocktail Bars in New York City.* Princeton University Press; Leitzel, Jim. 2007. *Regulating Vice: Misguided Prohibitions and Realistic Controls.* Cambridge University Press; Liempt (2015).

90 Tadié and Permanadeli (2015) study the politics of nightlife venues (i.e., bars, clubs and prostitution complexes) in Jakarta, and provide a comparative perspective on nightlife governance. They show "how informal agreements are central to ordering the night and to governance processes" and how the "appearances of order" are prioritized over effective urban planning (p. 471). Gentrification and the rezoning of dis-used buildings into entertainment areas similarly fall in line with these kinds of political economy studies (Tomkins 2005; Hae 2011). Tadié, Jérôme and Risa Permanadeli. 2015. "Night and the City: Clubs, Brothels and Politics in Jakarta." *Urban Studies* 52(3):471–485; Tomkins, Kevin. 2005. "Bouncers and Occupational Masculinity Contemporary Comments." *Current Issues in Criminal Justice* 17:154–161; Hae, Laam. 2011. "Dilemmas of the Nightlife Fix Post-Industrialisation and the Gentrification of Nightlife in New York City." *Urban Studies* 48(16):3449–3465.

91 Chatterton and Hollands (2002); Farrer (2008).

92 Hadfield et al. (2009:478).

93 Richardson, Laurel. 1990. *Writing Strategies: Reaching Diverse Audiences.* SAGE Qualitative Research Methods Series 21. Sage, p. 50.

5 Metropolis East money games

Whether you're a bartender, a musician that performs in the underground subway, or an exotic dancer, making a connection with a "big tipper" or "big spender" is something that is highly valued. When you work for tips, this is largely the entire point. As a general principle, bar staff are in the habit of following the jobs that will provide the highest earnings. When the earnings come in the form of cash gratuities, it warrants particular attention on the ways in which cash flows are both *socially* and *criminologically* configured, and how they reflect the movement of criminogenic capital.

In this chapter, I begin with a broad overview on the functional and symbolic role of currency. Cash is not only the lifeblood the nightlife economy, but also the circulatory system of licit and illicit economic activity writ large. As an anthropological and material record, currency also provides a potent representation of sovereign, or state, power and authority. Paradoxically, some readers in the Global North may not think about currency in this way, despite organizing our lives around how to best accumulate it! For readers who have actually worked in cash-intensive jobs, this section should nevertheless offer new ways of thinking about our social relationship with money.

After covering the overarching symbolic and material features of money, I'll return to the environment of study: The nightlife sector. You don't need to read this book to learn that under-reporting tips and employee theft is a common occurrence in the bars and nightclubs. Instead, I detail the various ways in which cash is individually and socially experienced in a white-collar crime context, and how various forms of blue-collar and white-collar crime are systematically normalized and engrained in normal industry practices.

This is important for connecting crimes of the powerful to crimes of the marginally powerful, or marginally powerless. Cash flows move upward in the nightlife hierarchy, with bartenders, barbacks, and security guards taking crumbs from the much larger pie. These larger pieces are far more interesting, and the third section of this chapter focuses on the way cash changes hands higher up the nightlife food chain.

Cash is king

Cash-intensive businesses, like casinos, exotic dance-clubs, and popular night-life strips, are notoriously stereotyped for being cash laundromats. In more mundane contexts, operating a restaurant is similar to operating a casino in that you have an active interest in mitigating loss prevention (e.g., employee theft). In cash-intensive bars and nightclubs, various mechanisms are put in place to guard against various forms of occupational – or *blue-collar* – crimes, like over-charging customers or under-ringing drinks, shorting barbacks their appropriate tip-out, or giving away product (e.g., liquor) for free in an unauthorized manner. Anyone who has worked nightlife jobs is familiar with the gray-shaded norms in this space. As one long-time manager put it, "There is a lot of money to go around and people want their share when they can get it." While I capture some of these garden-variety forms of white-collar crime, I also offer insights into practices that are less accounted for and harder to find – and that involve a wide variety of actors that are powerful in a contingent, temporary, and relational way, like city officials, law enforcement, mid-level managers, and business owner-investors.

Money and power are familiar bedfellows. As an anthropological technology, money – or physical symbols of value – reveals the power dynamics of a given time and place. Before the widespread adoption of paper notes and metal coins, there were other ways of physically trading relatively stable units of value. A common historical narrative, for example, involves the use of salt as acceptable payment to Roman soldiers – known then as *salarium*, which has evolved today to the word *salary*.[1]

Cash and currency are technological innovations. Physical currency, as it did thousands of years ago and through today, makes social and economic transactions far easier. Like any technology, there is no inherent moral direction to which it can be used. Cash is the material basis for facilitating both licit and illicit forms of commerce and exchange, making it the lifeblood of crimes of the powerful and powerless alike.

In short, cash is king. It is the material representation of state power. When you examine a currency note, it is not the symbolism of a private national bank that dominates the design, but the symbolism of the state. The phrase, *the business of government is business* is symbolically supported by the fact that most sovereigns – across monarchies, democracies, republics, and totalitarian regimes – have relied on physical currency to undergird economic activity. Think about it. A U.S. currency note is, quite literally, a promissory note. We use it because we trust that it will be socially recognized as valid when we seek to exchange paper currency. As a "global reserve currency," all this really means is that most financial institutions and actors are comfortable with assuming that the United States, as a coherent governmental entity, will continue to exist. When a state is failing, or its viability existentially threatened, currency starts to lose its meaning, as the world wars of the 20th century and other armed conflicts show.

Whoever controls the currency controls the nature and integrity of commerce. Similarly, whoever *threatens* the integrity of currency similarly threatens the integrity of commerce, and thus the very basis for having a state. What good is an elite military force if the people who are ostensibly being protected can't trust the basic units of economic exchange? For this reason, counterfeiting currency has long been a capital eligible offense. From this position, those who undermine the sovereign's currency by counterfeiting it are also undermining the very existential basis for the state to claim legitimacy. If economic exchange cannot be rationalized, and prices cannot be stable, and we cannot trust in the stability of a currency, then what "state" is there to regulate a meaningless "coin" or "dollar"?

Given the anonymous nature of physical currency, bribes and other acts of economic corruption have played a key role in facilitating actions that might be viewed as controversial or illegal in any given time. Bribes *grease the wheels*, goes the familiar expression. Such a metaphor acknowledges the functional – and therefore structural – role that acts of corruption play in the larger political economy.

> Money is the oil of our present-day machinery, and elected public officials are the pistons that keep the machine operating. Those who come up with the oil, whatever its source, are in a position to make the machinery run the way they want it to. Crime is an excellent producer of capitalism's oil. Those who want to affect the direction of the machine's output find that the money produced by crime is as effective in helping them get where they want to go as is the money produced in any other way. Those who produce the money from crime thus become the people most likely to control the machine. Crime is not a by-product of an otherwise effectively working political economy: it is a main product of that political economy.
> (Chambliss 1988:1–2)

To be able to successfully operationalize the power of this machinery, you need cash. Money is the ammunition that is most valuable for carceral systems. Cash is not merely a representation of state power, but a weapon system in itself.[2] In armed conflicts, bundles of cash notes are used as leverage to foster strategic relationships with other parties. Money has both exchange value and intrinsic psychological value. It is what gives us the feeling of confidence and a salient material advantage. For this reason, it is an end in itself and can be used to influence people. Funds are transferred around to get others to do things that are of strategic benefit for the paying party. Bribes, then, are simply forms of persuasion, and what makes them stigmatized is merely the understanding that bribes are transactions that are generally designed to be kept from public view, because awareness of the transaction would reveal a contradiction between prescriptive values and descriptive actions.

In today's digital and Internet-connected economy, physical cash has decreased in its relative importance. Salaries are not paid in physical things, be in salt, corporate tokens, gold, silver, or paper notes. Electronic direct deposits are a normal method of receiving our wages. For *spending* our money, we have paper checkbooks and plastic debit cards, and plastic credit cards if we're spending someone else's money. Yet cash remains the uncontested lifeblood of *all* commerce, licit or illicit. Whether it's the cash reserve requirements of regulated financial institutions, or the reams of $100 USD notes that are used to pay for illicit products or services, cash runs the show.

Cash notes are the lifeblood of any organized racket. For certain white-collar crimes, like embezzlement or money laundering, the existence of physical cash notes makes a world of difference. Cash provides anonymity. There are no bank statements, no credit card terminals, no text message alerts or online banking portals. Giving someone a dollar is like giving them a blade of grass. Nobody would have any reason to know where it came from or why you have it. Because cash facilitates commerce, it can be problematic when the commerce in question is legally prohibited. When state actors decide to prioritize such issues, there are levers of state power that reign in under-regulated commerce. In 2016, India's prime minister, Narendra Modi, sought to demonetize the two largest denominations of their rupee currency as part of an effort to address under-regulated commerce and rampant economic corruption.[3] Physical currency is the lifeblood of crimes of the powerful and crimes of the powerless. Since the nightlife economy is cash intensive, it would be reasonable to assume that both blue-collar and white-collar crimes are widely prevalent. In the following section, I focus on how particular kinds of white-collar crimes are practiced and negotiated by blue-collar workers in bars and clubs.

We ultimately live in a material world and have material interests, and this is reflected in the very elaborate systems humans have created to identify, accumulate, and protect the systems that produce what we need to survive. Whether it's accumulating reserves of seeds or protecting the supply chain distribution of petroleum, the human footprint around the world is consistently organized around these material interests. Whether it's livestock, arable land, minerals, means of transport, access to waterways, or prime hunting lands, a society that values such items will have symbolic representations of their importance.

We continue to use both simple and complex symbols to communicate our material status – or our class position. The way we dress, move, speak, and carry ourselves often reveals something about our class position. While historically there were firm barriers separating the haves from the have nots, money can purchase access to higher class locations. Old money and new money can rub elbows at the Kentucky Derby and while sitting courtside at an NBA playoff game.

Bars, clubs, and blue-collar crime

Paying in cash gives you anonymity. It also has immediate exchange value. In any industry where there are large amounts of undisclosed or under-reported cash, conditions are ripe for specific forms of white-collar crime. Data on white-collar crime is usually indicative of blue-collar actors, or people who engage in lower-level forms of fraud or deception to advance their material interests. In the nightlife economy, the ubiquity of under-disclosed sums of cash makes for a ripe environment for skimming and pocketing funds in a systematic way.

Following the money

Starting with the customer

The 360 Group had fraud-detection devices at each point-of-sale (POS) to mitigate against the risk of receiving counterfeit forms of payment, and one manager used a software patch to alert his cellphone when any gift card or temporary visa was swiped into the system. At the party bars, one bartender reported having been paid in counterfeit bills before and that $50 notes are the most difficult to detect, arguably because they are used with less frequency relative to other denominations. Other examples of lower level white-collar offenses included customer fraud, like the use of someone else's credit or debit card. At one venue, management strenuously enforced the collection of signatures on every credit card slip because there was a trend of customers calling their credit card companies to contest the charge. When this happens, the business must provide evidence that the customer was physically present in the venue and that they signed their receipt. Without the venue's copy, the credit card company will generally default to the customer and provide a refund.

Bar staff

Bartenders, starting at the blue-collar (i.e., occupational) level, can take advantage of this occupational environment by skimming funds in a variety of ways, and industry insiders are generally aware of the unwritten norms, rules, and expectations concerning these practices. Effective managers will know how to best mitigate these risks, but they will also participate in symbiotic practices that are of mutual benefit to both frontline and managerial employees in ways that I will describe below. With this in mind, I will now turn to how bartenders engage in what can be called blue-collar crimes, or low-level occupational crimes.

First and foremost, bartenders work for tips in a cash-intensive industry. For every dollar that is exchanged across the bar, the bartender has a direct incentive for it to be placed in the tip jar – which goes to employees – as opposed to the cash register, which goes to the business. When the bar is busy, "under-ringing" is one of the most effective ways of skimming small amounts. If a price of a drink is $5, and a customer orders two of these drinks and pays $10 in cash, a bartender can enter two drinks that have lower price points (e.g., $4 each) and then place the remaining $2 in the tip jar. This is a less stigmatizing form of skimming than, for example, a scenario where a customer orders a $4 beer, pays with a $5 bill, and the bartender places that $5 note directly in the tip jar. The idiosyncrasies are endless, but there are norms governing this behavior.

For example, skimming might be viewed as an essential part of the venue's culture in scenarios where the customer base is known to tip poorly. In one venue that I studied, the bar managers explicitly told their employees to place every fourth drink – assuming it's a cash transaction – directly into the tip jar, since this was a nightclub where the college student customer base was notorious for *not* tipping. The calculation by management was that they would not be able to keep quality employees if the bartenders were not making sufficient wages, and thus encouraged a predictable way of moving funds that would otherwise go in the cash register directly to the tip jar of the employees.

It is not a matter of *whether* bartenders steal from the venue, but how much and within what limits. These practices exist on a continuum. Being effective at skimming transactions throughout the night is one way of being a desirable person to work with. If there is a high volume of transactions, the sales data will be favorable and the amount that is skimmable will be high. Bartenders who work at premium venues take pride in their ability to generate high tips, in both legitimate and illegitimate ways, and at the end of each shift it will be a matter of pride (or embarrassment) to compare one's individual tip earnings to their counterparts of the night. As a result, not only does everyone benefit from under-ringing and skimming, but there is a structural incentive to support whatever system is most sustainable. This creates an incentive to *not* report, but also an imperative to directly participate. The last thing you want to do is be bad at making money.

In observing venues where managers were inexperienced, I observed that they were oblivious to these systemic practices. When everyone benefits from each additional tip dollar, each person has a vested interest in continuing the practice and mitigating the risk of detection. One industry manager understood these practices because they themselves had worked in the same capacity and under these same subcultural norms. They, too, responded to incentives. If sales were high, there was no need to play the role of police officer or detective. If the owners are happy with the sales numbers, and the bartenders are happy, and everyone is getting paid, there is no need to look behind the curtain or under the hood to examine how the money is generated. Nobody rocks the boat when times are good.

Another form of pocketing money comes from the making of shooters. For certain kinds of shooters, the actual amount of alcohol used is less than the amount that would coincide with a single unit pour of that same alcohol. In other words, five lemon drop shots might be comprised of three standard shot servings of citrus vodka. In the nightclubs surveyed in this study, the shooters were generally at the same price as the primary liquor ingredient, if not more. In this way, the customer is actually paying a premium for the labor added by the bartender, and the marginal costs of adding syrups, juices, mixers, and so on. Whereas the retail price of the dispensed liquor would be $30 ($10/ citrus vodka serving), the customer is charged for five shooters at $10/each, resulting in a $50 tab. If the customer pays in cash, the retail value of the dispensed alcohol is $30, and thus some bartenders might under-ring and pocket the remaining $20 for the tip jar. Bartenders commonly justified this mental rationalization by being able to confidently assert that the business didn't lose any money on the bottle, and the bartender's tip jar could benefit from the value-added labor.

More egregious forms of maximizing personal revenues are the modification of credit card slips. There were strong taboos against this practice in all the venues studied. It is also the most flagrant — if not the dumbest — of the methods for obtaining extra funds, because the risk-reward calculus is unfavorable. If a signed credit card slip is off by one cent, and the customer has retained their copy, the dispute process will generally favor the customer. Moreover, even when the customer loses or fails to keep their copy of the receipt, when they dispute a transaction, the venue can be asked to produce evidence of payment via the merchant's copy of the signed credit card receipt. This is why businesses will keep all credit card slips organized and secured for a standard length of time. Table 5.1 is not exhaustive, but it reflects a sample of occupational white-collar crime (or blue-collar crimes) in the nightlife work environment.

A separate form of occupational crime involved the selling of personal or unauthorized inventory. At two venues, there were cases where bartenders would engage in what is normatively regarded as a highly unethical activity within the occupation. In this one instance, two bartenders would split the cost of a handle (i.e., 1.75 liter-sized bottle) of Fireball (i.e., cinnamon whisky), and sell it at a discount price on college football game day. As the official game season bar for a top 25-ranked college football team, the bar would be jam-packed and filled with fans of university alumni. Shots of Fireball would be sold at $5 per unit, and the bartenders working together would pocket all of the money sold from their own bottle. Costs vary, but these individuals purchased the bottle for anywhere between $29.99 and $39.99 and, based on the shot glass size of 1.5 oz. at this venue, the 1.75L bottle yielded just a little over 39 drinks, yielding a return on investment of approximately $165. One bartender interviewed for this study was fired for this, as it was a practice that is nearly impossible to conceal since bars and clubs generally do not carry 1.75L containers of alcohol for direct service. Its mere existence behind the bar is a red flag to management.

Under-age consumption

One respondent recalled a scenario where a college student minor (over 18 but under 21) presented a fake Canadian ID. The bartender in this scenario noticed the customer's Florida driver's license in a visible slot of their wallet, confirming their suspicion that the Canadian ID was fake. The bartender looked at the patron and said, "It'll be $20 for these two beers." When the customer complained about the high price point, the bartender responded, "It'll be more expensive to fix your ID situation, so it's up to you." The bartender took the

Table 5.1 Crimes of the marginally powerful, or blue–collar crimes

Action/WCC type	Description and/or example	Effect(s)
Under-ringing cash transactions	A customer orders a drink that typically costs $9. The bartender takes a $10 bill from the customer, turns to the POS, and enters a $6 drink without the customer knowing. The bartender returns $1 to the customer. The remaining $3 will be placed in the tip jar.	Venue victimized through loss of revenue
Over-billing customer	When something that might otherwise be free is billed to the customer. For instance, a club soda or a cup of water is given to a customer, but the customer is told that it costs $3. The bartender places the $3 in the tip jar.	Customer is victimized, possibly without realizing
Under-billing shooters	Citrus vodka costs $10 per single serving, no matter how it is mixed or diluted. A customer orders four lemon drops, at $10 each – which would require approximately 2–3 servings of citrus vodka, instead of four. The bartender charges $40 for the four shooters, but only rings in two of them in the POS and pockets the remaining $20.	Opportunity cost to venue, but no inventory loss. No difference for the customer. Significant gains for bartender
Adding auto-gratuity	The bartender manually adds a percentage of the sales cost to be incorporated as a tip that is part of their take-home wages. This is done electronically through the POS software.	Victimizes the customer in a relatively transparent manner
Adding manual gratuity	The bartender manually adds a fixed amount to a subtotal, to be incorporated as a tip that is part of their take-home wages. This is done electronically through the POS software.	Victimizes the customer in a relatively transparent manner
Serving minors	Serving alcoholic drinks to minors, or those without the appropriate wristband signaling that their ID has been verified at the door; allowing for minors to purchase drinks at inflated prices.	Risks the liquor license of the business
Credit card slip adjustments	When a bartender writes (by hand) on a credit card slip to inflate the gratuity amount; forging signatures.	Victimizes the customer in a non-transparent manner. When detected, can result in the customer contesting the credit card charge.

$20, rang in a single beer, and placed the remaining $16 in the tip bucket. The under-age buyer was reportedly left alone.

The use of auto-gratuities is not the only way that bartenders can generate tips from credit card tabs. Multiple iterations of this scenario have occurred, with the following vignette serving as just one example.

A group of friends at the bar consume $100 worth of alcohol. Their tab comes out to $50, as opposed to a figure closer to $100. The paying customer knows that each drink costs anywhere from $9–14 each and notices how low the amount is after reviewing the bill. In most cases, the customer is pleased and feels as though a favorable outcome has taken place. The receipt, though, shows a $4 charge with a $46 auto-gratuity manually added on top.

This practice was common in one of the nightclubs included in the study and interviewees differed in their justification for when this was appropriate. One claimed to do this only if it was a slow night, while another claimed to do this regularly if they felt comfortable with the group.

Giving away the bar

Free drinks are a currency of their own in the nightlife setting. Giving away the bar – or a substantial loss of inventory from free or reduced-priced drinks – exists in an equilibrium that is specific to each venue and management style. On one end of the spectrum, having alcohol that can be "given away for free" is a necessary tool in the toolbox for a successful nightlife venue, and management will have clearly identifiable ways of facilitating the practice. On the other end, giving away the bar could result in the swift and certain termination of one's employment if it's done in a manner inconsistent with the venue's de facto norms and managerial rules.

At nightclubs especially, some people are unconventional employees of the nightclub, and that their wages are in the form of comped drinks. In today's influencer culture, popular socialites and verified Twitter and Instagram users can be "hired" to serve as effective marketing instruments for the business. Select promoters and friends of the business regularly have generous *comp tabs* that conventionally ranged anywhere from $50 to $300, under the general understanding that all drinks be logged into the point-of-sale system for inventory integrity. Closer friends of the owners or managers may have de facto unlimited tabs. Bartenders themselves can have comp tabs and spill tabs, allowing for considerable discretion in providing free drinks.

Comp tabs can be leveraged for personal gain as a bartender. To begin with, recipients of comp tabs will generally tip if they're familiar with industry culture and/or want to maintain a positive relationship with the staff. Moreover, a comp tab can be monetized rather effectively. As a bartender, if you had a $50 comp tab, and someone paid you $50 in cash for an order of drinks, you could put that money right into the tip jar and log the drinks in. This system can be readily gamed when high-volume cash transactions are handled by savvy bartenders who know the game. When you have 10+

people with 10+ forms of payment and a trained method of leveraging your short-term memory, the most efficient course of action is to make all the drinks as quickly as possible, get them in the hands of everyone who needs them, and collect cash and cards for processing. If drinks cost $8 or $9, it's common for someone to give you $10 and walk away. Over time, some become proficient in this strategy, and it is incredibly difficult to detect via conventional CCTV oversight measures. For this reason, experienced managers might emphasize an iterative form of the "action-transaction" model, where drinks should not be made in bulk, but by customer/party. To be clear, this prevents a scenario where a bartender takes orders for four different sources of payment, but only rings in three of them while pocketing the cash provided by the fourth party.

TL;DR: someone purchased a $10 drink and gave you $10 cash. Put the drink on the Spill Tab and put the cash in your bin.

Typically, comp tabs will not include premium liquors or other items defined by management. One way to get around this is to serve premium alcohol and ring it in as a lower-priced item. Another opportunity for exercising considerable discretion is when there is no computer key for a select product in the POS system, allowing for it to be given away for free or charged at prices that the bartender could, for all intents and purposes, make up on the spot.

From this perspective, the alcohol that is comped takes on an exchange value (or a symbolic currency) in its own right. It provides positive reinforcement for bachelorette parties, and it provides meaningful tokens of appreciation to friends, guests, and employees of the venue.

Inventory loss

Failing to ring up anything at all is the primary method by which product (liquor) is lost or stolen. From entire bottles to entire cases, there were the usual suspects of what would be commonly "lost" to the bar. Fireball, Red Bull, Grey Goose, Belvedere, Patron, Hennessy, and Jägermeister (all of which are brand-named spirits) could disappear without a memo from management. Some losses are idiosyncratic and predictable, associated with individual patrons of the bar. Some losses are not losses at all, since it presumes that there is accurate inventory data in the first place.

The loss of product/inventory was found to be commonplace in the venues studied, and management perspectives on this issue varied considerably, as did the methods employed to reduce inventory loss. It is important to note that sometimes these losses are just conventional spills or measurement errors. Not all inventory losses are stealing. The presence of comp tabs, alone, encouraged product loss, since not all drinks would be rung in accurately. A double (serving of) Ciroc might be entered as one rail vodka or a single serving. A Jäger or Fireball may be entered as a rail whisky. Reasons for doing this vary. For example, consumers may not return to your specific bar if each promoter that brings a lot of people in only has a $50 comp tab and you ring up every drink at full price/retail value. You may lose out on generating a consistent customer and tip base. Social capital is critically important and, for many bartenders, it hinges on the ability to provide free or discounted drinks as part of a strategy of building a customer base. Not all regulars will offer big tips for free. You have to give something to get something, and comped drinks or other ways of providing discounts (e.g., extending happy hour prices) help to facilitate a mutually beneficial relationship between the bartender and the customer. If a beer is normally $6 plus tip, and I'm selling it for $3, on average there will be people who will leave a higher tip.

Developing one's own list of regulars can be a precursor to securing higher wages and loyal customers, benefitting everyone. Ultimately, comp tabs are a tool for bartenders to better execute the emotional labor of making a patron feel special.

Management plays a significant role in providing conditions favorable or unfavorable to the existence of these practices. Some were meticulous with tracking inventory, whereas others seemed uninterested. There were managers who would only care about specific products, typically the more expensive items like Patron (premium-priced tequila) or Red Bull. Inventory loss due to staff drinking was commonplace and each venue had their own method of calibrating an acceptable loss amount. One manager stated:

> We have a worksheet that we use once a week for assessing the amount of used product. Our acceptable loss ratio is a lot more liberal here, at 22%. A hotel or a more tightly controlled place will have a loss ratio of about 9% or so. We give away a lot of product, but that's okay, it's part of our model. . . . I can look in [the software system] and see how much of a bottle was sold. Some places use metrics [weight or electronic pour counts] to get real specific, but again, we don't monitor it too closely.

In this venue, it was common for employees and management staff to drink generously while on the job. Rather than ringing in one's own drinks on their comp tabs, bartenders would only ring in non-rail drinks that they give out to others (e.g., friends, regulars, and the like). In my own experience,[4] Jameson was a popular drink among certain employee networks in the nightlife setting. As a medium-tier brand, Jameson also has a higher price point for the business. The following quote is an e-mail excerpt shared by a former bartender, showing how a bar owner reacted upon realizing a massive loss of brand-name inventory that presented a more significant financial cost.

> This is some FUCKIng bullshit!!! Im tired of you guys having a free for all on my dime! I try and take care of each of you, but if you don't respect me or this place then let me know. [Our team does] a great job trying to book parties to make you money and half the time you bitch about where you work and who you work with. I don't really bust balls like I should cause I want you guys to make money and have a good time. But if you keep

this shit up we will have a problem. Thursday alone I'm missing 4 bottles of fireball that is just one product. Let me look at Jameson and jäger. This is not a playground. It's your job. You make money I make money. U steal from me and my family we will have a issue.

Managers focused on sales data more so than inventory data, and inventory data was most trackable in aggregate unit sizes, like cases as opposed to bottles.

The 360 Group ebbed and flowed with its inventory loss policies. One of their nightclubs stopped carrying sugar-free Red Bull because it is an expensive product to obtain from the liquor distributor. The staff members were consuming more of it than they would sell. Another one of their venues implemented a mandatory ban on staff consumption of Red Bulls and later relaxed its policy by allowing staff members to consume house inventory at a discounted price. At one specific nightclub, sugar-free Red Bull was reportedly reserved only for police officers and first responders who would frequent the venue.

Under-reporting income

Under-reporting income in a cash-intensive economy of nightlife is so widespread that it is almost redundant to emphasize it as a substantive finding in this study.[5] However, some observations in this study include mid-level managers that were off the books as part of their agreement to work in a particular venue. This allowed for 100% of the income to remain free from tax liability. Similarly, two bartenders explicitly reported that some of their W-2s were omitted from their earnings when they prepared their taxes. They were confident that they have never been audited.

Moving up the food chain: management pressures

Up until this point, we have treated bartenders as workers who might take advantage of opportunistic conditions. However, the undisclosed sums of cash that move through a venue trickle *upwards*, and the skimming that occurs at the point of sale is just one minor process in a broader ecosystem of divvying up cash flows. The following practices reflect downward pressures exerted on nightlife employees.

Embezzlement and other money games

Porter fees

All venues pertaining to the 360 Group imposed a "porter fee" on all bartenders and cocktail waitresses. This fee, usually $20–$30, would be required from *each* individual at the end of their shift and would come directly from their cash tips. At one of the network's venues, this could result in as much as $250 in cash per night that was undisclosed cash revenue. The purpose of this fee and the direction or destination of these cash flows was never coherently specified. When employees reportedly asked what the porter funds were for, responses varied, and were often dismissed by the manager or owner that was providing the answer. The practice still meets preliminary criteria for embezzlement regardless of the destination of these cash flows.[6]

Ainsworth (2016; 2008) highlights how food service and other cash-intensive businesses can reduce their tax burden or under-report incoming cash flows using Zappers, or software patches that fulfill this function.[7] Prior to the existence of smartphones, smart apps, and similar technological tools, many bars, pubs, and saloons relied on the same vintage cash registers found in antique shops and at your old school (or hipster) bakery. As Ainsworth suggests, under-declaring income can be a potentially shared incentive on behalf of both front-line employees and upper-level management.

Bangers

Two venues that were included in this study relied on vintage mechanical cash registers that were referred to as *bangers*. The systematic use of bangers at two locations allowed for a continued revenue stream of undeclared and undisclosed cash. As one manager put it:

> Bangers are the best thing for business owners, and for scrubbing money. You use it to underreport earnings and use the unaccounted cash to pay for business expenses like DJ, fixtures, whatever.

The risk of audit is relatively low, given that the businesses that use bangers also have conventional point-of-sale (POS) software for processing food orders and accounting for more expensive items. The use of bangers was incorporated into the rule structure of the bar: rail drinks and all beers were to be processed through the bangers (when cash is the form of payment), whereas more expensive or loss-prone inventory (e.g., Patron, Grey Goose) would be entered into the POS, regardless of the form of payment, so that inventory data could be accurately monitored. The owner of one of these venues would occasionally drop in and request a certain amount of cash from the banger as if it were their personal ATM. Functionally speaking, it was. Other sources of undeclared revenue streams come in the form of cover charges. According to one of my interviewees, the owner of a bar that was affiliated with a prestigious local university had no idea that their staff were implementing a cover charge for over three years. When the owner attempted to account for where all that money went, there was no way to track it.

Stealing time

I observed the strategic use of clock-in and clock-out times by security staff at two venues. This venue paid its security based on amount of time worked and used a clock-in/clock-out system. Some security staff members would hang around and have a drink after hours with other co-workers on select nights. This was especially common in the summer months. Specific employees were consistently reprimanded by management for failing to clock out at the expected time. At the nightclubs, security was paid a flat amount per night, and while hours were accounted for via the same clock-in/clock-out process, the flat rate compensation structure did not provide an incentive to extend one's clock-out time. Similarly, being 30 minutes late for work would not cost you half of your hourly rate. Accumulating 0.25 hourly increments, over time, offer additional funds to wage workers who are already being paid less than a living wage.

More relevant to the managerial class, owners and supervisors also stole time. During the implementation phase of the Affordable Care Act, one business routinely adjusted the number of hours that any individual employee could work within a given week.

> I do two things routinely that could be criminal violations but are certainly civil liabilities. I edit the clock in/clock out times to save the company money, and I edit reported tips. One of these actions hurts the employees but the other one reduces their tax liability. That's the tradeoff.
>
> (Party Bar Manager)

Comparable to how a private employer can save money by having two or three part-time employees without benefits, instead of paying the associated costs of one full-time salaried employee with benefits, this bar made it clear that they would not allow for any employee to be reported as having worked the amount of hours that would require the provision of health insurance. Compliance with this mandate did not necessarily result in full-time workers having their workweek shortened: In some cases, an employee would clock in and formally work as a bartender and then work as a barback "off the books" for the remainder.

> Barbacks are often off the books. And sometimes you really need to hire this guy because he's better than anyone else you've found. This is common in kitchens and among minorities. If an immigrant applicant uses a faulty SSN, the payroll company will flag it and let the company know. Payroll companies won't notify law enforcement because that's not their job, but they let the business know that something is wrong. So, to avoid that, you just pay cash.
>
> (Party Bar Manager)

Conversely, even management members switched from being on the clock in a management capacity to working off the clock as a bartender, making up the difference in pay through inflated and undisclosed cash tips.

Those who make the rules are most aware of the caveats, loopholes, and limitations of their rule system's oversight mechanisms. For private nightlife industry actors, there is no right and wrong, there is only technical compliance within the regulatory landscape. Nightlife workers

> have the ability to become familiar with the business's use of surveillance and monitoring equipment, the work schedules of employees who might serve as guardians of the business's property, and other forms of guardianship. . . . A motivated employee's intimate knowledge of guardianship mechanisms presents an interesting twist on the relationship between the target and the offender, because the offenders – employees in the case of employee theft – typically have legitimate access to the targets of theft as a function of their job.
>
> (Kennedy 2016: 411)

Interpreted broadly, employee is to employee theft what public officeholder is to public corruption.

The further up the food chain one goes, the more routinized certain practices become. As one Metropolis East respondent put it:

> The most common inappropriate use of money is the underreporting of income and the evasion of taxes. There is LOTS of internal siphoning. I didn't take an offer to have a stake in a venue because I couldn't see the books myself. If you're guaranteed 15% of revenue, you're really getting 15% of 80% of 90% of the real revenue. We all know this happens so if you can't see the books yourself, it's not a smart investment. You don't want to receive whatever they want to give you, because it will always be less than what you are actually owed.

Symbiotic ties: the regulators and the regulated

One other activity observed in this study was a unique relationship that the local police (Metropolis East Police Department, or MEPD) had with a well-known nightclub (Levelz). Every Saturday, Levelz would have anywhere between five and seven trays of cupcakes for employees to consume after hours. Occasionally there would be one label on the cupcake trays, with a company logo. This company had an extraordinarily vague website, and their public Twitter account included local police officers, bar staff, and members of the network and promotions company that owned and operated Levelz and other nightclubs. One cocktail waitress reported that the business is operated by a spouse of an MEPD officer. Each Friday, these cupcakes are delivered by a uniformed officer. In a separate interview, one security officer said that the two security directors handed an envelope of cash to the police every weekend. This was independently corroborated by the general manager of this same venue, who was much more technical and legally conscious throughout our interview, being careful how to phrase his responses and reading and referring back to my IRB informed consent document throughout our meeting. This respondent said he knows that money does change hands between the regulators and the regulated, which would be consistent with the interview data of the security guard. Based on more informal conversations with employees of this venue, it seems likely that the cupcakes are the layer of insulation for any potential claims that the business is paying MEPD off the books, since whatever cash flows that are being given to the police each weekend can be plausibly attributed to the cupcake service.

Another occasion was shared to further illustrate the benefits of retaining prosocial ties to the local detail officers. During a late inspection by a fire marshal, the marshal ordered that the venue be closed immediately. Last call was scheduled for approximately 30 minutes after the fire marshal gave the command to the on-duty manager. The manager tried to stall, since this time period was when the venue was busiest and when tabs and sales were still of high interest to the business's profitability. When the fire marshal determined that his demand was not being immediately met, he asked six cops to come in off of the street, telling them to do their job and start arresting people because they were violating his order. The cops – all familiar and friends with one of my interview respondents – refused. The cops said they weren't going to stay up three extra hours to do paperwork until sunrise, and that it didn't really matter since the venue was about to close anyway.

In Washington, D.C., the local police have received negative press for the lack of transparency surrounding their reimbursable detail process.[8] In a hearing where a residential interest group was protesting the renewal of a liquor license, the residential representative claimed that there were motorcycles operating unlawfully outside of the nightclub, driving the wrong way in a one-way street, doing wheelies, revving engines, and engaging in related activities that would warrant a police intervention. One ABRA member said that this residential member should have contacted MPD, saying, "No way . . . there is no way I can see the MPD would allow that to happen every Sunday if they know and you know that [the motorcycle issue] is going to be occurring."[9] The residential protestor responded, "Well, actually . . . MPD was there, I believe in his role, you know, [in] this program that they have where they can [be hired as detail officers]". The ABRA member quickly switched topics, but the point had been made: MPD was strangely nonresponsive to activities that uniformed police are reasonably expected to address.

Law, order, and regulatory power

In *On the Take: From Petty Crooks to Presidents*, Bill Chambliss (1st edition in 1978) found that one of the primary ways that political capital retains its leverage over economic capital is through a hegemonic rule structure that allows for regulators (whether in licensing, zoning, or health, safety, or fire codes) to always have some kind of violation to use as a pretext for shaping the commercial landscape. I asked this respondent what they thought about how the regulatory structure provides leverage over any single business, sort of like the way a police officer can use minutiae in traffic and driving regulations to make a stop for motives that have little to do with failure to use turn signal or maintain whatever feet of distance.

> The regulatory process is a money game. Everything has a cost, and the process of yearly renewals alone reflects always needing to pay them for something. The rules are organized by priority category. . . . And [they] shouldn't be viewed as arbitrary either. Most of them are designed with things like public health and safety in mind. You don't want diseases or health issues emanating from a food or beverage establishment. But yeah, if they want to mess with you, they have the fine print that allows them to do so. Yeah, sort of like a pretextual stop.

In that same conversation, this respondent shared that he had recently observed something that was unprecedented in his 17 years of nightlife experience. An unscheduled visit took place, and this respondent, a nightclub manager, was coincidentally standing outside the venue to take notice of what he describes as something he "had never seen before." The Liquor Control Board, Food Safety and Hygiene (i.e., Health Inspector), and the Fire Marshal "were about 40 yards out, colluding, or discussing their game plan prior to approaching the business. This *never* happens, certainly not with us." In a staff meeting, he communicated that he believed the recent crackdown had something to do with the fact that this nightclub was one of the last remaining venues that allowed for 18+ customers to enter as part of their standard operating procedures, and that higher authorities wanted to edge out the practice.

One respondent is a manager of one of the upscale nightclubs in the city, who stood out from other participants on measures of education and direct experience as a bartender before entering management. When I asked whether there are certain kinds of crimes or deviant activities that are normal operating procedures within the nightlife economy, and if participants had to be comfortable operating in both legally and morally ambiguous spaces, their response was the following:

> Listen, you've got a bucket or situation where the currency is cash, and the venues house the popular images of sex, drugs, and alcohol. When money is tight, desperation trumps morality. So, it's a pitfall of corruption and deception, given all of these ingredients. . . . While there are people that do things by the book, yeah, it would be safe to say that anybody placed in this situation would be tempted with similar activities. Again, $1,000 cash is a lot for a city bureaucrat making $40,000 a year, who isn't respected all the time or treated nicely. There is a lot of money to go around and people want their share when they can get it.

As emphasized in Chapter 1, political capital and economic capital have symbiotic and interdependent relationships, but regulatory authorities generally always retain instrumental leverage over economic organizations. The caveat to this statement is campaign finance, where economic capital influences who might be a "viable" political candidate or office-holder. The state, through its regulatory institutions and the discretionary authorities therein, can exercise power over any individual corporation within an ecosystem of industries, but can buckle to the demands of an organized collective of businesses. For scholars of white-collar crime and corruption, this means that we should expect there to be a symbiotic understanding between the regulators and the regulated in cases where deviant or illicit activities are so widespread that they constitute core features of an industry, such as the nightlife economy. In accounting for whether corrupt, illegal, and/or normatively ambiguous activities are structurally incentivized as normal business operations, I have problematized – as many others have – the meaning of the word *corrupt* and the unstable relationship between what is illegal and what is socially and normatively expected across social groups and settings.

Conclusion

The nightlife economy is cash intensive. As cash notes circulate throughout the nightlife economy, we can figuratively trace their pathways through circuits of "normal" white-collar crime and corruption. At various stages, commercial and regulatory actors skim off the top, or take a little more than expected. From bartenders to city regulators, everyone – no matter their individual biographical details or psychological profiles – seems to be *on the take* in both mild and substantive ways. Regardless of whether the activities described in this chapter are explicitly legal or illegal, they all reflect attempts to maximize shared economic and material interests. When so many kinds of actors or players engage in the Metropolis East money games, the law itself becomes a game-like process, where people learn various kinds of rules, both official and unofficial, to keep the game going. Now that we've covered Metropolis East in descriptive detail, the next chapter provides an explanatory narrative for making sense of other cities and jurisdictions.

Notes

1 Hordijk, Wim. 2014. "From Salt to Salary: Linguists Take a Page from Science." *NPR* (www.npr.org/sections/13.7/2014/11/08/362478685/from-salt-to-salary-linguists-take-a-page-from-science).
2 Grable, Sam. 2010. "Cash as an Instrument of War." *Hoover Institution*. Retrieved December 26, 2019 (www.hoover.org/research/cash-instrument-war); Gilbert, Emily. 2015. "Money as a 'Weapons System' and the Entrepreneurial Way of War." *Critical Military Studies* 1(3):202–219.
3 Sunder, Shyam. 2016. "What are the Consequences of India's Currency Reform?" *Yale Insights* (https://insights.som.yale.edu/insights/what-are-the-consequences-of-india-s-currency-reform).
4 Anecdotally, party bars and college bars tend to have strong Irish-themes in their design or marketing, and Jameson is an Irish whiskey with relatively strong brand recognition.

5 See Morse, Susan Cleary, Stewart Karlinsky, and Joseph Bankman. 2009. "Cash Businesses and Tax Evasion." *Stanford Law & Policy Review* 20(1):37–67.

6 Embezzlement is the theft or misappropriation of funds placed in one's trust or belonging to one's employer. It differs from money laundering in that the latter requires converting *illegitimately* obtained funds into a usable form.

7 Ainsworth, Richard T. 2016. "Zappers – Technological Tax Fraud in New Hampshire." *Boston University School of Law, Law and Economics Research Paper No. 16-40.* Social Science Research Network (https://papers.ssrn.com/sol3/papers.cfm?abstract_id=2851110); Ainsworth, Richard T. 2008. "Zappers: Tax Fraud, Technology and Terrorist Funding." *Boston University School of Law, Working Paper Series, Law and Economics No. 08-07.*

8 Charlie Sheen received a police escort from Dulles International Airport, located 20+ miles away from the D.C. border, prompting many to question the integrity of the detail program. See Flaherty, Mary Pat and Paul Duggan. 2011. "D.C. Police Escort of Charlie Sheen Motorcade Under Investigation, Official Says." *Washington Post*, April 21 (www.washingtonpost.com/local/dc-police-escort-of-charlie-sheen-motorcade-under-investigation-official-says/2011/04/21/AFETJGLE_story.html).

9 Alcoholic Beverage Control Board. 2014. Protest Hearing in the Matter of: License No. 84847. Case No. 13-PRO-00169. September 17. District of Columbia.

6   Corrupt capital

Structural contradictions theory posits that many observable forms of crime are integral features of our political economy. Bill Chambliss was a pioneer for this perspective: "If crime and corruption were simply the action of an occasional government official, focusing on the individual would make sense[, but w]hen it is ubiquitous and institutionalized then we must seek our answer in structural characteristics of the political, economic, and social system."[1] When people engage in economically motivated crime, there are arguably acting in a manner that is consistent with the dominant belief system of the time (i.e., capital accumulation – or getting money – is the overarching goal) and yet prohibited by law. Our material conditions (or the way that our economic practices are organized) are predicated on making people do things in specific ways, like working for a wage but not owning the fruits of your labor; or taking on ever-increasing amounts of personal debt in order to get an education so that you can secure the privilege of working for specific industries that compensate you just enough to pay down that same debt while also meeting your ever-increasing cost of living expenses. In short, being "money hungry" is not limited to the stereotypical corporate fat cats or robber barons that are always in the pursuit of more. Whether you fundamentally *need* to make ends meet, or you are simply socialized and incentivized to pursue material advancement, we find evidence of this culturally embedded value system everywhere we choose to look, from Peloton commercials to *Billboard* Top 100 lyrics; from status-conferring wireless headphones to Instagrammable plates of food. The good life is a function of upward economic mobility, or the accumulation of capital, and yet we know that our social structure fundamentally *requires* that larger portions of the population be located near the bottom of a triangular pyramid where they will not be able to *legally* accumulate enough capital to enjoy the things they are encouraged to obtain.[2] It is here where bribe-giving and bribe-taking make the most sense. And, indeed, there is nothing particularly special about Metropolis East.

Between 1990 and 2002, there were 10,000 federal prosecutions of U.S. government officials for acts of official corruption, including fraud, campaign-finance violations, and obstruction of justice.[3] In Washington, D.C. alone, every mayoral administration in the past 30 years has been the subject of corruption probes. When Lincoln Steffens published *Shame of the Cities* in 1904, his over-arching thesis was to show the parallels between localized corruption in cities big and small. The places and names vary, but the facts have told the same story across time and space. It's not a matter of whether a city has any corruption-related issues, but a question of degree. There are well-known and obscure jurisdictions, including Chicago;[4] Manitowoc County, Wisconsin;[5] Crystal City, Texas;[6] the Boston taxicab industry;[7] Seattle;[8] Philadelphia's Department of Licenses and Inspection;[9] and the storied corruption sagas of the NYPD.[10]

Nightlife-specific examples are plentiful and a sample list includes:

- According the Department of Justice and the *Los Angeles Times*, two former officials in California's liquor agency pleaded guilty for their involvement in a systematic bribery scheme.[11] Payments ranging from $2,000 to $5,000 were used to direct Alcohol Beverage Control board officials to engage in disciplinary enforcement against competing businesses and to expedite liquor licensing for in-network partners.[12] One of the defendants "accepted more than $28,000 in bribes and kickbacks from Seo, a former ABC employee who owned a consulting business that targeted Koreatown bars that needed help navigating the state's stringent liquor laws and licensing requirements."[13]

- The owner of a Los Angeles nightclub was indicted in 2015 on federal charges that he laundered hundreds of thousands of dollars as part of a Mexican-drug trafficking network.[14]

- In 2016, a Milwaukee strip club owner was indicted in "a sprawling racketeering case that targeted the Russian mob operating in the U.S."[15] The case involved money laundering and cocaine dealing that was uncovered as part of an investigation dubbed "Russian Laundry."

- In 2015, the FBI issued a press release announcing the arrest of seven businessmen and associates charged with racketeering, money laundering, and drug-trafficking-related crimes. Two of the businessmen were associated with The Gold Club franchise, with nightclub and strip club locations in South Carolina, Delaware, and New Hampshire.[16]

- In 2012, a downtown Minneapolis nightclub surrendered its liquor license while being investigated for tax fraud, which the owners claimed was the result of being targeted by city leaders for having an "undesirable" customer base.[17]

- The owner of a party bar in Lake George, a lake town northward of Albany, New York, was investigated in 2014 over suspicious financial transactions in potential violation of banking laws.[18]

- A federal indictment was issued in 2001 for Steven Kaplan, who allegedly skimmed millions in revenue from Gold Club coffers to pay for protection from the Gambino crime family.[19] John Gotti, a prisoner at this time, was transferred to Atlanta to testify on the extent to which he knew Steven Kaplan and his business activities or locations, ranging from Boca Raton, Florida to New York City. Kaplan was also managing strip club locations in Atlanta. In investigations of Kaplan, a convicted drug dealer testified that Kaplan secured a fake ID for a man wanted for stealing diamonds in a United Parcel Service heist, and that he himself had used cocaine with Kaplan at the Gold Club opening in Jacksonville in 1994.[20]

- Khadem al-Qubaisi was investigated over suspected embezzlement from Malaysia's government wealth fund, 1MDB, allegedly responsible for "fraud, money laundering and corruption." Al-Qubaisi was chairman of Hakkassan prior to the investigation and runs elite restaurants and nightclubs in several locations including Vegas, London, and the United Arab Emirates. He was also the former head of Abu Dhabi's state oil investment firm.[21]
- In a federal corruption probe, eight city regulators were arrested and charged with crimes related to their participation in a scheme to extort cash payments from a South Beach nightclub and participate in cocaine trafficking.[22]

As is the case with all major cities in the United States, there is a rich history of fraud, waste, abuse, and corruption that has been extensively documented in investigative journalism.[23] While the over-arching narratives are similar, every jurisdiction has important nuances and characteristics that make each city worthy of a separate case study. For our purposes, I'll focus on Washington, D.C., to demonstrate how private and public institutions – and the individual agents who work in these organizations – are embedded in political-legal arrangements that underscore the utility of structural contradictions theory.

The regulators and the regulated of Washington, D.C.

In the case of D.C. nightlife, the primary regulating authority in the D.C. nightlife economy is the Alcoholic Beverage Control Board, also known as ABC.[24] This entity is an independent body that meets once each week to adjudicate, administer, and enforce alcoholic beverage laws. Board members are appointed by the Mayor and confirmed by the D.C. Council for a four-year term. There may be as many as seven members on the Board, with three members constituting a quorum. As posted on their website, The Board is responsible for:

- Approving all applications for new alcoholic beverage licenses, renewals, transfers of ownership or location, substantial changes, suspensions, revocations, the safekeeping of licenses, and voluntary agreements.
- Enforcing District alcohol laws.
- Issuing new alcoholic beverage regulations and policies related to the sale and distribution of alcohol.
- Referring violations of the law to the Office of the Attorney General and other legal authorities for investigation and prosecution.
- Overseeing the Alcoholic Beverage Regulation Administration (ABRA).

The Alcohol Beverage Control Board (ABC) and the Alcoholic Beverage Regulation Administration (ABRA) are functionally equivalent, as the appointees chosen to serve as officials of the former are also judicial officers for the latter. In practice, ABRA is the investigatory arm of ABC. ABRA's mission is to support the public's health, safety, and welfare through the control and regulation of the sale and distribution of alcoholic beverages. In December 2016, ABRA oversaw approximately 1,970 liquor licenses, which includes restaurants, hotels, liquor stores, grocery stores, and virtually any private business that sells or serves an alcoholic beverage of any kind. Gauging the size of the nightlife economy can be done through a database that categorizes licensees by venue type.[25] The D.C. nightlife economy is home to 334 taverns,[26] 43 nightclubs,[27] and 39 clubs.[28] Those who serve in ABRA positions are nominated by the Mayor and confirmed by the D.C. Council, as per § 25–205 of the D.C. Official Code Title 25 and D.C. Municipal Regulations Title 23. ABRA is an extension of the city's executive branch of government, but is formally accountable to – and in regular communication with – the D.C. Council, or the legislative body of city government.

City council

The D.C. Council's mandates

> also include oversight of multiple agencies, commissions, boards and other instruments of District government. Led by the Council Chairman, the 13 members of the Council work to improve the quality of life in District neighborhoods by ensuring safer streets, furthering education reform, developing a vibrant economy, and implementing groundbreaking programs. Working with the Mayor and the executive branch, the Council also plays a critical role in maintaining a balanced budget and the fiscal health of the District of Columbia government.[29]

The D.C. Council formulates legislation and responds to constituent concerns on a wide range of issues, ranging from the regulation of backyard chickens to bike zones, from zoning and licensing contracts to investing in infrastructure. Serving in the role of Councilmember is the highest level of political office that one can attain unless they become mayor. Vincent Gray is one of the few people to rotate between these top positions in the legislative and executive branch. A former mayor of the city, Vincent Gray is a Ward 7 Member of the Council, representing base constituents from previous mayoral races. Many political figures have been found guilty of campaign-related felonies,[30] but Vincent Gray is particularly notable since many people in his campaign and inner circles have plead guilty to federal charges involving illicit campaign contributions and political corruption.[31]

The influence that any individual Councilmember can have is notable, including in how individual office holders can shape the nightlife landscape of the city.

Former D.C. Councilmember Jim Graham served four terms (16 years) on the D.C. council and was a well-known (albeit not always well-received) figure in the local political scene of D.C. After retiring from public office, Graham had a new investment and operations stake in the opening of a new all-nude gay nightclub, "embarking on a new career," as described by the *Washington Post*.[32] His interest in nightclub operations, however, was anything but new, and his involvement in nightlife and other sectors of the local D.C. economy make for a fitting illustration of political corruption. In 2013, while Graham was serving on the D.C. Council, his colleagues publicly reprimanded and stripped him of his power to oversee District liquor licenses and alcohol issues as head of the Human Services Committee,[33] "an assignment Graham has long cherished."[34] Graham responded to these actions by filing a lawsuit claiming that his due process rights had been violated through this public punishment without a chance to adequately defend himself. In the preceding three years alone, Graham had been investigated for three separate instances where he allegedly engaged in ethical violations and breaches of his authority. When he was a representative on the Washington Metropolitan Area Transit Authority Board, he allegedly "proposed that businessman W. William Jr. drop out of a Metro land deal in return for Graham's support on the council for [a separate] lottery contract bid."[35] While he may have been publicly reprimanded, this was a political punishment, not a legal one.

In a separate corruption probe by the Federal Bureau of Investigation (FBI), Graham's Chief of Staff, Ted G. Loza, was sentenced to prison after being part of a bribery scheme on behalf of a taxicab businessman.[36] Ted Loza took the fall for accepting $1,500 from an FBI informant, insulating Graham from the investigation. Councilmember Jim Graham introduced legislation that was favorable to the informant and did so the day after meeting with the bribe-giver, according to a federal indictment.[37] When Graham introduced a bill to limit the number of taxis that operate in the city and transition to a hybrid medallion system, it was the current mayor, Muriel Bowser, who co-sponsored the bill. Jim Graham is not the only one who benefitted from a layer of insulation represented by a staffer taking the fall for the shadow activities of a legislative official.

Graham allegedly used his authority and influence over ABRA-related functions and liquor licenses to facilitate the gentrification of nightlife spaces. He was claimed to have selectively targeted minority-owned bars and nightclubs to find ways to push them out of their venues, which would in turn facilitate new incoming waves of commercial investors. On the record, Jim Graham never admits to any wrongdoing, and referred to his actions as standard political "horse trading" which he presented as a staple part of the legislative process.[38] Graham, the subject of many probes and investigations, was never indicted, prosecuted, or found guilty of any criminal wrongdoing.

Thomas Gore, assistant treasurer for Vincent Gray's 2010 mayoral campaign, pled guilty to obstruction of justice and the destruction of evidence. He was secretly recorded telling another campaign aide that he destroyed a notebook containing records of illegitimate payoffs.

> In court papers, Gore admitted to participating in the scheme to pay candidate Sulaimon Brown to levy verbal campaign attacks on Fenty, the

mayor at the time. Gore purchased money orders and gave them to the other aide, Howard L. Brooks, who gave them to Brown.[39]

These are just some of the documented instances of political corruption, all of which reflect the culturally shared goal of maximizing capital accumulation. In this case, the objective is to use cash to advance instrumental political goals. In an electoral system that favors the candidate with the most financial resources, cash serves the symbiotic purpose of helping candidates win at the cost of having their financiers' interests well represented at the decision-making table. One of the foremost structural contradictions is that political arenas are ostensibly organized around some representative democracy structure where one person equals one vote, at least in theory. In practice, however, we might reconfigure this orientation and cast it as *one dollar, one vote*. The more dollars you bring to bear, the more votes you have. This is ultimately symptomatic of our political economic framework that relegates economic decisions (and the control over the means of production) to the *private* sphere while superficially placing political representatives in the ostensibly democratic *public* sphere. In the case of Washington, D.C., motives for – and documented cases of – economically motivated corruption can be found even at the most granular, local level of government, which is the focus of the next section.

Advisory Neighborhood Councils

Advisory Neighborhood Councils (ANCs) are the ground-level political units of the city. There are 37 ANCs, clustered into eight larger geographic units known as Wards. ANCs consider a wide range of policies and programs affecting their neighborhoods, including traffic, parking, recreation, street improvements, liquor licenses, zoning, economic development, police protection, sanitation and trash collection, and the District's annual budget.[40] Those who serve on ANCs are known as Commissioners, who each serve two-year terms without pay.

In theory, commissioners are said to individually represent approximately 2,000 residents in their immediate area (anc.dc.gov). In practice, however, the ANC commissioners may not necessarily represent the interests of those who reside in their geographic space. ANC Commissioners have been characterized as being ostensible protectors of the community and as if they represent community interests, but in reality, they are just a handful of individuals that exercise influence on topics that they take issue with. But in the nightlife economy, the ANCs have considerable clout in their relationship with the Alcoholic Beverage Regulation Administration. Since the ABRA Board is appointed by the mayor, they are invested in getting the mayor reelected. Their jobs depend on it. As such, ANCs offer a potential ally or adversary if any nightlife economy matters become topics of contention, as the ANC reflects local voting blocs.

Because ANCs are the most grassroots level of conventional political organizing, there is wide variation in the kinds of issues any individual Commissioner may be preoccupied with. In non-commercial areas, the most pressing
issue may be about the presence or absence of sidewalks or the design of a
future park. In more mixed-use sections of the city, there are so many residential interests that ANCs are further supplemented – or sometimes supplanted –
by alternative residential units of political mobilization. One in particular, the
Dupont Circle Citizens Association, has an active stake in the regulatory framework of nightlife and other commercial space, since high population density
and mixed-use zoning, paired with extensive transit routes and tourism stops,
make this area especially sensitive to the impacts of regulation. To illustrate,
this Citizens Association formally created a DC Nightlife Noise Coalition,[41]
known to patrol nightlife areas by taking decibel-measurements to ensure commercial nightlife venues are in compliance with noise restrictions. In response,
there have been sporadic occasions where the restaurant, bar, nightclub, and
hospitality industry have organized to lobby on behalf of their business interests,[42] as was the case when an indoor smoking ban (now in effect) was being
proposed for all restaurants and bars.

Because there is a lot of competition within nightlife economy sub-
categories (i.e., competition between restaurants, nightclubs, and so on), not
all pro-nightlife voices are heard equally. Given the relationship between mayoral administrations and ABRA Chair appointments, one company attended a
mayoral fundraiser and donated $5,000 to the campaign. In doing so, they also
expressed their distaste for the current ABRA chair and suggested that someone else chair the board. Upon successful reelection, there was a new ABRA
Chair in that position.

Two ANC commissioners were strongly criticized in the media for what
some might view as influence peddling, attempted extortion, and blackmail.
An owner of a prominent and popular venue in Adams Morgan was contacted
in 2002 and asked by an ANC Commissioner for an $1,800 loan, claiming that
her financial situation might affect her decision as an ANC member.[43] Another
owner of a restaurant and music venue claimed that two ANC Commissioners
entered her business and asked for three to four months' rent. A third businessmen came forward with another revelation that one of these Commissioners
asked for over $1,000. ABRA has a yearly renewal process where community
members can protest the renewal of a liquor license, which, in turn, can set off
a process where the business has to comply with demands from community
stakeholders in order to have its liquor license renewed. In response to this story,
Jim Graham – Ward 1 DC Council Member at the time of the incident – said,
"I think we've got to get to the bottom of this very quickly. These are serious
charges of corruption." Nothing ever came of this story, but when these three
venues had their liquor license renewals, the ANC voted unanimously to protest
the renewals.[44] These news reports are consistent with independently provided
claims made by interviewees about how local city regulators, ranging from the

city council and the liquor control board and down to the local units of government, all had their own discreet stakes and interests in different nightlife networks. Referring to the governance structure of Metropolis East, one interview respondent offered the following perspective:

> Just remember that you have regulators who are making pennies on the dollar. They have no money through their job, but they have power . . . . and so that combination allows for some of the regulator to think about how they can get their piece of the pie. . . . $1,000 is a lot of money for someone who makes $40,000 a year, and $1,000 is nothing to a bar or nightclub.

Metropolitan Police Department (MPD)

State agents – like an occupational grouping or class position – are not automatons. Police officers are not mindless drones that enact whatever the state wishes. They are human beings trying to make sense of their social world and navigate it as best as they can. With that caveat in mind, we can get a sense of the probabilistic tendencies that can be measured and observed in any occupational context. MPD has a robust history related to corruption and misconduct, and it is important to historically situate specific scandals as part of the consequences of hiring and recruitment decisions. In the late 1980s, Congress mandated that MPD hire 1,800 officers.[45] In less than two years, approximately 1,500 applicants in the 1989–1990 recruitment cohorts were "pushed through" academy training and placed in patrol shifts.[46] Within four years' time, over 200 of these officers would be arrested for a wide range of misconduct and criminal activity, including robbery, rape, homicide, extortion, and drug trafficking.[47] To best describe the law enforcement culture of this time, the following excerpt is taken from two *Washington Post* staff writers:

> The rigors of a police training institute often were nowhere to be found. Many trainees arrived late and talked loudly in the halls. A few drove cars with bullet holes in the doors, and some bragged about former exploits as drug dealers. One flashed his own gun in the parking lot, and another complained to instructors that someone had rifled a large bag of cash stored in his academy locker.[48]

In 1993, an FBI investigation uncovered "one of the largest police corruption cases in Washington's history," with a dozen MPD officers being indicted on charges that they took bribes to protect Federal agents who they thought were drug dealers and helped them transport cocaine.[49] To reinforce the notion that the 1989–1990 cohort was fundamentally flawed, consider the following excerpt from *The New York Times*:

> Most of the defendants are in their 20's and have served on the police force for less than four years, all of that period in the Fifth District, which

covers part of the northeast section of Washington between the Capitol and Anacostia River.[50]

While the names of the officers are published in the story, the Metropolitan Police Department is never mentioned by name, and the article only specifies "Capitol officers" in the headline and "Washington" as the location. At the time of this report, MPD had 113 officers under indictment or with felony charges.[51]

Police for hire

In this case, the reimbursable detail program reflects a structural mode of commodifying a public service. Police, in essence, are available for hire as part of the broader governance structure in the nightlife economy. The MPD works in tandem with ABRA and the D.C. Council to enforce public safety provisions and provide important investigative and report-related functions to support ABRA's mission. Most ABRA investigations hinge on a police report known as the 251, and MPD Chief of Police has the authority to order any nightlife establishment to be closed for up to 96 hours if the Chief believes that venue presents a significant threat to public order or public safety. ABRA's budget was expanded within the past decade to provide a subsidy for the Reimbursable Detail Program, to which we now turn. "There are two prongs to any protection racket. There's getting rid of the competition and there's forcing people who may or may not think they need your services to hire you anyway."[52]

The Reimbursable Detail Subsidy Program allows for restaurants, taverns, nightclubs, hotels, and multipurpose facilities to hire Metropolitan Police Department Officers to police the surrounding areas of an establishment or an outdoor event that is registered with the Program.[53] The ABRA pays 65% of the costs associated with hiring these police officers, with the alcohol licensee paying the remaining 35%. Certain alcohol licensees are *required* to participate in the Reimbursable Detail Subsidy Program as a function of the requirements for renewing their liquor license.

A similar program has existed in Metropolis East. As one nightclub manager put it during an interview:

> The detail system has been falling out of favor. The major problem with uniformed detail is that you have businesses paying substantial money to anchor an officer in front of the business. It is against their mandate to respond to crimes that are occurring in the general vicinity, and yet if a crime is occurring and the cop can see it, they are obligated to respond, thereby leaving the contracted business without their detail. If having a detail officer is part of the security protocol, the business is liable in the event that an [liquor control board] investigator checks in. Detail used to cost $3,000/month, but the prices have changed and gone up.

In Washington, D.C., other issues have been identified regarding the detail program. Martin Freeman – a former MPD officer – was involved in a whistleblower lawsuit against the MPD for what Freeman describes as retaliatory actions for his claims that the reimbursable detail program was a legally sanctioned protection racket.[54] Before the D.C. Council imposed new rules in 2000, many MPD officers moonlighted at nightlife venues as security personnel (e.g., bouncers, doormen). When the D.C. Council originally introduced a new MPD detail structure, it was highly lucrative for the MPD and city budget generally, since venues were charged upwards of $50–60 per hour.[55]

Around 2004, Freeman was seeking work along with a handful of other MPD officers to provide off-duty security services for a mall in downtown D.C. (Gallery Place). MPD "swooped in, somehow convincing the mall to install a reimbursable detail," which effectively displaced Freeman and his group from obtaining supplemental employment. Freeman spoke to the media and "blew the whistle on the department because the department was involved in illegal activity."[56] Freeman's then-Commander, Cathy Lanier, was reportedly not pleased with this media coverage, and Freeman believed Lanier planned to retaliate for his actions. Approximately one year later, three officers affiliated with Freeman were suspended, and Freeman himself was fired and unable to obtain similar employment due to negative references from MPD (Ibid.). The Fraternal Order of Police (FOP) helped to finance Freeman's lawsuit against MPD, as FOP's formal stance on reimbursable detail programs is that they interfere with the ability of rank-and-file officers to secure private contract work elsewhere and without undue interference from their law enforcement employer. In November of 2012, the District of Columbia Court of Appeals ruled in favor of the MPD, and Freeman's whistleblower lawsuit was dissolved.[57]

In the nightlife industry of Metropolis East, the police detail program did very little to address the historic coziness that existed between law enforcement and private commercial interests. According to one general manager:

> A lot of bar owners have close relationships with high-ranking officials in MPD. . . . After a while of doing this, you get to learn who the cops are, and in some cases, selectively choose which cops get assigned to you. As you learn about them, you comp them some food, beverages, whatever. There are benefits to doing this, you know.

Of these benefits, there was a reported occasion where a bouncer aggressively threw someone out of a popular party bar. The bouncer reportedly met the criteria for assault and battery, considering how they physically picked up and launched the body of another person through the air and onto the sidewalk. This incident occurred in the presence of the police detail officer and would have normally constituted an arrestable offense. The general manager of this venue, who had a close relationship with the detail police, came outside and verbally said to the officer, "I know you didn't see anything, right?" The cop's response was, "What are you talking about?" While the ejected patron was demanding that the police take some sort of action, no arrest or police report took place.

There is a mutually beneficial relationship – or a symbiosis – that comes to emerge between private businesses and police units. This symbiotic dynamic is further legitimized via detail programs such as the one found in Metropolis East or the ones in major cities like Washington, D.C. During the course of my fieldwork, I observed an instance where the Metropolis East Police (MEPD) detail and supporting/back-up officers entered a separate nightclub to remove an aggressive patron. This customer was belligerent and hostile to the night-club security staff, who followed the protocol of calling for MEPD assistance when a hostile and physically capable patron makes clear that they are looking for a fight.[58] (Contrary to common tropes and media depictions, bouncers are not paid to accept invitations to fist fight with violent customers.) Within two minutes, a minimum of seven officers swarmed the patron and wrestled him to the ground. The intoxicated individual resisted in a manner that could be best described as a grappling match. The end result was a bloodied arrestee and an injured officer; the latter slipped and fell to the floor and suffered a lacera-tion to their head. The inebriated customer fared much worse. After a quick visit by a "white-shirt" supervisor,[59] a lower-ranking officer passed out witness statements to all who remained after hours. One of the veteran security staff members simply said, "Be sure to write that this guy [the unruly customer] was violently resisting," suggesting that any potential claims about excessive use-of-force are unwarranted.

When interviewing a manager of the network that jointly owns and operates this venue, they offered the following perspective:

> On the police misconduct side, I've definitely seen a lot of excessive force. Just unnecessary reactions. People getting roughed up, that kind of thing. But generally, you gotta think of them as people who are working a double shift. Think about working a double, and how you just want everything to go smooth and without problems so you can get through the shift and go home.

The physical control of space in a nightclub is central to the identity of bounc-ers and business owners alike. The police aren't called to engage in emotional intelligence de-escalation techniques or negotiate with an unruly patron, but to use the kind of violence and force that the private sector bouncers are not legally authorized to apply. As enforcement arms of their corresponding juris-diction, police are asked to navigate a series of legal and social contradictions. Their mandate is not to actually eliminate certain categories of crime (e.g., prostitution, drug markets, bars and clubs that serve to under-age patrons), but to selectively control and manage those markets. Independent of the specific identities of the police officers, their occupational role is one where the objec-tive is to minimize legal and political liabilities and, in a perfect scenario, regu-late illicit or deviant markets in such a way that they remain available but largely out of sight. We can apply this same logic to excessive use-of-force instances, whereby the objective is not to eliminate the existence of overwhelming uses of force against individuals but reduce the liabilities (and negative press coverage) associated with their continued occurrence. Phrased differently, we can ask a related question: Who benefits from cops using excessive force on nightclub patrons? Bar and club owners are the primary beneficiaries, although this comes at a cost that is accounted for in both licit and illicit ways. Legally, the reimbursable detail program offers compensations for this kind of symbiosis. Illegally, there are discrete payoffs and perks given to police, which I have covered in the preceding chapter.

Nightlife corruption

Beyond the more symbolic actions like participating in the city's Adopt a Block program – where venues proactively sweep and clean the street segment that their business occupies at the end of each night of business – they were also highly engaged in local politics. In 2006, Abdul Khanu donated $1,500 to Vincent Gray's campaign for council chairman, $500 for A. Scott Bolden's At-Large run, and $1,000 to Mayor Adrian Fenty.[60] Marc Barnes contributed $500 to Mark Long's campaign for the Ward 7 council seat.[61] The Group allegedly contributed to a mayoral gala, as well. In Metropolis East, having political connections to local regulators was viewed as a critical factor in a nightlife venue's success, *especially* if the venue was to be associated with large crowds or specific target audiences. As one nightlife manager offered:

> If you're new to the industry, it is more likely that you'll NEED to have a shortcut. If you know someone that "knows a guy," you can be likely to circumvent, omit, or move quickly through the application process of entering the industry.

Two other long-time manager-owners in the nightlife economy specifically referenced liquor control board regulators as being in "their pocket" – referring to the relationship between regulators and a well-known association of bars and nightclubs. *Washington Post* data can partially corroborate these interview statements. In 2011, ABRA was in the *Washington Post* for allegedly receiving gratuities and favors from a high-profile nightlife venue. Jermaine Matthews, a supervisory investigator for ABRA, was suspended with pay pending the outcome of a probe into a cocktail waitress's allegations that he was given four bottles of ultra-premium vodka at Josephine lounge and nightclub, a venue operated by a well-known business group.[62] The waitress filed complaints with three agencies after a fight at the nightclub left her on crutches. In her complaint, Kelley questioned the impartiality of J. Matthews and other inspectors who allegedly receive free alcohol, a practice that she, another club employee and a former inspector interviewed by the *Washington Post*, described as commonplace. Each of the four bottles that this investigator was provided costs paying customers $320, resulting in a total of $1,280, plus 30% in tax and gratuity that was comped by the business network. Kelley, the cocktail waitress, claimed that ABRA Investigator Matthews was a "frequent flier" at the Josephine nightclub.[63] In text messages revealed to the *Washington Post,* the cocktail waitress messaged, "Liquor board dude wants goose instead of belv[edere]," to which the manager responded, "Sure, np," meaning no problem.[64]

ABRA inspectors have been accused of accepting free alcohol before and, in a whistleblower lawsuit, an ABRA official (Felicia Martin) who used to report to a supervisor named Jermaine Mathews claimed that ABRA employees were engaged in "corruption, fraud, waste and abuse, employees consuming alcoholic beverages on the job, inside influence, cronyism, abuse of authority and discriminatory treatment of licensees."[65] Josephine would continue to operate without repercussion until voluntarily closing its doors years later and nothing more ever came of the story. While most of the top-level operators of the network have never been implicated in any wrongdoing, not everyone in this network is untouchable. In 2019, both industry and regulatory agents were arrested as part of a federal bribery and fraud investigation.[66] Abdul Khanu was convicted on two counts of tax evasion.[67] Khanu's nightclubs were absorbed by the 360 Group network, retaining several of Khanu's social capital and staff, four of which contributed to this study. Gholam Kowkabi, owner of Tuscana West in downtown D.C., Ristorante Piccolo in Georgetown, and Home Nightclub was also indicted for tax evasion.[68] A less serious punishment was faced by Marc Barnes, known as an influential figure for his affiliation with the Park nightclub, who was arrested over the destruction of an ID.[69] The language used to describe Barnes (i.e., kingpin) is coincidentally consistent with the racial bias commonly observed in criminal justice data: Barnes, Khanu, Kowkabi, are all Black.

For some historical context, ABRA has had intermittent bad press since its creation in 2001 when it spun out of the DCRA (Department of Consumer and Regulatory Affairs). A former chief alcoholic beverage control (ABRA) investigator was suspended with pay after an inquiry by the D.C. Inspector General was launched in 2001. This investigation involved allegations that Maurice Evans, the ABRA chief investigator, had colluded with a nude dancing club (strip club) owner to circumvent and superficially meet the regulatory requirements imposed by the D.C. health inspector after an inspection visit resulted in sanctions for the business.[70] In 2004, a convicted cocaine dealer secured an alcohol-beverage license and operated a nightclub whose rear windows overlooked the MPD's fifth district headquarters, and laundered proceeds and drug deals worth as high as $100,000 through the nightclub's record-keeping (see *Washington Times* 2007). The negative press surrounding this incident involved confusion as to why this formerly convicted drug dealer – A. Jones – was able to secure a license when all applicants are required to undergo a "Clean Hands" background check that mitigates against the possibility that these exact cases (nightclubs as drug-market laundromats) will occur.

In further discussing the role that certain businesses play in influencing regulators, this interviewee pointed to a neighboring high-end nightclub.

> Do you think these Greeks are throwing urban parties because they like the music? Ozio has had two stabbings in the past three weeks, and when they had someone seriously hit on Saturday night, they were still open for Sunday brunch! The only explanation that makes sense is that Ozio either has a city councilmember or an ABRA member in their pocket.

Jermaine Matthews, the same ABRA supervisory investigator that was relieved of duty for negative press surrounding the gratuities received from one nightlife business, reenters the story of nightlife corruption. Felicia Martin – the same ABRA investigator who used to report directly to J. Mathews, her supervisor, is on the record stating that in 2012, J. Mathews instructed her to evaluate compliance with the reimbursable detail program – which is the agreement held between the Metropolitan Police Department and the private business. When Investigator Martin arrived, she was met by a well-known nightlife manager with firm network connections to both the public and private nightlife sectors. ABRA Investigator Martin asked an on-duty officer, who was in front of this establishment, if they were part of the reimbursable detail program. The officer responded, "No." Functionally speaking, this police officer was acting as though they were, in fact, participating in the reimbursable detail subsidy program, which is what the general manager attested to. Investigator Martin asked to see invoices for the detail to verify whether there was some miscommunication or misfiled paperwork on behalf of MPD, but the general manager claimed that those invoices were at their northeast headquarters and could not be contacted at that time. ABRA Investigator Martin stated, "So once my investigation was over, I still did not get a clear answer as to what is their position on the MPD reimbursable detail, [and] why they were not there on that night."

In this same ABRA hearing, investigator Martin did not yield anything new or noteworthy. The owner of the Irish Pub was politely questioned by the board, and the transcript ends without any wrongdoing attributed to the business, the MPD, or any of the participants that night. It may be just a matter of coincidence that Jermaine Matthews instructed Felicia Martin to specifically inquire about the pub's reimbursable detail on that one night, but Matthews has a record of inappropriate use of office, and Martin has been involved in a whistleblower and workplace discrimination and retaliation lawsuit in which she claims – among other things – that ABRA employees were engaged in "corruption, fraud, waste and abuse, employees consuming alcoholic beverages on the job, inside influence, cronyism, abuse of authority and discriminatory treatment of licensees."[71]

Structural contradictions, manifested wherever you look

Across all levels of city government and mayoral administrations, claims of fraud, abuse, waste, corruption, and outright incompetence have never been in short supply.[72] A former tax examiner for the city was sentenced in 2012 to a 30-month prison term on federal wire fraud charges related to a scheme involving more than $400,000 in fraudulent tax refunds.[73] The perpetrator, Mary Ayers-Zander, "treated the D.C. treasury like her personal piggy bank," according to U.S. Attorney Ronald C. Machen Jr.[74] Whether it's the tax examiner or public works employees accepted bribes to fix parking tickets, corruption exists at all levels of the local government.[75]

D.C.'s current mayor was linked to a scheme involving Tom Lindenfeld and the funneling of $1 million to the campaign coffers of a Democratic big, Chaka Fattah, for Philadelphia mayor. Lindenfeld "is a former partner of David Axelrod, President Obama's political guru" and an adviser to Muriel Bowser.[76] Lindenfeld is a political operative for the Democratic party known to be able to execute both at national levels and local office races, having advised "the successful D.C. mayoral campaigns for Anthony A. Williams and Adrian M. Fenty" (DeBonis & Sullivan 2014). A "cloud of corruption" has followed every D.C. mayor that has served since its mayoral election system was implemented in the 1970s.[77]

Yet prosecutorial data does not fairly represent the scope and extent of crimes of powerful or the illicit conduct of political elites. This is due, in part, to the difficulty of successfully prosecuting instances of public corruption when they are actually detected. When words are chosen very carefully and public regulators shield themselves through the use of their subordinates, proving elements of an offense beyond reasonable doubt becomes exceedingly difficult as active measures are taken to integrate reasonable doubt into the process of bending the rules to one's liking. Conceptually this makes sense; who better to skirt the rules than the population that makes them? According to a longtime general manager of a major nightclub, word choice is particularly telling when assessing alternative remedies for otherwise potentially dangerous liabilities for the business. "So how do you wanna handle this?" If an ABRA inspector says that, it can be interpreted as a signpost that perhaps some kind of payout or gratuity can avoid formal sanctions. This kind of data, obtained in a confidential interview, is consistent with themes found in cases that are formally investigated by federal agents.

In 2007, Yitbarek Syume offered Leon Swain, the chairman of the D.C. Taxicab Commission, $20,000 in cash.[78] Syume claimed that he and other businessmen "in the taxi industry wanted to give Swain $20,000 to help him build 'community support.'"[79] Syume knew that Swain spent two decades with the metropolitan police and was a high profile and respected figure in local D.C. community affairs and was even floated as a potentially attractive competitor for a seat on the D.C. Council. As Wilber (2012) writes:

> Syume provided Swain an envelope with $14,000 in cash, telling him he wanted to purchase licenses to operate cab companies. The next day, he gave Swain $8,000 explaining that he wanted to expedite the licensing process. He also said he thought the certificates would become increasingly valuable if the city limited the number of cab companies as expected.[80]

This exchange underscores how there are fundamental contradictions between what the legal criteria for establishing that a bribe took place versus the real practice of providing and accepting bribes. Despite the insistence at the highest levels of judicial expertise that bribes be legally relevant *only* if there is an explicit *quid quo pro*[81] exchange, not even stuffed envelopes of cash are given with specific directions or itemized requests that are fundamentally tied to the "gift."

These examples barely skim the surface. An exhaustive study of political corruption in any specific city would only be able to document activities that are detected and captured in newspaper headlines, investigative reports, or after extensive, arduous mining of public records to tie events together. It would be reasonable to assume that corruption is routinized and deeply embedded so as to be entirely mundane and uninteresting, sort of like the way campaign finance laws or tax havens make occasional waves, but remain largely uninteresting and relegating to "how things are" or "how the world works." Whether the business is liquor licenses, or taxi medallions, or strip clubs, or recreational cannabis dispensaries, the relationship between money and power is one that requires symbiotic interdependencies between the licit and illicit sectors of the economy. Organized criminal enterprises and routine acts of corruption are symptoms of larger structural contradictions, and the criminal law itself serves as an instrument to give order and predictability to the symptoms of these contradictions without ever addressing their root causes. No matter where you choose to conduct a study or investigation, there is systematic waste, fraud, abuse, and corruption to be found. The question is not whether it exists, but to what degree.

What next?

Structural contradictions theory is especially useful for connecting fundamental, embedded features of our political economy to specific empirical events. Crime events, and the networks of individuals and institutions that both participate and benefit from such events, are reflective of attempts to reconcile contradictory forces. Laws and regulations are, themselves, reflective of such attempts to promote equality and fairness while political and economic interests are misaligned if not opposed to those same values.[82] So long as capital (and cash) remain the lifeblood of our political economic systems, we can expect that the dilemmas and conflicts will take on iterative forms, but the driving contradictions will remain the same.

> We can remove patronage from the liquor boards, but the bigger problem is a regulatory scheme tilted toward entrenched players who reinforce their position through generous contributions to politicians – usually legal ones given to campaigns but at least occasionally of the cash-in-an-envelope variety. Maryland's alcohol laws date to the post-Prohibition era and are ostensibly designed to protect public health. But as this scandal shows,

they have been transformed into a tool to protect individual economic and political interests. The whole system needs to be changed.[83]

Whatever shape the system ought to take is beyond the scope of this book and is certainly not for any one person to authoritatively declare. But as I stated in the beginning of this book, my obligation is to describe things as best as I can, given the limitations of my own subjective lens for making sense of the world around me. How should we make sense of this chapter? Perhaps if we fail to account for the embedded nature of criminogenic capital in both state and corporate realms, we'll risk not knowing how to explain the continued disenchantment with liberalist views on democracy and rule of law. If our legal system is one that robustly defends criminogenic capital, perhaps then we'll have less xenophobic or displaced narratives for making sense of the logical consequences of that arrangement. As the population of haves is increasingly dwarfed by the have-nots, and if those who are most invested in social science fail to integrate the study of crime and its control to the study of state-corporate power and coercion, then crimes-of-the-powerful scholars have failed to share their messages.[84] If there is evidence that crime, as operationalized by the institutions of criminal justice, are accurately described as "those actions which the wealthy have no desire to commit,"[85] the criminological project requires that we connect our concepts of crime, deviance, and victimization to the "growing monetary inequalities and asymmetries of political and economic power," particularly when these same power structures are directly responsible for some of the most widely felt and demonstrably injurious (and preventable) impacts in the modern world.[86] In both licit and illicit settings, the contradictions are to be found in the corrupting nature of our political economy or, as the title of this book suggests, in *corrupt capital*.

Moving beyond the critiques: ultra-realism

The global economy is characterized by significant and increasingly rising levels of economic trickery, fraud, and crime in many business sectors.[87] Whether or not these economic practices are labeled as *corrupt* is a political, ideological, and cultural matter. The most incisive critique of criminology is that we have failed to both prevent and explain both crime and social harm. What are we to do about this? For academic readers, I believe the ultra-realism perspective offers both a principled and pragmatic way forward.

There are "strong empirical and theoretical grounds for believing that an economy based on dispossession lies at the heart of what capital is foundationally about."[88] If one views capital – both the economic model of capitalism and its ideological underpinnings of liberalism – as being central to U.S. law, political philosophy, and history, then there are salient gaps between prescriptive value systems and descriptive realities that require careful sociolegal analysis. With corruption receiving renewed vigor in public and scholarly discourse,[89] ultra-realism offers a platform for integrating past and present forms of criminological perspectives "in a coherent critique of the whole advanced capitalist way of life, its competitive-narcissistic culture, its subjectivities and its harms."[90] Ultra-realism advances this position while still taking seriously the core mandate that we have as *criminologists*: Advancing empirical and explanatory understandings of harmful behavior – much, though not all, which may be formally designated as *crime*.

Steve Hall, a leading scholar on ultra-realism in criminology, articulated how the majority of

> articles in the allegedly "top" criminology journals are superficial quantitative studies testing some outdated idea or producing findings that have little political bearing on broader structures or processes. These findings might help cops to respond to incidents a little faster – the sort of research that before neoliberal budget cuts was once done more effectively by the cops themselves – but have no bearing on the big economic, cultural and political issues that underlie today's rapidly mutating forms of crime and harm.[91]

This was not always the case. Following the watershed of political mobilization in the 1960s and 1970s, a critical criminology emerged in a variety of American colleges and universities, including UC–Berkeley.[92] Many of these earlier pioneers laid a foundation for connecting criminological research to the political economy of capitalism and the hegemonic force of state-corporate power, highlighting "linkages between the operations of post-war monopoly capitalism and social injustices such as class domination, economic inequalities, racism, sexism, and particularly racial and class disparities in justice system practices."[93]

For criminologists who might identify – or be identified – as being outside the conventional orthodoxy, many scholars within the critical[94] criminology sub-field have focused on class and economic structure, empirically and conceptually linking a broad range of crimes, including state-corporate harms, to the dilemmas and contradictions of capitalism.[95] Yet the bulk of critical scholarship on "state-corporate crime" – while politically aligned with ostensibly speaking truth to power – focuses on symptoms or iterative effects of the basis of such power. In other words, the work focuses descriptively on how power manifests itself in ways that are raced, classed, and gendered, but does not always center the colonial legacies and neocolonial realities that undergird and condition the very phenomena found in the nominal categories of "racial capitalist harms," "corporate crime," "crimes of the powerful," "transnational organized crime," "patriarchal violence," and so on. This suggests that the time to entertain a radically different approach to crime and justice research is both overdue and now.

It is a worthwhile use of our time to carefully and persuasively unpack the ways in which colonialism, imperialism, neoliberalism, and Western liberalism are all part of a broader historical process of capital accumulation and forceful dispossession, and how patriarchy and racial projects are embedded therein. After all, "the accumulation of capital determines a nation's power, wealth, and survival today, as it did 300 years ago."[96] However, that still does not help answer the basic question of why some people engage in harmful activities, whereas others do not. To move beyond these critiques, ultra-realism invites us to take part in these shared projects.

Embracing political economy and political locations

Right-wing and left-wing liberalism (or the contemporary discursive climate between Democratic and Republican platforms) have starved the political imagination, and researchers should connect their empirical claims to some broader political project. Ideally, such a project should stimulate ideas that escape the narrow confines of liberalist political discourse. It also would be virtuous to specify – as the Schwendingers might say – which side you are on and whether one's scholarship aligns with defending the existing order, as opposed to advancing some articulable notion of human rights.[97]

Getting out in the field

Conventional criminological theory and methods have grown stagnant. But a rich world awaits us and ethnography is the most direct pathway for reimagining ideas related to crime, justice, and human-made systems. Because the methodological and the political are inseparable,[98] it is a political location in and of itself to conduct ethnographic work, and to be clear about why and how you decided to go about it. To stay relevant beyond our obscure CCJ silos, criminologists *must* incorporate the perspectives that have long been advanced by black feminist scholars, critical criminologists from the Global South and the Global North, and both historians and sociologists of punishment who have illuminated various shortcomings of criminological inquiry. Particularly for readers of this series, *crimes of the powerful*, as a subfield, risks becoming somewhat parochial if we do not provide compelling responses to the interdependent systems of racial, classist, and gendered matrices of oppression in a way that centers the material and lived experiences of variously constituted subjects – or in plain English: People who are both perceived and treated differently for reasons outside of their control.[99]

Do you dress like they did in the 1700s? Do you have wooden teeth, will you die of dysentery, and spend time churning your own butter? Among all the things we've left behind in the name of technological and socio-cultural advancement, the fact that we seem to have no issues referencing European literature from the 1600s and 1700s should mean something *beyond* Euro-centric supremacy. Perhaps it speaks to contemporary concerns and critiques of power and authority. Perhaps we are repurposing some of the language and discourse of the Enlightenment Era to look upward at the power structures of our time. Rather than writing about alternatives to the abuses and excesses of the church and crown, today we draw from the texts of this time-period and adopt them as analytic tools to understand – and critique – the current iteration of concentrated power: The state-corporate nexus personified by C. Wright Mills (1956) in *The Power Elite*. But this isn't really about crimes of powerful *people* at all. It's about how people make sense of the systems that they inherited, and whether they decide what parts, if any, are worth keeping. The ratio of those who like things as they are and those who want something else – or need something else to survive – is presumably changing at a faster rate.

The Enlightenment was a period when the church and crown, and the related abstractions on which their legitimacy was perpetuated (e.g., primogeniture; divine right) were not only called into question but met with compelling alternative blueprints and proposals. When John Locke wrote *Treatise* (1689), the death knell of feudalism was ringing ever stronger with the Tenures Abolition Act of 1660, and broader historical forces during "the long 18th century" were prompting many to question the very essence of sovereign power and citizenship at a time when European nation-states were competing for primacy in the new political economic world system they were creating for themselves. These ideas did not come about at random or in a vacuum. Collectively, writers were responding to the existing conflicts and dilemmas of their time. Many of them died not knowing that their written works would still be known 300 years later, or appear on the reading list of someone's comprehensive examinations. Presumably, some of them died with cynicism, pessimism, or existential dread. In short, the fact that we are increasingly using our professional and personal outlets to raise social critique is, itself, a sign that something tectonic in scale is happening in our social world and we are trying to make sense of it beyond the obscure discourses that help very few people, like ruminations on *the Lacanian real* or the obscure sociological high-brow of *Bourdieusian fields*, among other things, we were told were important in graduate school. Ultra-realism asserts that even after we've done all the right readings, the conferencing in the right panels, and the virtue signaling through citing the right works, it is time to get back out into the field to find better ways of describing and explaining what is actually happening, as opposed to using the theories and words that are currently in vogue but that will soon change. While there is much to continue studying about crimes of the powerful, such scholarly attention – just like mass social movements – must move beyond after-the-fact responses, but produce a sustained focus on recalibrating the political and economic structures that make state-corporate crime so routine.[100] As a shared project, auditing the full scale of how powerful systems and corrupt capital condition our lives and livelihoods seems like a worthy use of our time.

Conclusion

Had I followed the trends and advice of the field, my dissertation might have yielded tables of coefficients crafted to fit a socially (and intellectually) sterile theory about criminal offending –but then I would've had neither the inspiration nor a viable pathway for producing a book. As researchers increasingly recognize, our own relative class position and account for these evolving forms of systemic harm and corruption that affect variously situated criminological orientations, it might be then that criminology transcends its historical baggage as managerial cop shop sciences, and takes seriously what some (certainly not all) radical and critical criminologists have been pointing to for quite some time: The corrosive, racializing, and patriarchal nature of capital. In promoting the privileges that I was fortunate to receive, I ask those readers within academe to consider the merits of encouraging their colleagues and graduate students to take to the field and reduce the social distance between the researcher and the researched. After all, some of us could not build careers, compete in the tenure track or McUniversity rat race, or pay our bills without extracting or commodifying the experiences of "human subjects" in a way that convinces academic gatekeepers that such experiences are worth sharing. I am grateful that Routledge and the readers of this book found my own auto-ethnographic approach to be a story worth sharing, and I respectfully encourage educators and students alike to put their own biographical concerns and experiences at the center of how and why they research and write about their topics of interest. Criminological research, and especially research into crimes of the powerful, should increasingly come from people who have seen or experienced it themselves. It is time to put the social back into social science, and specify the broader political project that our research and writing serves.

Notes

1 Chambliss, William J. 1988. *On the Take: From Petty Crooks to Presidents*. 2nd ed. Indiana University Press, p. 208.
2 See Chambliss (1988:210).
3 Glaeser, Edward L. and Raven E. Saks. 2006. "Corruption in America." *Journal of Public Economics* 90(6–7):1053–1072.
4 Bentley, Chris and Jeremy Hobson. 2019. "How Chicago Politics Produced a Deeply Entrenched Culture of Corruption." *WBUR Public Radio*, February 28 (www.wbur. org/hereandnow/2019/02/28/chicago-politics-corruption).
5 See Davey, Monica. 2016. "'Making a Murderer' Town's Answer to Netflix Series: You Don't Know." *The New York Times*, January 28 (www.nytimes.com/2016/01/29/us/ making-a-murderer-town-netflix-steven-avery.html).
6 Kaplan, Sarah. 2016. "FBI Arrests Nearly All of the Top Officials of Crystal City, Tex." *The Washington Post*, February 8 (www.washingtonpost.com/news/morning-mix/ wp/2016/02/08/theres-only-one-person-left-on-this-texas-city-council-after-fbi-arrests-top-officials-on-corruption-charges/?utm_term=.694d638b723a).
   Zapotsky, Matt. 2016. "This Might be the Most Corrupt Little Town in America." *The Washington Post*, March 5 (www.washingtonpost.com/world/national-security/ this-might-be-the-most-corrupt-little-town-in-america/2016/03/05/341c21d2-dcac-11e5-81ae-7491b9b9e7df_story.html?utm_term=.02d4ce6e5ea0).
7 Glaeser, Edward L. 2013. n.d. "Excessive Regulation Turns Boston Taxi Industry into Shadowy, Corrupt Sphere." *The Boston Globe.Com*. Retrieved October 3, 2016 (www. bostonglobe.com/opinion/2013/04/04/excessive-regulation-turns-boston-taxi-industry-into-shadowy-corrupt-sphere/cQbYTEaNsBOtH1abtRde7J/story.html).
8 Chambliss (1988).

9 Orso, Anna. 2015. "Bribes, Strippers, Corruption and Red Tape: Philadelphia's Department of Licenses and Inspection." *Billy Penn*, July 14 (http://billypenn.com/2015/07/14/bribes-strippers-corruption-and-red-tape-philadelphias-department-of-licenses-and-inspection/).

10 Czitrom, Daniel. 2016. "The Origins of Corruption in the New York City Police Department." *TIME*, June 28 (https://time.com/4384963/nypd-scandal-history/); see also Pileggi, Nicholas. 2008. "The Mob and the Machine." *New York Magazine*, April 30 (https://nymag.com/news/features/crime/46610/index1.html).

11 Department of Justice. 2018. "Koreatown Consultant and Ex-California Dept. of Alcoholic Beverage Control Official Plead Guilty in Long-Running Bribery Scheme." *U.S. Attorney, Central District of California, News*, November 29 (www.justice.gov/usao-cdca/pr/koreatown-consultant-and-ex-california-dept-alcoholic-beverage-control-official-plead).

12 Department of Justice (2018).

13 Rubin, Joel and Victoria Kim. 2018. "A State Official Overseeing Koreatown Bars Was on the Take for Years, Prosecutors Say." *Los Angeles Times*, October 19 (www.latimes.com/local/lanow/la-me-koreatown-bribes-20181019-story.html).

14 Rocha, Veronica. 2015. "Club Owner Indicted on Charges of Laundering Money for Mexico Drug Trade." *Los Angeles Times*, March 7 (https://www.latimes.com/local/lanow/la-me-ln-nightclub-owner-indicted-20150306-story.html).

15 Diedrich, John and Mary Spicuzza. 2016. "Milwaukee Strip Club Owner Indicted in California." *Milwaukee-Wisconsin Journal Sentinel*, August 25 (www.jsonline.com/story/news/investigations/2016/08/22/milwaukee-strip-club-owner-indicted-california/88615080/).

16 Federal Bureau of Investigation. 2015. "Gold Club Owner among Those Indicted for Using Business to Operate Elaborate Money Laundering Scheme." March 19 (www.fbi.gov/contact-us/field-offices/sanfrancisco/news/press-releases/gold-club-owner-among-those-indicted-for-using-business-to-operate-elaborate-money-laundering-scheme).

17 Gilbert, Curtis. 2012. "Envy Nightclub Surrenders Liquor License; Owners Investigated." *MPRnews*. August 31 (www.mprnews.org/story/2012/08/31/business/envy-nightclub-surrenders-liquor-license-owners-investigated).

18 Rulison, Larry. 2014. "Feds Investigating Lake George Night Club Owner." *Times Union*, April 24 (http://blog.timesunion.com/business/feds-investigating-lake-george-night-club-owner/59880/).

19 Harris, Art. 2001. "Judge Gives Gotti a Pass in Strip Club Trial." *CNN*, May 18 (http://edition.cnn.com/2001/LAW/05/18/gotti.gold.club/index.html?related).

20 Times-Union Associated Press. 2001. "Convict Says Club Provided Sex, Betting." *The Florida Times-Union*, June 1 (http://jacksonville.com/tu-online/stories/060101/met_6322404.html).

21 Moshinsky, Ben. 2016. "The Former Chairman of the Hakkasan Restaurant Group is Allegedly Being Investigated in a Global Embezzling Case." *Business Insider*, August 15 (www.businessinsider.in/The-former-chairman-of-the-Hakkasan-restaurant-group-is-allegedly-being-investigated-in-a-global-embezzling-case/articleshow/53708095.cms).

22 Federal Bureau of Investigation. 2012. "Eight Individuals Charged and Arrested in Two Separate Corruption Investigations." *FBI* (www.fbi.gov/miami/press-releases/2012/eight-individuals-charged-and-arrested-in-two-separate-corruption-investigations).

   Weaver, Jay. 2012. "Miami Beach Fire Inspector Pleads Guilty in Federal Club-Extortion Racket Case." *The Miami Herald*, June 8 (www.miamiherald.com/latest-news/article1940441.html).

23 Austermuhle, Martin. 2019. "A Brief History of Legal and Ethical Misdeeds by Some D.C. Lawmakers." *WAMU*, July 9 (https://wamu.org/story/19/07/09/a-brief-history-of-legal-and-ethical-misdeeds-by-d-c-lawmakers/).

24 All descriptive statements regarding ABC/ABRA's form and function are replicated directly from https://abra.dc.gov/page/about-abra.

25 https://abra.dc.gov/node/1209342; 2019 update here: https://abra.dc.gov/node/1415756.

26 Taverns are generally defined as an establishment that 1) serves food and alcoholic beverages, 2) plays recorded or background music, and 3) possesses a dance floor, not to exceed 140 square feet, without an entertainment endorsement.

27 Nightclub means a space in a building, and the adjoining space outside of a building, regularly used and kept open as a place that serves food and alcoholic beverages and provides music and facilities for dancing.

28 Clubs are defined as any organization that 1) is incorporated for 3+ months; 2) owns, leases, or occupies a building; and 3) has a main source of operational revenue that is NOT from alcoholic beverage sales. Definitions are replicated from p. 20 of the revised March 2016 update to the D.C. Official Code, Title 25, available here: https://abra. dc.gov/sites/default/files/dc/sites/abra/publication/attachments/DCOfficialCode-Title%2025DCMRTitle23_0.pdf.

29 Council of the District of Columbia. 2016. "About the Council." (http://dccouncil. us/pages/about-the-council).

30 King, Colbert I. 2016. "The Painfully Slow Corruption Probe of Vincent Gray." *Washington Post*, August 7 (www.washingtonpost.com/opinions/the-painfully-slow-corruption-probe-of-vincent-gray/2015/08/07/05165b7a-3c55-11e5-b3ac-8a79 bc44e5e2_story.html).

31 See Emery, Theo. 2014. "Washington Businessman Pleads Guilty Over Illegal Contributions." *The New York Times*, March 10 (www.nytimes.com/2014/03/11/us/ washington-businessman-pleads-guilty-over-illegal-contributions.html).

32 Hesse, Monica. 2015. "Jim Graham Served Four Terms in the D.C. Council. Now, He Promotes All-Nude Stripper Nights." *The Washington Post*, April 23 (https:// www.washingtonpost.com/lifestyle/style/jim-graham-served-four-terms-in-the-dc-council-now-he-promotes-all-nude-stripper-nights/2015/04/22/92776550-e77c-11e4-8581-633c536add4b_story.html).

33 Craig, Tim. 2012. "D.C. Alcohol Board Adds Bars to Late-Open List (Posted 2012-11-09 20:35:48)." *The Washington Post*, November 9 (https://www.washingtonpost. com/blogs/dc-wire/post/dc-alcohol-board-adds-bars-to-late-open-list/2012/11/09/ 90b91730-2a92-11e2-bab2-eda299503684_blog.html).

34 Craig, Tim and Mike DeBonis. 2013. "D.C. Council Member Jim Graham Fights Back against Resolution." *The Washington Post*, February 21 (www.washingtonpost. com/local/dc-politics/dc-council-member-jim-graham-fights-back-against-resolutio n/2013/02/21/7539f732-7c6c-11e2-9a75-dab0201670da_story.html).

35 Madden, Patrick. 2012. "D.C. Council Member Jim Graham Violated Metro Code of Conduct." *WAMU* 88.5. (http://wamu.org/news/12/10/12/dc_council_member_ jim_graham_violated_metro_code_of_conduct).

36 See Zapana, Victor. 2011. "Former D.C. Council aide Sentences to 8 Months in Prison." *The Washington Post*, June 28 (www.washingtonpost.com/local/former-dc-council-aide-sentenced-to-eight-months-in-prison/2011/06/28/AG8Y0mpH_story. html); Wilber, Del Quentin. 2012. "D.C. Taxi Industry Insiders Sentences in Bribery Scheme." *The Washington Post*, February 10 (www.washingtonpost.com/local/crime/ dc-taxi-industry-insiders-sentenced-in-bribery-scheme/2012/02/10/gIQApuH04Q_ story.html).

37 Wilber, Del Quentin, Lena H. Sun and Tim Craig. 2009. "Graham Aide's Arrest Rooted in Probe of D.C. Tax Industry." *The Washington Post*, September 26 (www. washingtonpost.com/wp-dyn/content/article/2009/09/25/AR2009092503648.html).

38 Madden, Patrick. 2013. "Jim Graham Fights Back against Reprimand from D.C. Council." *WAMU*, February 22 (https://wamu.org/story/13/02/22/jim_graham_ fights_back_against_reprimand_from_dc_council/).

39 DeBonis, Mike and Tim Craig. 2013. "Howard Brooks Pleads Guilty in Probe of Mayor Gray's 2010 Campaign." *The Washington Post*, May 24 (www.washington post.com/local/dc-politics/howard-brooks-pleads-guilty-in-probe-of-mayor-grays-2010-campaign/2012/05/24/gJQArf9snU_story.html).

40 See https://anc.dc.gov/page/about-ancs

41 Stein, Perry. 2014. "Dupont Circle Citizens Take on Loud Nightclubs, One Decibel Reading at a Time." *Washington City Paper*, March 26 (www.washingtoncitypaper.com/ food/blog/13130845/dupont-circle-citizens-take-on-loud-nightclubs-one-decibel-reading-at-a-time); see also http://dcnightlifenoise.com/.

42 See Ankarlo, Kris. 2015. "D.C. Nightlife Pushing Back on New Legislation." *CBS DC*, November 4 (https://washington.cbslocal.com/2015/11/04/dc-nightlife-pushing-back-new-legislation/).

43 Fahrenthold, David A. 2002. "3 Say D.C. Officials Solicited Funds." *The Washington Post*, July 27 (www.washingtonpost.com/archive/local/2002/07/27/3-say-dc-offi cials-solicited-funds/9b928d93-57eb-49cb-b9b2-5746ef040733/).

44 Fahrenthold (2002).

45 Flaherty (1994).

46 Flaherty, Mary Pat and Keith A. Harriston. 1994. "Police Credibility on Trial in D.C. Courts." *The Washington Post*, August 30 (www.washingtonpost.com/archive/ politics/1994/08/30/police-credibility-on-trial-in-dc-courts/a07131f2-81fd-45d4-8e7b-2e1ad64ae45f/).

47 Flaherty, Mary Pat. 1994. "After Rookie Got Role Model, He Lost Job." *The Washington Post*, August 29 (www.washingtonpost.com/wp-srv/local/longterm/library/dc/ dcpolice/94series/trainingday2_side.htm); Harriston, Keith A. and Mary Pat Flaherty. 1994. "D.C. Police Paying for Hiring Binge." *The Washington Post*, August 28 (www. washingtonpost.com/wp-srv/local/longterm/library/dc/dcpolice/94series/training day1.htm).

48 Harriston, Keith A. and Pary Pat Flaherty. 1994. "Standards Eased in Rush to Expand Force." *Washington Post*, August 29 (https://www.washingtonpost.com/wp-srv/local/ longterm/library/dc/dcpolice/94series/trainingday2.htm).

49 Labaton, Stephen. 1993. "Ex-Official Is Convicted In HUD Scandal of 80's." *The New York Times*, October 27 (https://www.nytimes.com/1993/10/27/us/ex-official-is-convicted-in-hud-scandal-of-80-s.html).

50 Labaton (1993, web).

51 Harriston, Keith A. and Hamil R. Harris. 1993. "12 on D.C. Force Arrested in Corruption Probe." *The Washington Post*, December 15 (www.washingtonpost.com/ archive/politics/1993/12/15/12-on-dc-force-arrested-in-corruption-probe/d8fd4e74-a481-4609-9cac-a154caabc301/).

52 Smith, Rend. 2010. "MPD's Private Security Branch." *Washington City Paper*, August 6 (www.washingtoncitypaper.com/news/article/13039342/mpds-private-security-branch-how-the-district-can-force-bars).

53 See Alcoholic Beverage Regulation Administration (https://abra.dc.gov/page/ reimbursable-detail-subsidy-program).

54 Smith (2010).

55 Smith (2010).

56 Smith (2010).

57 See Freeman v. District of Columbia (http://caselaw.findlaw.com/dc-court-of-appeals/ 1615807.html).

58 At this venue, the security staff is its own unit worthy of sociological inquiry. The members of this team exist in a hypermasculine working environment, with members from all walks of life. Represented in this group are members of the military (reserve and active duty), a former police officer, a parole officer, and former inmates. Some security staff are inclined to self-select into physical confrontations, but the protocol

to call MPD exists to mitigate against the outcome of having multiple security staff responsible for an intoxicated customer's injuries.

59 The uniform of the lieutenant rank and above consists of a white shirt. Sergeants and below wear navy blue shirts. Sergeants have considerable clout in nightlife interactions, and can be easily identified by their badge, which is gold like all other ranks above the sergeant. Patrol officers wear silver badges, and a single chevron or the lack of insignia meant, for all intents and purposes, that the cop was a cog in the nightlife machine.

60 Gould, Jessica. 2007. "The Death of the Party." *Washington City Paper* (www.washington citypaper.com/news/article/13004859/the-death-of-the-party).

61 Gould (2007).

62 Stewart, Nikita. 2011. "Club's Attorney Says Free Liquor Went to D.C. Inspector's Friends." *Washington Post*, December 1 (www.washingtonpost.com/local/dc-politics/clubs-attorney-says-free-liquor-went-to-dc-inspectors-friends/2011/12/01/gIQAu3 CVIO_story.html).

63 See Stewart (2011).

64 See Stewart (2011).

65 See Stewart (2011); See also Stewart, Nikita. 2011. "ABC Inspector Suspended in D.C. after Allegation of Free Liquor." *Washington Post*, November 30 (www.washington post.com/local/dc-politics/abc-inspector-suspended-in-dc-after-allegation-of-free-liquor/2011/11/30/gIQAnBcXEO_story.html).

66 U.S. Department of Justice. 2019. "Four Men Indicted in Schemes to Corrupt and Defraud District of Columbia's Office of Tax and Revenue." *U.S. Attorney's Office, District of Columbia* (www.justice.gov/usao-dc/pr/four-men-indicted-schemes-corrupt-and-defraud-district-columbias-office-tax-and-revenue).

67 No. 10-3039 (D.C. Cir. 2011); 09-087 – USA v. Khanu; see also Cherkis, Jason. 2009. "DC Live/Platinum/VIP Club Owner Indicted On Tax Charges." *Washington City Paper*, April 1 (www.washingtoncitypaper.com/news/city-desk/blog/13058045/dc-liveplatinumvip-club-owner-indicted-on-tax-charges); Smith, Rend. 2010. "Convicted Club Kingpin Abdul Khanu Gets Three Years in Jail." *Washington City Paper*, May 11 (www.washingtoncitypaper.com/news/city-desk/blog/13061563/convicted-club-kingpin-abdul-khanu-gets-three-years-in-jail).

68 Leonnig, Carol D. 2005. "Tax Fraud Alleged At D.C. Restaurants." *Washington Post*, April 16 (www.washingtonpost.com/archive/local/2005/04/16/tax-fraud-alleged-at-dc-restaurants/c0047eea-2f42-4f06-b6e8-e56cc3ed7f2e/).

69 See Alexander, Keith L. 2014. "Marc Barnes, Owner of D.C. Nightclub Park at 14th, Charged over Destruction of ID." *Washington Post*, November 8 (www.washingtonpost. com/local/crime/marc-barnes-owner-of-dc-nightclub-park-at-14th-faces-charge-over-destruction-of-id/2014/11/07/4079ba02-6606-11e4-836c-83bc4f26eb67_story.html).

70 See Santana, Arthur. 2003. "Liquor Control Official Faulted by D.C. Inquiry." *Washington Post*, February 22 (www.washingtonpost.com/archive/local/2003/02/22/liquor-control-official-faulted-by-dc-inquiry/df33df12-d5f5-4202-81ac-02d6f1874b33/); see also MAURICE EVANS V. DISTRICT OF COLUMBIA ET AL. Civil Action No. 03-2331 (PLF). United States District Court for the District of Columbia (www. govinfo.gov/content/pkg/USCOURTS-dcd-1_03-cv-02331/pdf/USCOURTS-dcd-1_03-cv-02331-1.pdf).

71 See PR Web. 2020. "Whistleblower & Discrimination Lawsuit Moves Forward Against DC's Alcoholic Beverage Regulation Director Fred Moosally and Former Director Maria Delaney Among Others." May 19 (www.prweb.com/releases/2012/2/prweb9227777.htm).

72 Nnamdi, Kojo. 2012. "How D.C. Became a District of Corruption." *Washington Post*, July 13 (www.washingtonpost.com/opinions/how-dc-became-a-district-of-corruption/2012/07/13/gJQA1ZhiiW_story.html).

73 FBI. 2012. "Former D.C. Tax Examiner Sentenced to 30 Months in Prison in Scam Involving More Than $400,000 in Refunds." *Federal Bureau of Investigation – Washington Field Office* (www.fbi.gov/washingtondc/press-releases/2012/former-d.c.-tax-examiner-sentenced-to-30-months-in-prison-in-scam-involving-more-than-400-000-in-refunds).

74 Cenziper, Debbie. 2012. "Problems Lingered at D.C. Tax Office for Years after 2007 Scandal, Audits Show." *Washington Post*, October 8 (www.washingtonpost.com/investigations/problems-lingered-at-dc-tax-office-for-years-after-2007-scandal-audits-show/2012/10/08/236f14a0-0cbe-11e2-bb5e-492c0d30bff6_story.html).

75 See Harriston and Harris (1993).

76 DeBonis, Mike and John Sullivan. 2014. "Tom Lindenfeld, Consultant to D.C. Mayors, Implicated in Phila. Corruption Scheme." *Washington Post*, September 3 (www.washingtonpost.com/local/dc-politics/tom-lindenfeld-consultant-to-dc-mayors-implicated-in-phila-corruption-scheme/2014/09/03/6bafdd20-32f1-11e4-9e92-0899b306bbea_story.html); DeBonis, Mike and Matt Zapotosky. 2014. "Ex-Bowser Adviser Admits to Pa. Corruption Scheme." *Washington Post*, November 5 (www.washingtonpost.com/local/dc-politics/ex-bowser-adviser-lindenfeld-admits-to-corruption-scheme-in-philadelphia/2014/11/05/c4dcc72a-650d-11e4-836c-83bc4f26eb67_story.html).

77 Davis, Aaron C. 2015. "As Cloud of Corruption Passes in D.C., Regular Dysfunction Back in Spotlight." *Washington Post*, August 2 (www.washingtonpost.com/local/dc-politics/as-cloud-of-corruption-passes-in-dc-regular-dysfunction-back-in-spotlight/2015/08/02/c1006fb2-37ad-11e5-9739-170df8af8eb9_story.html).

78 See Wilber, Del Quentin. 2012. "D.C. Taxi Official Turned FBI Informant Recalls Role in Corruption Probe." *Washington Post*, April 2 (www.washingtonpost.com/local/crime/dc-taxi-official-turned-fbi-informant-recalls-role-in-corruption-probe/2012/04/02/gIQAErYhrS_story.html).

79 Wilber, Del Quentin. 2012. "D.C. Taxi Industry Insiders Sentenced in Bribery Scheme." *Washington Post*, February 10 (www.washingtonpost.com/local/crime/dc-taxi-industry-insiders-sentenced-in-bribery-scheme/2012/02/10/gIQApuH04Q_story.html).

80 Wilber, Del Quentin. 2012. "D.C. Taxi Official Turned FBI Informant Recalls Role in Corruption Probe." *Washington Post*, April 2 (www.washingtonpost.com/local/crime/dc-taxi-official-turned-fbi-informant-recalls-role-in-corruption-probe/2012/04/02/gIQAErYhrS_story.html).

81 Department of Justice. 2020. "834. Intent of the Parties." *The United States Department of Justice Archives.* (https://www.justice.gov/archives/jm/criminal-resource-manual-834-intent-parties).

82 Chambliss (1988:216).

83 *The Baltimore Sun.* 2017. "Liquor and Corruption." January 13 (www.baltimoresun.com/news/opinion/editorial/bs-ed-prince-georges-liquor-20170113-story.html).

84 See Barak, Gregg, Paul Leighton and Allison Cotton. 2015. *Class, Race, Gender, and Crime: The Social Realities of Justice in America.* 4th ed. Rowman & Littlefield, p. 527.

85 Godwin, William. 1793. *An Enquiry Concerning Political Justice.* Vol. II. London.

86 Tombs, Steve and David Whyte. 2015. *The Corporate Criminal.* Routledge.

87 See Whyte, David and Jörg Wiegratz. 2016. *Neoliberalism and the Moral Economy of Fraud.* Routledge.

88 Harvey, David. 2014. *Seventeen Contradictions and the End of Capitalism.* Oxford University Press, p. 54.

89 Doshi, Sapana and Malini Ranganathan. 2018. "Towards a Critical Geography of Corruption and Power in Late Capitalism." *Progress in Human Geography* 43(3):436–457. https://doi.org/10.1177/0309132517753070.

90   Hall, Steve and Simon Winlow. 2017. "Ultra-realism." In *The Routledge Companion to Criminological Theory and Concepts*, edited by Avi Brisman, Eamonn Carrabine and Nigel South. Routledge.

91   Interview with Prof Steve Hall on Ultra-Realist Criminology. Web (www.injustice-film.com/2018/01/02/interview-prof-steve-hall-ultra-realist-criminology/).

92   Koehler, Johann. 2015. "Development and Fracture of a Discipline: Legacies of the School of Criminology at Berkeley." *Criminology* 53(4):513–544; Barak, Gregg. 2020. *Chronicles of a Radical Criminologist: Working the Margins of Law, Power, and Justice.* Rutgers University Press.

93   Michalowski, Raymond J. 2016. "What is Crime?" *Critical Criminology* 24:181–199, p. 193.

94   Critical criminology and radical criminology are also differentiated on important grounds, foremost of which is that the latter is framed as being synonymous with Marxist criminology, whereas the former is far more diverse in its ideological and political assumptions. For a comprehensive overview on the distinction between conflict and radical criminology, see Bernard, Thomas J. 1981. "The Distinction Between Conflict and Radical Criminology." *The Journal of Criminal Law and Criminology* 72(1):362–379. See also Friedrichs, David O. and Martin D. Schwartz. 2007. "Editors' Introduction: On Social Harm and a Twenty-First Century Criminology." *Crime, Law and Social Change* 48(1):1–7.

95   Greenberg, David F. ed. 1981. *Crime and Capitalism: Readings in Marxist Criminology.* Mayfield; Pearce, Frank. 1976. *Crimes of the Powerful: Marxism, Crime and Deviance.* Pluto Press; Bittle, Steven, Laureen Snider, Steve Tombs and David Whyte. 2020. *Revisiting Crimes of the Powerful: Marxism, Crime and Deviance.* Routledge.

96   Chambliss, William J. 2009. "State-Organized Crime." In *Crimes of the Powerful: A Reader*, edited by David Whyte. McGraw-Hill, p. 152.

97   This phrasing is directly from the Schwendingers. See Schwendinger, Herman and Julia Schwendiger. 1970. "Defenders of Order or Guardians of Human Rights?" *Issues in Criminology* 5(2):123–157.

98   DeKeseredy, Walter. 2011. *Contemporary Critical Criminology.* Routledge.

99   Moosavi, Leon. 2018. "Decolonising Criminology: Syed Hussein Alatas on Crimes of the Powerful." *Critical Criminology* 27:229–242.

100 Kramer, Ronald C. 2016. "State-Organized Crime, International Law and Structural Contradictions." *Critical Criminology* 24(2):231–245; Michalowski, Raymond. 2013. "The Master's Tools: Can Supranational Law Confront Crimes of Powerful States?" In *State Crime and Resistance*, edited by E. Stanley and J. McCulloch. Routledge, p. 221.

Epilogue

The standard format of a conclusion is to offer a summary of the text and conclude with a forward-looking, cautiously optimistic tone, or perhaps some prescriptive *future directions* agenda. Writing in the midst of the spring 2020 COVID-19 (coronavirus) pandemic, my personal relationship to crimes of the powerful scholarship has become more intimate. I like to think that this is a time where we replace the question of "When will things go back to normal?" with a deeper question, like "What, exactly, do we think is normal?" or "What is it about our institutional arrangements that are worth keeping?" The pandemic will surely pass, but the state-corporate forces that we are seeing through new angles are likely to remain unchanged. On the flip side, some of us are realizing that the patterns and routines (or systemic and institutional practices) we once thought were stable and permanent are just matters of social custom, and could radically change in short order. We worked and lived and commuted and related to each other in patterned ways not because we had a divine revelation that this was *the* way to do things, but because these systemic practices have been cultivated and maintained so as to benefit specific groups and institutions. In short, things appear to be "set up a certain way" until they are not, and such things are not "set up" at random. There are powerful forces – economic, ideological, political, and social – that will shape what emerges on the other side of this pandemic.

Somewhat paradoxically, there is no shortage of work in studying powerful practices and institutions, even though there are few institutions that reward us doing so. But unlike the freelance journalist or precariously employed field reporter, it is a unique privilege for tenure-track academics to have jobs that allow us to have material security (e.g., a consistent salary) while we research and teach on topics that are mostly within our control, and in ways that are legible to various audiences and constituencies. As such, if academia generally (and criminology specifically) fail to take seriously crimes of the powerful, we will be complicit in obfuscating the impact and extent of harmful systems. (Who else is in a position to study these issues full time?) It is not self-evident that criminology and criminal justice scholarship should remain on a trajectory that often feels like we're rearranging chairs on the titanic, measuring the impact or efficacy of policies and institutions that need not exist as they currently do. (The answer to racism and patriarchy in the workplace will not be found in a business school curriculum that endorses more non-white and women CEOs.)

As corruption and the legitimized and routinized production of social harms increasingly permeate our daily lives and rhythms, this area of research is becoming increasingly necessary. Criminologists can learn a lot from how other disciplines have approached related forms of inquiry, and decide to open up some bandwidth beyond the bread-and-butter fare of cops-courts-corrections research. In a decade or in a century from now, what paradigm of scholarship will our work be categorized in? What kind of institutional arrangements did our writings assume as natural, stable, or even desirable? I respectfully urge that researchers consider getting back out into the real world, ditching the stale and restrictive parts of the disciplinary canon, and contribute to the shared project of describing and explaining crimes of the powerful.

★★★

No matter how good we think we have it, there is a carceral underpinning to our political economy that affects us all. Some readers have known this in deeply biographical terms, while others find this claim unjustified, polemical, or simply awkward. Nevertheless, in the absence of seriously engaging with the nature and operation of powerful systems, we risk – among so many other things – being woefully unprepared for the possibility that criminogenic capital and carceral regimes might no longer exist for your general benefit, but instead become directed against you. A more politically conscious approach to criminology and criminal justice scholarship is not only possible, but necessary.

Index

Note: Page numbers in **bold** indicate a table on the corresponding page.